I'M JUST
SAYING!

I'M JUST SAYING!

Daily Devotional Inspiration and Insight for Men and Women

NATALIE A. FRANCISCO, ED. D.

I'M JUST SAYING! Daily Devotional Inspiration and Insight
by Natalie A. Francisco, Ed. D.

© Copyright 2012

SAINT PAUL PRESS, DALLAS, TEXAS
First Printing, 2012

The name SAINT PAUL PRESS and its logo are registered as a trademark in the U.S. patent office.

ISBN-10: 0-9854258-3-0
ISBN-13: 978-0-9854258-3-8

Printed in the U.S.A.

DEDICATION

This book is dedicated to my precious Lord and Savior, Jesus Christ, in whom I have found salvation, purposeful living, and eternal life; my family of birth (The Gatling Family) from which I received my spiritual foundation; my immediate family (my husband, Leslie, our wonderful daughters: Nicole, Lesley and Lauren and the rest of the Francisco Family) with whom I joyfully live, work, and play; Ralph Marston (who, although we have never met personally, graciously responded to and accepted my inquiry to write the foreword for this book which he inspired); and the many people across the United States and around the world who have granted me so many opportunities to share biblical principles and life lessons with them face-to-face as well as through email and social media. If I could, I would name them one by one in an attempt to count my many blessings. However, there are so many people that it would be an impossible feat to name them all.

For the past three years, I have been inspired by Ralph Marston, the author, and publisher of *The Daily Motivator*, to write my own column titled "I'm Just Saying!" to share with others the perspective God has given me as a result of loving and applying biblical principles to my life while encouraging those who read them to do the same. Every Monday through Friday for years, I read *The Daily Motivator* and as a result, I decided to return the blessing by creating a database of my own which included family, friends, Women of Worth & Worship Institute graduates, co-workers, spiritual leaders, parishioners, business owners, and associates. The list continued to grow as people asked to be added for the sake of receiving "I'm Just Saying!" email communications. Consequently, I began to receive wonderful responses from those who eagerly anticipated each new email stating how profoundly touched they were by the words I shared which were exactly what they needed at the time. *I'm Just Saying! Daily Devotional Inspiration and Insight for Men and Women* is a compilation of many of the emails sent to those included in my weekly distribution database list each Monday through Friday over the years.

I appreciate each of you, along with Ralph, who have both inspired and propelled me to pursue the publishing of this book to expand the sphere of influence that it will reach for generations to come. May the blessing of giving and receiving inspiration and insight each day continue as it is shared with others in your circle of influence.

FOREWORD

Author and Publisher of *The Daily Motivator*

We are, by and large, what we repeatedly think. Our lives are built by the actions we take, and those actions are the intentional results of our most consistent thoughts. If your thoughts are constantly focused on life's problems and shortcomings, your actions will tend to enlarge and perpetuate those problems. When, on the other hand, you make it your practice to tune in to life's goodness and positive possibilities, you will, over time, notice a dramatic beneficial difference in your life. In more than fifteen years of publishing daily motivational messages on the web, I've seen over and over again how brief, positive daily reminders of life's goodness can lead to life-changing results.

That's why I'm so excited about this book. It is filled with a whole year's worth of positive daily reminders. They are particularly powerful because they combine the timeless wisdom of selected Bible quotations with practical, relevant insights on dealing with life's daily challenges and opportunities. Each insight by Dr. Natalie Francisco has the feel of a brief, positive sermon and inspiring motivational seminar, all rolled into an easily accessible form that will give a quick boost to anyone's day.

Your life has so very many beautiful possibilities that you'll never even come close to knowing them all. What you can do, however, is thankfully, enthusiastically and joyfully explore and fulfill as many of them as you can imagine. The positive, uplifting messages in this book will encourage you, over and over again, to do just that.

INTRODUCTION

I am extremely grateful for the opportunities to meet countless people as a result of my travels. Although I have been invited to speak to a variety of audiences in churches, conferences, schools, colleges, and corporate settings to add value to those attending each event, my own life has been made the better by simply availing myself as a conduit to share the wisdom and resources with which God has blessed me with others along my journey. This book is another avenue and channel of blessing to share with the world.

In March of 2012, I had another wonderful opportunity to share what I have learned with others as I was invited to visit South Africa for the third time. This time, the route to get there was unlike any other international itinerary I had ever encountered. Although I departed from my local airport at 2:34 p.m. on a Wednesday afternoon, I did not reach my final destination of Durban, South Africa until the following Friday morning at 7:30 a.m., after which I retrieved my luggage and was picked up by Pastors Flinn and Karen Ranchod (Senior Pastors of Calvary Community Church in South Africa) to travel about 65 miles to Pietermaritzburg. The destination was worth the time and effort expended in flying from Norfolk, VA to New York City to Amsterdam in the Netherlands to Johannesburg, spending eight hours in the Johannesburg Tambo Airport Thursday night, and then flying to Durban early Friday morning. What a journey!

Many people desire to travel, achieve greatness through their accomplishments, or reach a particular destination in their spiritual, personal or professional life. However, desire alone is not enough. We must decide what we want in life and ensure that it is God's will, and then embody the discipline and expend the necessary energy to manage our God-given time, talents, and treasures to stay the course until we reach the destination. The journey along the way is just as valuable as the destination itself, and should be viewed as incredible opportunities to enrich others, enhance ourselves and enjoy every moment we are given to the fullest.

The process of time from the beginning to the end of our lives (also referred to by some as "the dash" in our epitaph) is an amazing gift from God; however, what we do with it is our gift back to Him, others, and ourselves. We each must choose to become accountable and responsible not just for reaching the final destination of our dreams on earth or an eternal home in Heaven, but for being wise, resilient, and patient enough to endure and enjoy the journey of life every day as we empower ourselves by seeking God's wisdom, becoming good stewards of our resources, and sharing what we know and have with others.

I'm Just Saying! Daily Devotional Inspiration and Insight, is my gift to you in your quest to acquire and apply wisdom from its pages each day in your life. I encourage you to use it as a motivational resource to enhance your life and empower the lives of those who cross your path 365 days a year.

Enjoy!

Dr. Natalie A. Francisco
Author of *Wisdom for Women of Worth and Worship*,
Parenting and Partnering with Purpose, and *A Woman's Journal for Joyful Living*
(Saint Paul Press)
Founder/Executive Director,
Women of Worth & Worship Conference / Institute
www.NatalieFrancisco.com
Co-Pastor, Calvary Community Church (Hampton, VA)
www.CalvaryCommunity.org

DAY 1

Inspiration:

"It is of the LORD's mercies that we are not consumed,
because his compassions fail not. They are new every morning:
great is thy faithfulness."
Lamentations 3:22-23, King James Version

Insight:

Every new day and year offers God's gift of mercy -- a second chance and time to begin again not just with the dawning of a new day or year, but with the awakening of a new attitude to fulfill every dream and desire to excel within our sphere of expertise and influence. Peace, prosperity, and possibilities are within our reach and up to us to grasp. Opportunities to dream and achieve what we desire in our personal and professional lives abound in abundance. However, the actualization of our dreams requires deliberate dependence upon God, strategic thinking, goal-setting, faith, fortitude, and the determination to follow through with actions that are purpose-driven and productive.

It is absolutely necessary to do the following if we really mean business and want to see results each day and throughout the year:

1. Eliminate excuses and replace them with a spirit of excellence.
2. Instead of pointing the finger to blame others for a lack of progress, choose to become accountable and responsible for our own success.
3. Trade in timidity for tenacity and allow bold confidence to override fear.
4. Prepare to replace procrastination with a plan of action.

Adopting this attitude and applying these action steps will make every dream a reality.

Ready...set...get to it and do it!

Prayer to Ignite Action:

Father, I commit myself to You anew today. I pray that You will forgive me for missing the mark in any area of my thoughts and actions. I receive Your mercy and forgiveness and apply it to my life and freely give it to others who need it from me. Infuse me with Your wisdom and power that I may think and act in ways consistent with Your plan for my life today. In Jesus' name. Amen.

DAY 2

Inspiration:

"By an act of faith, Abraham said yes to God's call to travel to an unknown place that would become his home. When he left he had no idea where he was going. By an act of faith he lived in the country promised him, lived as a stranger camping in tents. Isaac and Jacob did the same, living under the same promise. Abraham did it by keeping his eye on an unseen city with real, eternal foundations--the City designed and built by God. By faith, barren Sarah was able to become pregnant, old woman as she was at the time, because she believed the One who made a promise would do what he said."
Hebrews 11:8-11, The Message Bible

Insight:

During one of the lessons I taught for Wednesday Women's Noonday Bible Study at Calvary Community Church in Hampton, Virginia, I spoke about the love that Abraham and Sarah had for each other, and the even greater love and obedience that was evident in their devotion to God. That is not to say that their life's journey was without difficulty and doubt. Although they faced negative situations and experienced times of testing, God promised to make Abraham and Sarah the father and mother of a multitude of nations which was fulfilled in the birth of Isaac, Jacob, their descendants, the lineage of Christ (Matthew 1:1) and ultimately the inclusion of Gentiles years later who would accept Christ and be called the seed of Abraham and heirs of the same promise. Abraham and Sarah's determination to believe God and to love one another transformed their situation, moving them from a place of pain to pleasure, from a mood of melancholy to mirth, and from barrenness to breakthrough.

In essence, we can receive the same breakthrough blessing in every area of our lives when we focus on the positive promises of God rather than the negative nuances of our problems. Focusing our faith on God and lavishing our love on Him and others, are two keys that will unlock the door of unlimited opportunities, endless possibilities and abounding abundance in our lives.

Prayer to Ignite Action:

Father, today I receive the gifts of faith and love in my life. Let my faith be evident in my actions as I place my total trust in You and choose to follow the path You have set before me. I pray that all doubt, worry and fear will be dissipated and displaced by my love for God and the people placed in my life today. In Jesus' name. Amen.

DAY 3

Inspiration:

"For the kingdom of heaven is as a man traveling into a far country, who called his own servants, and delivered unto them his goods. And unto one he gave five talents, to another two, and to another one; to every man according to his several ability..."
Matthew 25:14-15, King James Version

Insight:

All of us are faced with choices each day that can either lessen or greatly lengthen the quality of life for ourselves and those closest to us. Completing tasks undertaken and fulfilling promises previously made require much more than having good intentions alone. A determined attitude and deliberate ability are necessary to exhibit excellence and realize results in all of life's affairs and relationships.

In what is known as "The Parable of the Talents" in Matthew chapter 25, two of the three servants who had received talents which represented money, increased what they were originally given by having a determined attitude and showing deliberate actions to make a profit for the owner of their household. However, the third servant was apathetic in his attitude and procrastinated on purpose by giving excuses as to why he did not put forth the effort to be productive with the talent he was given. The words spoken by Jesus in this parable were promising to those who were purpose-driven and productive in verses 20-23, but punitive to the unprofitable and unproductive servant in verses 24-30.

Today, we can choose to be purpose-driven and productive when we decide to have a determined attitude and deliberate actions to back up our words and good intentions. As a result, we will be able to enjoy the fruit of our labor in this lifetime and hear the affirming words of Jesus echoing throughout eternity: 'Well done, good and faithful servant; you were faithful over a few things, I will make you ruler over many things. Enter into the joy of your lord.'

Prayer to Ignite Action:

God, please help me to recognize the potential You have placed within me and to respond by using my gifts and talents to honor You and bless the lives of others. Open my eyes that I may see the needs of those closest to me and fill those needs by offering words of encouragement and love in tangible ways. In Jesus' name. Amen.

DAY 4

Inspiration:

"Let us hear the conclusion of the whole matter: Fear God, and keep his commandments: for this is the whole duty of man."
Ecclesiastes 12:13, King James Version

Insight:

The unexpected death of well known entertainer, Whitney Houston, reminded us all that life is but a vapor--a brief stint of time that cannot compare to eternity. My prayers were extended to her family in their time of grief. She was an incredible talent whose gifts were definitely a result of the rich musical heritage in the family from which she hailed.

We cannot take life for granted, but rather, we must treasure every moment and relationship by adding value with our words and deeds. All we have is today, and to make the most of it requires living with intentionality (knowing our God-ordained purpose and pursuing it unapologetically), authenticity (being genuinely ourselves), specificity (being strategic about our life's choices and mission), and simplicity (knowing who and what is truly important in our lives and prioritizing accordingly).

May we all remember how truly precious life is, and that we must be good stewards of our spirit, mind, and body, as well as our relationships.

Prayer to Ignite Action:

Heavenly Father, today I thank You for the ability to see and hear You in my daily activities so that my life will be a representation of Your light shining through me into the darkest of places around me. I will not be consumed by dark thoughts, choices or actions, but I choose to overcome them with Your power and presence living in me. In Jesus' name. Amen.

DAY 5

Inspiration:

"And whatever you do, do it heartily, as to the Lord and not to men, knowing that from the Lord you will receive the reward of the inheritance; for you serve the Lord Christ."
Colossians 3:23-24, New King James Version

Insight:

Every time I read Colossians 3:23-24, I am encouraged to think, speak, act, and live in ways that reveal the true nature of my heart's desires. Desire begins as a seed planted in the fertile ground of the heart as God's clue of what we were originally created to do. To do anything "heartily" according to Merriam Webster's Dictionary requires acting "in a hearty manner, with all sincerity wholeheartedly, with zest or gusto." Consequently, you and I are called to exhibit enthusiasm and joy not for the sake of pleasing people, but for the sake of pleasing our audience of One, God. As a result, we will be rewarded for a cheerful disposition as we serve Him with the right motive--not just with our actions, but with our attitudes as well.

Prayer to Ignite Action:

God, You are the source of every good and perfect gift in my life. Today, use me to the fullest so that my ability to serve others is motivated by a passionate mission to serve You with all that I am and all that I have. In Jesus' name. Amen.

DAY 6

Inspiration:

"Hope deferred makes the heart sick,
But when the desire comes, it is a tree of life."
Proverbs 13:12, New King James Version

Insight:

Hope is the propeller of faith, while faith causes our vision to have vitality as we work towards transforming our desired vision into reality. There is nothing like putting in the sweat equity necessary to accomplish a God-given goal and basking in the accomplishment of it as a long awaited dream manifests right before our eyes. What is gained in the end makes all the hard work worth the effort even though challenges may have risen along the way. It is infinitely more important and inspiring to focus on the fruitfulness and fulfillment rather than the frustration and fatigue of every effort. By doing so, the motive of every mission becomes the vision for all effort undertaken--to work with purpose while enjoying life.

Prayer to Ignite Action:

God, I place all of my hope and expectation in You today. I ask that You will give me clarity of thought, purpose, and vision for my life. Show me the plan that You have for me today, and give me directions for setting strategic goals so that the vision You have given me will become reality in the right time and season. In the meantime, I thank You for the patience and plan I have today to follow through with appropriate actions as I enjoy the life and work You've given me. In Jesus' name. Amen.

DAY 7

Inspiration:

"Ye are of God, little children, and have overcome them: because greater is he that is in you than he that is in the world."

1 John 4:4, King James Version

Insight:

Although we are living in this world, we do not have to allow the world to live in us. Being a Christian does not exempt us from the pressures of life, the temptations of sin, or the negative opinions and actions of others. However, because "GREATER is He that is in [us] than He that is in the world," we have the power to overcome all that is contrary to God's Word and will for our lives. There is no pressure, temptation or negative force that we cannot resist because of the Spirit that lives within us — the same Holy Spirit that leads, guides, directs, counsels, comforts, and convicts us when we yield ourselves to Him.

Refuse to allow people or circumstances to disturb your peace and to deter your destiny. God has already given you double because He is with you to both outweigh and outnumber your troubles.

Prayer to Ignite Action:

God, I thank You that I am called Your child. I acknowledge and appreciate the presence of Your Holy Spirit dwelling in me, and I invite You to transform me into who You originally created me to be — a person with greatness and vast creativity waiting to be unleashed. I thank You that I am called to impact the world for Your glory, others' benefit, and my fulfillment. In Jesus' name. Amen.

DAY 8

Inspiration:

"So teach us to number our days, that we
may apply our hearts unto wisdom."
Psalm 90:12, King James Version

Insight:

Today is the day that God has made, and as such, we have reason enough
to make the choice to rejoice. We can celebrate each moment by having
an attitude of gratitude for the time that God has given us to start each
morning anew with mercy and grace to live and love life with zeal and
fervor. With the dawning of each new day comes brand new opportunities
and possibilities that are tailor-made to fit the plan that God has for us,
the personality that He has given us, and the particular skill set that we
possess for the purpose of touching the lives of others. Each second,
minute, and hour carries with it the chance for us to maximize it in a way
that no one else can do on our behalf. We are the gatekeepers of each
day, and we will only be productive as a result of valuing and prioritizing
the time that God gives.

Prayer to Ignite Action:

Heavenly Father, You are Alpha and Omega - the Beginning and the
End. You created time and measured it out today as a gift to me and
others so that we can use it effectively. Teach me to be a good steward
of my time and daily activities. Let me not waste time, but face time
with an attitude of respect in the way I respond to prioritize and organize
my day. In Jesus' name. Amen.

DAY 9

Inspiration:

"I know you inside and out, and find little to my liking.
You're not cold, you're not hot--far better to be either cold or hot!"
Revelation 3:15, The Message Bible

Insight:

These lyrics to a classic song, paint the portrait of positive thinking which results in positive living: *You've got to accentuate the positive, eliminate the negative, latch on to the affirmative...don't mess with Mr. In-Between.* Whereas these lyrics are certainly not scriptural, I can't help but think of Revelation 3:15-16 written to the Laodicean Church giving them a choice to be either hot (on fire for God, and therefore positively producing fruit and influencing others) or cold (nonchalant and negative, and consequently, unproductive and apathetic towards God, others and life in general). The scripture went on to state that those who were lukewarm (in-between and indecisive) would be spewed out of the mouth of God. Wow...what revelation!

In essence, the lesson we learn from relating Revelation 3:15 to the lyrics of the familiar song above is to choose to let the light of God shine in our thoughts, words, and actions in such a way that the fervency of God can be clearly seen and felt by those who encounter us on a daily basis. Positive thinking alone is not the answer. Rather, it is the choice to positively influence the lives of others by becoming transformed by God ourselves. In the process, we reject all that is contrary to the Word and will of God for our lives which would cause us to grow cold in our Christian walk. And of course, we dare not "mess with Mr. In-Between" because we can't play both sides of the fence and expect to be productive today and in the future.

Prayer to Ignite Action:

God, please forgive me for not being in hot pursuit of my relationship with You and Your purpose for my life. I repent for allowing my own plans and purpose to dictate the paths I've taken. I commit myself to You today, and pray that Your voice will speak to my mind and heart as I walk in Your ways. I submit my thoughts, plans, and will to You today. In Jesus' name. Amen.

DAY 10

Inspiration:

"I returned, and saw under the sun, that the race [is] not to the swift,
nor the battle to the strong, neither yet bread to the wise,
nor yet riches to men of understanding, nor yet favour to men of skill;
but time and chance happeneth to them all."
Ecclesiastes 9:11, King James Version

Insight:

We never know what a day will hold, but we do know who holds the day. God is able to give us grace, peace, and strength not only to endure, but to prevail and prosper in the midst of the unknown variables and vicissitudes of life. There is nothing too difficult for God, and there is nothing impossible to us when we trust and believe in Him and do our part to participate in His plan. In fact, God empowers us to fulfill the desires of our hearts by giving us the choice and the chance to make the most of every moment by living each day with purpose, on purpose. Let's make full use of each opportunity by exerting the best of our energies and efforts each day while expecting the best results in return.

Prayer to Ignite Action:

Heavenly Father, today I thank You for another time and chance to enjoy life because of Your grace, peace, and strength. I accept the fact that You have given me grace to function in ways that are consistent with who You created me to be and what I am capable of doing. I allow Your peace to permeate in the recesses of my soul (which includes my mind, will, intellect, emotions, and imagination) so that all anxiety is removed. And finally, I anticipate Your power working in and through me to accomplish great things today. In Jesus' name. Amen.

DAY 11

Inspiration:

"To whom also he shewed himself alive after his passion by many infallible proofs, being seen of them forty days, and speaking of the things pertaining to the kingdom of God."
Acts 1:3, King James Version

Insight:

Jesus allowed His passion to serve others in His life, death and resurrection. His zeal for obeying the will of His Father (God) and His love for serving people (including you and me), fortified His resolve to significantly influence and impact the entire world.

Many people are in search of the formula for success in relationships, ministries and businesses around the world. I have found that it is much easier to strive for significance rather than success, for in so doing I am determined to set goals and follow through with them because they add value to those whom God assigns to my sphere of influence. As I seek God in daily prayer, Bible reading and establishing my checklist of "things to do," I ask Him for wisdom to prioritize and plan with purpose and passion. He honors my request simply because He knows that my heart's desire is to serve as a channel and conduit of blessing to others.

There are a plethora of books on leadership, success, and prosperity, but I have simplified the process of choosing to live a significant life by meditating on this mantra: Today is a gift for us to treasure and share, and time is a gift for us to measure with care. Decide to spend your day and time with those you love, accomplishing the things that you are passionate about. What a wonderful way to live!

Prayer to Ignite Action:

God, I am awed by Your love for me and the entire world in that You sent Your only Son to earth to live, die, and be resurrected for a purpose that supersedes what our minds can fathom. Thank You, Jesus, for showing me how to live with purpose, on purpose. May the same passion that ignited You to fulfill destiny now ignite me to follow the passion and fulfill the purpose that God has given me. In Jesus' name. Amen.

DAY 12

Inspiration:

"Don't become so well adjusted to your culture that you fit into it without even thinking. Instead, fix your attention on God. You'll be changed from the inside out. Readily recognize what He wants from you and quickly respond to it. Unlike the culture around you, always dragging you down to its level of immaturity, God brings the best out of you, develops well-formed maturity in you."

Romans 12:2, The Message Bible

Insight:

Whether we choose to acknowledge it or not, we are all leaders in some capacity with the capability of influencing those who are watching and listening to us daily. As a result, we must be mindful of our orthodoxy (belief) and orthopraxy (behavior). Our thoughts certainly determine our conversation, conduct, and the consequences that follow. Consequently, if we desire to have a better quality of life then we must evaluate the musing of our mind and the muttering of our mouths. Living abundantly is fully possible, but it begins with transforming the way we think, speak, and act with the intent to please God and the integrity to lead by example.

Prayer to Ignite Action:

Father, I desire to please You today. Forgive me for the times I've allowed my desire to please people to override my desire to please You. I know that my life is to serve as a living letter for others to read and follow. May my motives be pure in Your sight so that my thoughts, words, and deeds may be sincere as well and yield results that will honor You and add value to others. In Jesus' name. Amen.

DAY 13

Inspiration:

"I will praise thee; for I am fearfully and wonderfully made: marvellous
are thy works; and that my soul knoweth right well."
Psalm 139:14, King James Version

"For we are His workmanship, created in Christ Jesus unto good works,
which God hath before ordained that we should walk in them."
Ephesians 2:10, King James Version

Insight:

Too many people are trying to keep up with "the Joneses" in what they
wear, drive, do, and say, as well as in where and how they live. How
preposterous! Psalm 139:14 and Ephesians 2:10 remind us that we are
fearfully, wonderfully, and uniquely created to do good works that God
planned for us to accomplish before we were ever born. Since that is the
case, there is no need to compare ourselves to others or to covet what
they have. When we realize just how extraordinary we already are, then
we dare not measure our success against that of others, nor should we
exchange our authenticity and originality for a carbon copy of someone
else.

If we are to add value to the people and the world around us, we must
choose a life of significance over success and meaningful purpose over
material possessions. Besides, when we seek God's kingdom and His will
for us first, all of the things we may desire will be given to us as a result
of pleasing God and having our priorities in the right place.

Prayer to Ignite Action:

Father, I am created in Your image and likeness, and yet wonderfully
crafted in a way that is as unique as my fingerprints, personality, and
abilities. Thank You for loving me so much and entrusting me with inner
and outer resources to be used for a greater purpose. Accomplish good
works in and through me today. In Jesus' name. Amen.

DAY 14

Inspiration:

"But what happens when we live God's way? He brings gifts into our lives, much the same way that fruit appears in an orchard--things like affection for others, exuberance about life, serenity. We develop a willingness to stick with things, a sense of compassion in the heart, and a conviction that a basic holiness permeates things and people. We find ourselves involved in loyal commitments, not needing to force our way in life, able to marshal and direct our energies wisely. Legalism is helpless in bringing this about; it only gets in the way."
Galatians 5:22-23, The Message Bible

Insight:

One of the most important lessons we can ever learn is not to give up when times seem tough and the going gets rough. We must not allow ourselves to be controlled by our environment or emotions which may change as often as the weather. The even-tempered man and woman with a steady will keeps going in the midst of challenging circumstances, cynics, critics, and crisis. In fact, the optimistic person who keeps his or her faith focused on what can be rather than what is, will surely transform obstacles into opportunities for growth, development and productivity. Having God's Spirit gives us access to love (unconditional acceptance of and compassion for others despite their response to us), temperance (self-control), meekness (intestinal fortitude and strength under control), and mental toughness (inner peace and soundness of mind that is unaffected by outward conditions). When we determine to stand and to keep on standing, and to go and to keep on going, we possess the key to unlock the best that life has to offer because we have learned to give the best of ourselves as God handles the rest.

Prayer to Ignite Action:

Heavenly Father, today I ask that You would cultivate the fruit of the Holy Spirit in my life. I accept and apply Your love, joy, peace, patience, goodness, gentleness, faith, meekness and temperance. I know that I am only responsible for my own decisions and actions as I am led by You, and I will not allow the decisions and actions of others to blemish my character or bruise the fruit of the Spirit working in me. I pray in advance for others who do not know You, and ask that Your Spirit would draw them into relationship with You as the God who loves and desires to provide for their needs. Use me as a conduit of Your love. In Jesus' name. Amen.

DAY 15

Inspiration:

"God created human beings; he created them godlike, reflecting God's nature. He created them male and female.
God blessed them: 'Prosper! Reproduce! Fill Earth!
Take charge! Be responsible for fish in the sea and birds in the air, for every living thing that moves on the face of Earth.'"
Genesis 1:27-28, The Message Bible

Insight:

We are fully capable of being creative, imaginative and innovative because we were and are made in the image and likeness of God our Creator. Throughout the first two chapters of Genesis, we see the methodology of God which serves as our pedagogy. Before anything was created, it first began as a thought painted on the canvas of God's mind. Each thought was then translated to spoken word (i.e., "Then God said...") which was uttered as a result of what was initially created and seen as a mental image. The lesson for us in this is to embrace the creative power of God by using our imagination to see what is possible in our minds and speak what will be (as though it is already manifested) with our mouths. When we follow God's pattern by utilizing this pedagogy, we will be creative, imaginative, innovative and productive in all we think, see, say, and do.

Prayer to Ignite Action:

God, I want to reflect Your nature and creativity today in my home, workplace, church, and community. I realize that my words are the force that will create the environment where I live, work, rest, and play. Season my words with love, grace, peace, encouragement, and correction for myself and others so that productivity and prosperity will prevail in and around me. In Jesus' name. Amen.

DAY 16

Inspiration:

"Yea, a man may say, Thou hast faith, and I have works: shew me thy faith without thy works, and I will shew thee my faith by my works."
James 2:18, King James Version

Insight:

We've heard it said that "nothing beats a failure but a try." However, there is something that supersedes a try, and that is "the will to succeed." Trying alone, although it is certainly a step above failing, simply serves as an attempt not to fail. It takes more than that to actually realize and materialize results. The power to turn dreams into reality resides within us so that we may live out our destiny. However, our will must be resolute enough to transform our seeds of thought (faith) into deeds wrought (works). Possibilities and opportunities are presented to us daily to make our dreams come true. We don't have to wish upon a star, but we do need to initiate and activate a plan of action if we truly desire to succeed in any area of our lives.

Prayer to Ignite Action:

God, my faith is in You and also in what You can and will do when my faith becomes active with my actions. I know that faith and works fit together like a hand in a glove. Strengthen and steady my will today so that I may be disciplined enough to manage my life, relationships, daily tasks, and resources well. In Jesus' name. Amen.

DAY 17

Inspiration:

"The serpent was clever, more clever than any wild animal GOD had made. He spoke to the Woman: 'Do I understand that God told you not to eat from any tree in the garden?' The Woman said to the serpent, 'Not at all. We can eat from the trees in the garden. It's only about the tree in the middle of the garden that God said, 'Don't eat from it; don't even touch it or you'll die.' The serpent told the Woman, 'You won't die. God knows that the moment you eat from that tree, you'll see what's really going on. You'll be just like God, knowing everything, ranging all the way from good to evil.' When the Woman saw that the tree looked like good eating and realized what she would get out of it--she'd know everything!--she took and ate the fruit and then gave some to her husband, and he ate."
Genesis 3:1-6, The Message Bible

Insight:

It is amazing how we often times focus our attention on what we think we want (although we don't really need it), rather than on what we already have within our reach and at our disposal. Eve, the mother of all living, did this when she partook of the fruit from the Tree of the Knowledge of Good and Evil in the Garden of Eden (reference Genesis chapters 1-3). She and Adam wanted and ate the forbidden fruit, and failed to enjoy the fulfillment of the freedom they already possessed to enjoy each other and the paradise in which they were already placed.

Today, let's purpose in our hearts to be grateful for the goodness of what we already have in and around us to enjoy. As we focus on what God has placed in our heart and hands now in terms of loving family, friends, talents, skills, and resources, we will realize that we possess and are blessed with everything at this present time to live a rich and rewarding life of abundance.

Prayer to Ignite Action:

God, I thank You that I am blessed by You so that I may be a blessing to others. Forgive me for taking what I have been given for granted. Help me to be more grateful and responsible in sharing what I know and have when given the opportunity to do so today. I appreciate and am content with what I have now, and I trust You, knowing that the plans You have for my future will unfold for my good. In Jesus' name. Amen.

DAY 18

Inspiration:

"Looking unto Jesus the author and finisher of [our] faith; who for the joy that was set before Him endured the cross, despising the shame, and is set down at the right hand of the throne of God."
Hebrews 12:2, King James Version

Insight:

Life is all about forward movement and maturity. Although we remember our past, it doesn't do any good to rehearse it repeatedly, particularly when what is remembered and reiterated causes regression rather than progression. Experiences and events from the past should be memorialized only when lessons can be extracted for us to learn and pass on to others to promote growth.

Living life in the past is like trying to drive a car forward while looking only in the rearview mirror. Accidents and mishaps can be avoided as a result of paying attention to the current conditions, maintaining control of the vehicle, and staying focused on the road ahead.

Let's take our cue from Jesus who "for the joy that was set before Him" not only endured the cross, but kept His gaze on the glory of fulfilling His purpose as His Father commanded. Even the Rev. Martin Luther King said, "I've been to the mountaintop and I've seen the Promised Land...Mine eyes have seen the glory of the coming of the Lord!" We have also received instructions from God to stay focused on our purpose and to "keep it moving" no matter what. Many are depending on us, and a better life--a legacy to leave for others--awaits!

Prayer to Ignite Action:

Father, I release my past to You. Forgive me of my sins and help me to focus on the glorious promises that will determine the quality of my present and future. I choose to dwell on what lies before me rather than on what lingers behind me. Thank You for redeeming, restoring and renewing me today. In Jesus' name. Amen.

DAY 19

Inspiration:

It pleased Darius to set over the kingdom one hundred and twenty satraps, to be over the whole kingdom; and over these, three governors, of whom Daniel was one, that the satraps might give account to them, so that the king would suffer no loss. Then this Daniel distinguished himself above the governors and satraps, because an excellent spirit was in him; and the king gave thought to setting him over the whole realm. So the governors and satraps sought to find some charge against Daniel concerning the kingdom; but they could find no charge or fault, because he was faithful; nor was there any error or fault found in him."
Daniel 6:1-4, New King James Version

Insight:

I overheard the wisdom of my mother-in-law, Naomi, in her conversation with someone years ago that still echos in my hearing today: "If you complain, your situation will remain; if you praise, your situation will raise!" Now, I know that praise alone can be thought of and used by some as a mechanism to escape reality, but the truth of the matter is, our thoughts which precede our words really do determine how we perceive and respond to people and predicaments around us. She was simply using a rhyming phrase to drive home the point that murmuring and complaining about what we do not like or agree with is useless, for it will not change the person or the problem confronting us. However, if we change what we think and speak by having a positive perspective, our words and actions will be in agreement and our personal level of excellence will not allow us to respond inappropriately. Excellence does not yield to excuses or complaints; rather, it requires a personal level of participation that supersedes the status quo of being average or mediocre. Those who are excellent in thought, word and deed will always counteract complaints with the attention to detail that gives way to maximum performance and promotion in life.

Those who complain most certainly will remain, but those who praise by speaking well of God and the people, places, and predicaments in their lives will be raised to a new level. Those in positions of prominence always take notice of the spirit of excellence. God will see to it that our praiseworthy mentality, conversation, and conduct is rewarded when we are faithful and fruitful in cultivating excellence in our lives.

Prayer to Ignite Action:

Father God, today I pray that You will allow opportunities to come my way that will cause excellence to be cultivated within and around me. Help me not to complain, but to commit myself to thinking and acting in a manner that pleases You. Empower me to eliminate excuses and to put forth the effort that will cause me and those I influence to excel in every area of life. In Jesus' name. Amen.

DAY 20

Inspiration:

"'Before I shaped you in the womb, I knew all about you. Before you saw the light of day, I had holy plans for you: A prophet to the nations--that's what I had in mind for you.' But I said, 'Hold it, Master GOD! Look at me. I don't know anything. I'm only a boy!' GOD told me, 'Don't say, 'I'm only a boy.' I'll tell you where to go and you'll go there. I'll tell you what to say and you'll say it. Don't be afraid of a soul. I'll be right there, looking after you.' GOD's Decree."
Jeremiah 1:4-8, The Message Bible

Insight:

Don't ever shrink back from a task or an assignment because you think or feel that you can't do it. Many biblical patriarchs and matriarchs were called to do great things such as Gideon, Moses, Joshua, Jeremiah, Sarah, Esther, Hannah, and Mary the mother of Jesus. They were human and like us, sometimes frail and fickle in their thoughts and emotions. Although they responded to God's call with self-doubt, fear, intimidation, and inadequacy, God reassured each of them that He had equipped them for the task regardless of their age, gender, or self-perceptions. It has been said that, "God does not call the qualified; He qualifies the called." Simply put, each person has the ability to do whatever he or she has been uniquely created and called to do. Personalities and gifts that are both spiritual and natural are just as distinct as every individual's fingerprints and DNA. Jeremiah 1:4-8 serves as food not just for thought, but for consumption so that we can see ourselves as God sees us.

Prayer to Ignite Action:

Father, forgive me for doubting You, myself, and the abilities You've given me. Replace my feelings of fear, intimidation, and inadequacy with courage and confidence in Your call upon my life. I willingly surrender all that I am and ever will be to You by saying yes to Your plan for my life today. In Jesus' name. Amen.

DAY 21

Inspiration:

"It is the same with my word. I send it out, and it
always produces fruit. It will accomplish all I want it to,
and it will prosper everywhere I send it."
Isaiah 55:11, New Living Translation

Insight:

What are you believing God to do in and through you today? Are your dreams and desires big enough to inquire of, include and inspire God as you seize the possibilities that come your way? Merriam Webster's Dictionary defines possibility as the condition or fact of being possible; one's utmost power, capacity, or ability; something that is possible; and potential or prospective value. What you believe will become fact not just because God breathed an idea, dream or vision into your mind, heart, and spirit, but because He has already spoken it and empowered you with the capacity, ability and potential to make it possible. Is anything possible? The answer is, yes, as long as what you desire requires God's intervention and your full participation in order to add value to the world around you. The difference between a dream and a selfish ambition is this: a dream invites others to participate for the good of the whole which increases the value and releases the potential of everyone involved, whereas a selfish ambition seeks only to promote one's own agenda without including God and others in the process.

Today, we can choose to dream bigger and to do greater things that need God's approval and action working in and through us for His glory and the good of others including ourselves. Whatever God has spoken shall come to pass because it is not only possible; it is a fact!

You see, the dream really isn't about what we want at all. It is about what God wants for us. Today is full of possibilities, productivity, and prosperity. Confess it and partner with God to perform it. It's possible!

Prayer to Ignite Action:

Heavenly Father, expand my capacity to dream bigger and to do greater works for the sake of expanding Your kingdom on earth. Let my dreams mirror the reflection of Your vision for my life so that selfish ambitions are erased and the desire to honor You with the way I live and the service I give are embraced. In Jesus' name. Amen.

DAY 22

Inspiration:

"Great [is] our Lord, and of great power:
His understanding [is] infinite."
Psalm 147:5

Insight:

We serve an Omnipotent (All-Powerful) God whose nature also resides within those who acknowledge, believe in and serve Him. That same power is extended to us to dream and discern God's will in setting goals to fulfill our deepest desires and therefore, our destiny. The will of God is made manifest to us through prayer, reading, and applying His Holy Word in our lives, and following the leading of the Holy Spirit in our every day activities. The power of God is dispensed to us so that we can accomplish all that is in agreement with the dreams and plans that are inspired by Him. Therefore, we must take advantage of every opportunity that resonates with our deepest dreams and desires. There is absolutely nothing impossible to those who are faith-believers, dream-perceivers, and destiny-achievers.

Prayer to Ignite Action:

Dear God, You are the source of all power, and I thank You that great power dwells in me today that I may believe, perceive, and achieve the dreams You have given me. I pray for discernment and understanding so that I may serve You with my heart and hands. In Jesus' name. Amen.

DAY 23

Inspiration:

Without good direction, people lose their way;
the more wise counsel you follow, the better your chances."
Proverbs 11:14, The Message Bible

Refuse good counsel and watch your plans fail;
take good counsel and watch them succeed."
Proverbs 15:22, The Message Bible

Insight:

This is our year to take advantage of every opportunity and possibility to make a connection with new people and plans on our pathway of purpose. Whomever and whatever resonates the strongest with our sense of adding value to the world should become a part of our circle of influence. Networking with people who possess experience and expertise that we need is an essential ingredient needed as we partake of the smorgasbord of inspiration, ideas, and ingenuity to ignite us to take action as never before--action that is strategically aimed towards the fulfillment of daily, weekly, monthly, and yearly goals. Executing specific plans and placing ourselves in the company of others who are purpose-driven, will keep us motivated and moving in the right direction.

Prayer to Ignite Action:

God, I appreciate the support system of people you have surrounded me with--family, friends, spiritual leaders, mentors and business associates. Help me to better appreciate and glean from those with experience and expertise so that I may continue to develop my spiritual, intellectual, physical, social, and financial goals. I thank You for the wisdom to implement that which will add value to my life so that I may add value in the same way to others. In Jesus' name. Amen.

DAY 24

Inspiration:

"God spoke: 'Let us make human beings in our image,
make them reflecting our nature so they can be responsible for the fish
in the sea, the birds in the air, the cattle, and, yes, Earth itself,
and every animal that moves on the face of Earth.'"
Genesis 1:26, The Message Bible

Insight:

Each person is created in the image and likeness of God, and as such, reflects the beauty and uniqueness of character, personality, gifts, and abilities that stem from Him. Since we are His creation, we must consult God and His Word to discover the vast treasures that are within us for the purpose of making an indelible mark upon others and our part of the world to represent Him and reveal the essence of what we are equipped and empowered to do naturally. That is not to say that what we are passionate about accomplishing will come so easy that there will be no challenges. Rather, the obstacles that come our way should actually help to bring out the best (and not the worst) of our character and capabilities as we are strengthened and sharpened along the way. We are created to be the difference that we desire to see in the world.

Prayer to Ignite Action:

Father, I am so very grateful for the opportunity to reflect Your nature today through my personality and talents. I am empowered and equipped to effectively manage every situation that comes my way, for I know that You will use it to shape and mold me into the person I am predestined to become. I commit myself to becoming the change and the difference that I desire to see in my home, community and world. In Jesus' name. Amen.

DAY 25

Inspiration:

"Not that I have already obtained it or have already become perfect, but I press on so that I may lay hold of that for which I was laid hold of by Christ Jesus. Brethren, I do not regard myself as having laid hold of it yet; but one thing I do: forgetting what lies behind and reaching forward to what lies ahead, I press on toward the goal for the prize of the upward call of God in Christ Jesus."
Philippians 3:12-14, New American Standard Bible

Insight:

Procrastination is a weapon that many of us intentionally and habitually use, whether consciously or subconsciously, in our arsenal without realizing that it sabotages success and forward progression. In order to experience a higher level of living, we must elevate our level of thinking and respond accordingly by translating good intentions into better practices. The power to choose is always within our grasp, but the ability to follow through with the choices we make to secure the future we desire requires an unrelenting desire to pursue purpose and to press on to accomplish what is necessary now (today) so that we can have a better tomorrow.

Don't allow procrastination to lead to your own stagnation. Never put off for tomorrow what you know needs to be focused upon and finished today. There's nothing like the feeling of fulfillment that settles upon us once a worthwhile goal or task has been accomplished. Carpe diem (seize the day)!

Prayer to Ignite Action:

Dear God, I am sorry for missing the mark by procrastinating and putting off what I should have completed. Please help me to reevaluate my priorities beginning with my relationship with You, my loved ones and the tasks that are urgently vying for my attention. I will develop a list of what I must do in order of importance today and work towards completing all that is within my power with the authority and ability You've given me today. In Jesus' name. Amen.

DAY 26

Inspiration:

Today I have given you the choice between life and death, between blessings and curses. Now I call on heaven and earth to witness the choice you make. Oh, that you would choose life, so that you and your descendants might live! You can make this choice by loving the LORD your God, obeying Him, and committing yourself firmly to Him. This is the key to your life. And if you love and obey the LORD, you will live long in the land the LORD swore to give your ancestors Abraham, Isaac, and Jacob."
Deuteronomy 30:19-20, New Living Translation

Insight:

We have the power to take perceived experiences and limitations of the past, whether good, bad or indifferent, and transform them into lessons and a launching pad of possibilities for our present and future. The difficulties of days gone by can either diminish us, define us or draw us closer to our dreams as we glean from what we have learned to move forward and become the best we can be in our relationships and areas of responsibility. No one can take away our power to choose but ourselves, nor can anyone keep us from progressing in life unless we abdicate that responsibility by allowing them to do so.

Jim Rohn once said, "Happiness is not something you postpone for the future; it is something you design for the present." Choose to design your present by eliminating unhappiness and pursuing joy today. As we wave goodbye to yesterday and yesteryear and bid hello to today and our future, let us prepare ourselves for greater areas of responsibility, accountability, opportunity and possibility to do what we've never done and to go where we've never gone before. God and countless others are waiting for us to stop spectating and to start participating by giving the best of ourselves and living our best lives.

Prayer to Ignite Action:

Father God, You created us with "free will" and the power to choose.

Today, I willingly choose to love You, obey Your Word and live my life fully for the sake of those who will one day follow in my footsteps as I continue to follow You. I choose life and blessings by embracing joy over sadness, health over sickness, prosperity over poverty, and friendliness over loneliness. In Jesus' name. Amen.

DAY 27

Inspiration:

"And the angel came in unto her, and said, Hail, [thou that art] highly favoured, the Lord [is] with thee: blessed [art] thou among women. And when she saw [him], she was troubled at his saying, and cast in her mind what manner of salutation this should be. And the angel said unto her, Fear not, Mary: for thou has found favour with God. And, behold, thou shalt conceive in thy womb, and bring forth a son, and shalt call His name JESUS...Then said Mary unto the angel, How shall this be, seeing I know not a man? And the angel answered and said unto her, The Holy Ghost shall come upon thee, and the power of the Highest shall overshadow thee: therefore also that holy thing which shall be born of thee shall be called the Son of God...
For with God nothing shall be impossible."
Luke 1:28-31, 34-35, 37, King James Version

Insight:

When the virgin Mary was told by the angel that she would birth the Savior of the world, she questioned how this would happen. The angel replied that the Holy Spirit would come upon and overshadow her, "for with God, nothing is impossible." This response is good news to all of us as well, for it reminds us that anything that is to be accomplished for God's purpose and the benefit of others requires supernatural ability because our natural ability alone is not enough. That which seems to be difficult or impossible is made easier and possible when we allow the work of the Holy Spirit to overshadow our finite mentality and frail humanity. There is nothing too hard for God to handle on our behalf. He has a storehouse filled with knowledge, wisdom, strength, mercy, grace, favor, and peace that are only a prayer away, and therefore, at our disposal at a moment's notice. As we prepare ourselves by accomplishing what we are capable of, God will see to it that the rest is taken care of to ensure that the dreams He has incubated within us are birthed to full term.

Prayer to Ignite Action:

Heavenly Father, I know that with You nothing is impossible. Today, I thank You for transforming my mind to believe You for what otherwise would be impossible without Your power working in and through me. My faith looks up to Thee, oh Lamb of Calvary, for the fulfillment of every God-ordained dream and vision for me and those closest to me. I pray that You will bring to completion every plan that is in agreement with Your purpose for my life in the right season and timing. In Jesus' name. Amen.

DAY 28

Inspiration:

"'I know what I'm doing. I have it all planned out--plans to take care of you, not abandon you, plans to give you the future you hope for. When you call on me, when you come and pray to me, I'll listen. When you come looking for me, you'll find me. Yes, when you get serious about finding me and want it more than anything else, I'll make sure you won't be disappointed.' GOD's Decree."

Jeremiah 29:11-14a, The Message Bible

Insight:

An old adage says, "I don't know what the future holds, but I know who holds the future." In the midst of uncertain economic environments, unstable emotions, unreliable relationships, and undisclosed information, we can be sure that God has all the answers that we need if we only seek Him for wisdom and direction. Our confidence lies in God who knows the plans He established for us and the world before time began. Even though we may not understand all of the events that unfold before our eyes, we must trust that God is in complete control and that He will guide our will, words and ways despite what we see, hear or feel. Our hope and guarantees rest in God, and God abides with and resides in all who receive Him.

Prayer to Ignite Action:

God, You hold my future in Your hands. I trust You completely, knowing that You will not leave, forsake or disappoint me because You are the One who knows what is best for me. Even when all around me seem to be sinking sand, upon Christ the solid rock I'll continue to stand. All of my hope rests in You. In Jesus' name. Amen.

DAY 29

Inspiration:

"[A Psalm of David.] The LORD [is] my shepherd; I shall not want. He maketh me to lie down in green pastures: he leadeth me beside the still waters. He restoreth my soul: he leadeth me in the paths of righteousness for his name's sake. Yeah, though I walk through the valley of the shadow of death, I will fear no evil: for thou [art] with me; thy rod and thy staff they comfort me. Thou preparest a table before me in the presence of mine enemies: thou anointest my head with oil; my cup runneth over. Surely goodness and mercy shall follow me all the days of my life: and I will dwell in the house of the LORD for ever."
Psalm 23:1-6, King James Version

Insight:

One of my most favorite passages of scripture learned during my childhood years was Psalm 23. As I grew older, I came to appreciate the many ways in which God, as the Good Shepherd led me through the green pastures of fertile, fruitful, lush landscapes of life as well as through the dark, dismal valleys of death's shadow. One thing was certain: "Surely goodness and mercy followed me all the days of my life!"

No matter what encounters we experience, and regardless of the people who cross our path, we must choose to embrace the goodness and mercy of God that is always present, for it carries and stays with us through all the vicissitudes of life. Being grateful for the twin blessings of goodness and mercy keeps us focused on God's promises, provisions, protection and peace.

Prayer to Ignite Action:

Dear God, I call You Shepherd because You lovingly care for, look after, and provide for all of my needs. I confess that there is nothing missing, lacking, or broken in my life today. I have the assurance of knowing that You are with me every moment to protect me and to fill me with Your peace in every situation that I face today. Thank You that goodness and mercy are with me always. In Jesus' name. Amen.

DAY 30

Inspiration:

"Behold, God [is] mighty, and despiseth not [any: he is]
mighty in strength [and] wisdom."
Job 36:5, King James Version

Insight:

Life is full of surprises, certainties, pleasure and pain. Whether expected
or unexpected, explainable or unexplainable, we can gain much from all
these experiences by learning and valuing what we can from each moment
with the use of our rake and pitchfork. No matter what comes our way,
we have the choice like Job of raking in that which is relevant and pitching
out what is irrelevant or of no use whatsoever. Using this method to
manage the moments that ebb and flow through our lives allows us to
respond rather than to react to what happens around us as God continues
to grant us grace, strength, and wisdom.

Prayer to Ignite Action:

Heavenly Father, this is another day that You have blessed and kept me.
I thank You that I am still here in spite of the challenges I've faced. My
prayer today is that You will grant me the wisdom to discern the difference
between what is needed for my destiny and what must be discarded. I
will rake in everything that is useful and pitch out all that is irrelevant so
that I can focus more clearly and serve You more faithfully. In Jesus'
name. Amen.

DAY 31

Inspiration:

"For the Son of man is come to seek and to save that which was lost."
Luke 19:10, King James Version

Insight:

According to Merriam Webster's Dictionary, to persist means "to go on resolutely or stubbornly in spite of opposition." In this way, stubbornness can be used for a good purpose as we remain fixed and focused in our present position which will determine our life's future condition. When we know that God is guiding our steps, then we can continue in the direction of His leading even when others do not understand or agree. The passion of our heart will continue to fuel the fire that burns within us to press on while remaining true to our God-given purpose and our authentic selves.

There is no greater example of persistence than that of Jesus Christ who, despite persecution, fulfilled His purpose of coming to earth to seek and save those who were and are lost through His birth, life, ministry, death, and resurrection. May the Spirit of Christ and the persistence He possesses also reside within you today.

Prayer to Ignite Action:

Dear God, I adore You and am grateful that the persistence of Your Son, Jesus Christ, caused Him to fulfill the mission of coming to earth to seek and save all who were and are lost. Thank You for living in my heart and saving me from my sins. Today, I pray for those who are still lost and need to be redeemed and renewed. Please use me to draw those closest to me into a loving relationship with You. I pray that through the confession of sin and belief in the life, death, burial and resurrection of Jesus Christ, many will be sought after and saved today. In Jesus' name. Amen.

DAY 32

Inspiration:

"You are the light of the world. A city that is set on a hill cannot
be hidden. Nor do they light a lamp and put it under a basket,
but on a lampstand, and it gives light to all who are in the house.
Let your light so shine before men, that they may see your good works
and glorify your Father in heaven."
Matthew 5:14-16, New King James Version

Insight:

No person is insignificant, nor is any gift or talent that each
person possesses. Sadly, some people belittle or use others to make
themselves look better, shine brighter, or appear bigger. In reality, such
behavior is detrimental for it diminishes character, integrity, and trust.

Everyone has the ability to shine in our respective areas of expertise and
influence and to make life richer by intentionally seeking to better ourselves
and the sphere of persons assigned to our stewardship. There are a myriad
of ways to add value by recognizing the good that resides in the people
around us and the capabilities of our minds and hands, for in so doing,
we will bring out the best in ourselves and those closest to us.

Prayer to Ignite Action:

God, You are the light of my life. Your light provides direction, clarity,
and manifested purpose for me. Today, I will let Your light shine through
me to reflect Your glory and excellence everywhere I go in the midst of
everyone I meet. Let my character, integrity, and abilities exemplify who
You are in my life. In Jesus' name. Amen.

DAY 33

Inspiration:

"Every good gift and every perfect gift is from above,
and cometh down from the Father of lights, with whom is no
variableness, neither shadow of turning."
James 1:17, King James Version

Insight:

It is wonderful to receive counsel and advice from others who have both education and experience in matters that pertain to our personal or professional lives. There are also other resources that can sharpen our edge. Nevertheless, we cannot rely on human and natural resources alone to assist in defining who we are and in determining our destiny. These important details must be discovered as we search and find our identity and destiny in God--the Omniscient One who knows all and possesses all wisdom. He has the answers to all of our questions and will guide us by His all-seeing eye in the direction that we should go, instructing us along the way. There are times when others will come alongside us and share valuable pearls of wisdom, but the mystery, mission and motives of our mind, heart and soul can only be revealed to us by our Maker whose desire is to give to us every good and perfect gift. The greatest gift that we can receive other than salvation through Jesus Christ is wisdom, understanding, and discernment of life.

Prayer to Ignite Action:

God, I thank You for those who have given me wise counsel as needed in my life, and I ask Your blessings upon them as they continue to mentor others. I especially am grateful that I can depend upon You first as the source of infinite wisdom and the giver of every good and perfect gift. I pray that the gifts I have been given will be developed to full maturity in me for the sake of building Your kingdom and blessing the lives of others. In Jesus' name. Amen.

DAY 34

Inspiration:

"It's what we trust in but don't yet see that keeps us going."
2 Corinthians 5:7, The Message Bible

Insight:

An old adage says, "Seeing is believing." However, I have found the converse of this comment to be true, especially in the life of Christians. The Bible clearly states that "we walk by faith, not by sight" (2 Corinthians 5:7). It is important to visualize goals and dreams, but we will never see what we do not first believe. Before we see anything, the mind must firmly take hold of what the heart hopes for to conceptualize it, and then, visualize it. The desires of our hearts cannot manifest until our thoughts process those desires into mental images that motivate us to move into action. Believing, then, is seeing. And seeing a thing before it materializes takes faith, which is useless without works according to James 2:18, 20 and 26. Visions are inspired by thinkers who become doers.

Prayer to Ignite Action:

Father, today I pray that I will be encouraged by what I believe despite what I see. Strengthen my faith so that it sustains me and keeps me going with the expectation of seeing what You have promised me. I will be led forward in hot pursuit of Your perfect will for me as I keep my eyes fixed upon and my faith firmly grounded in You. In Jesus' name. Amen.

DAY 35

Inspiration:

"Then He said, 'What is the kingdom of God like? And to what shall I compare it? It is like a mustard seed, which a man took and put in his garden; and it grew and became a large tree, and the birds of the air nested in its branches.'" ~ Luke 13:18-19, New King James Version

Insight:

Every acorn has within itself an oak tree that will provide the surety of shade, shelter, sustenance, and security once it has been safely planted in fertile soil. The potential of the acorn resides in its seed which will only be nourished and nurtured in the proper environment. When the acorn seed establishes its root system in the earth, the potential of the oak tree will be released to become what it was meant to become even though atmospheric conditions may not always be ideal.

Like the acorn, we each possess potential that is in alignment with our original purpose which is God's predestined intent for our lives. We must ensure that we are rooted and grounded in the proper environment by nurturing our relationship with God, reading and applying biblical principles to our lives, and using our gifts and talents for God in our service to Him and those we are called to reach. When we focus on maintaining the root system of our faith, we will continue to enjoy the benefits of continued growth and expanded opportunities to give the best of who we are and what we possess to serve a greater purpose for the sake of God's kingdom.

Prayer to Ignite Action:

Dear Lord, I recognize that the life You have given me on this earth is akin to a seed that is planted in the ground. My desire is to be nurtured, instructed, and even corrected as I continue to grow through the pruning process that is necessary for my maturity. I thank You that I am planted in the fertile soil of a good church that teaches Your Word without compromise to strengthen my foundation. As I grow, I will share what I have learned and mastered with others in my circle of influence to expand Your kingdom. In Jesus' name. Amen.

DAY 36

Inspiration:

"So, dear brothers and sisters, work hard to prove that you really are among those God has called and chosen. Do these things, and you will never fall away. Then God will give you a grand entrance into the eternal Kingdom of our Lord and Savior Jesus Christ." ~ 2 Peter 1:10-11, New Living Translation

Insight:

What is it that we can do that uniquely utilizes our areas of strength while adding value to our life and those around us at the same time? When we discover that, we'll uncover our passion which serves as the motivation for doing that which brings us and others joy and fulfillment. In fact, the passion that we have is a seed planted in our hearts by God to lead us to and keep us on the path of purpose. No matter how much effort is needed, our passion continues to drive us forward to exert the energy necessary to accomplish what is in alignment with our highest ideals and strongest talents. When our dreams coincide with our deepest desires and best gifts, what we do to fulfill them becomes a natural part of who we are and what we are called by God to do. When we embrace our calling, we'll never "work" again because purpose becomes our vocation (a divine call to yield to God's service and our destiny) as opposed to our occupation (usual or principal work as a means of earning a living).

Prayer to Ignite Action:

Father, I answer Your call upon my life to do those things that are in alignment with the path of my purpose. Today, I freely yield my gifts to be used for Your service in the places where You lead me. I choose to accept my vocation as a high calling from You and not as an occupation to merely receiving a paycheck. I realize that You have divinely ordered my steps and I will represent You with humility and gratitude in all I think, say, and do. In Jesus' name. Amen.

DAY 37

Inspiration:

But God, who is rich in mercy, because of His great love with which He loved us, even when we were dead in trespasses, made us alive together with Christ by grace you have been saved), and raised us up together, and made us sit together in the heavenly places in Christ Jesus, that in the ages to come He might show the exceeding riches of His grace in His kindness toward us in Christ Jesus. For by grace you have been saved through faith, and that not of yourselves; it is the gift of God, not of works, lest anyone should boast." ~ Ephesians 2:4-9, New King James Version

Insight:

A favorite hymn of all time is Amazing Grace, for it reminds those who sing and hear it of the mercy of God who, despite our wretched human nature and willful disobedience at times, still extends to us an opportunity to repent and to receive redemption through His Son, Jesus Christ. This same amazing grace removes the shackles from our eyes so that we can see and comprehend the limitless love of our Savior not only for us, but for an entire world of saints and sinners alike. An appreciation for the grace of God also allows us to see life and mankind from a different perspective with eyes of wonder and attitudes of awe. Today, God, we thank You for Your grace, for it is still absolutely and altogether amazing!

Prayer to Ignite Action:

Father, I know that I am undeserving, but I thank You that I am saved today because of Your grace that abounds in my life. Your grace is unfathomable, unsearchable, and indescribable. I rejoice in Your love, grace, and mercy that are measured to me in the exact portion that I need today. Although I do not deserve these wonderful gifts, I freely receive them and will make them known to those who need them as well. In Jesus' name. Amen.

DAY 38

Inspiration:

"Every one who comes to me and hears my words and does them, I will show you what he is like: he is like a man building a house, who dug deep, and laid the foundation upon rock; and when a flood arose, the stream broke against that house, and could not shake it, because it had been well built." ~ Luke 6:47-48, Revised Standard Version

Insight:

My husband used to own a construction company years ago. In fact, this was his full-time occupation and passion—a dream that began shortly after he graduated and decided to go into business for himself. His drive to offer quality work including roofing, renovations and new home construction for deserving clients was the fuel that ignited him to awaken each morning, leaving at what he called "dark thirty" and returning home after the sun set with a sense of accomplishment and fulfillment. He knew that he was building something that his clients would live in and love, and he did it well.

After operating Francisco Construction Company successfully for many years, my husband and I heeded God's call to exchange our passion to build quality homes for a mandate to build quality lives. In October of 1990, we entered full-time ministry and have never regretted that decision. We definitely moved out of our comfort zones and witnessed the transformation of countless lives, including our own. Serving others has a way of bringing out the best in us when we strive for excellence that others can emulate. Seeking avenues for continued spiritual, personal, and professional development for ourselves keeps us on the cutting edge so that we can sharpen those whom God assigns to our sphere of influence. The quality and quantity of time we spend investing in our own growth has a direct impact on our desire to build the lives of others for a better today and a brighter tomorrow.

Prayer to Ignite Action:

Father, I thank You for the firm, secure foundation of Christ upon which

I stand. Because of the stability of my spiritual foundation, I have confidence in the fact that when the storms of life rise, I shall not be moved or swept away. Let my life be a testimony of Your presence, power, and provisions so that I may lead others to You. In Jesus' name. Amen.

DAY 39

Inspiration:
'Come, follow me,' Jesus said, 'and I will make you fishers of men.'" ~ Matthew 4:19, New International Version

Insight:
Countless opportunities to make a difference in the lives of others cross our path each day. Whether we realize it or not, people who we know personally as well as those whom we encounter on a daily basis who are unfamiliar, are watching and listening to us to ascertain how we will respond not only to them, but to life. With that knowledge, we must accept the fact that each of us are leaders within the context of our circle of influence, and as such, we must intentionally invest what we have learned into the lives of others. In an effort to do so, we must first ensure that we invest in ourselves. We cannot give what we have not received. We cannot add value unless we first recognize that there is value in us.

There is greatness in each of us which can only be seen as we share it with others. Our works or achievements are never to gratify ourselves alone; rather, they are simply the avenue to lift ourselves and others to the height of our greatest potential so that God is honored with our time, talents, and treasures and value is multiplied to the people with whom we connect. In this way, we will be sure to make a difference in the world in which we live.

Prayer to Ignite Action:
Heavenly Father, I recognize that I was created to honor You and to make a difference in this world. Let the purpose for which You created me shine through the words I speak and the work I do. Today, I will enjoy my time and existence, knowing that my life is inextricably connected to others who will follow me because I have chosen to follow You. In Jesus' name. Amen.

DAY 40

Inspiration:

But the LORD said to Samuel, 'Do not look at his appearance or at the height of his stature, because I have rejected him; for God sees not as man sees, for man looks at the outward appearance, but the LORD looks at the heart.'" ~ 1 Samuel 16:7, New American Standard Bible

Insight:

Our family went to see the Broadway production of Disney's Beauty & The Beast in New York as well as at a local venue in our vicinity. We all remembered seeing the movie years ago when our daughters were very young, but the actors who played Belle and the Beast brought the story to life by taking the audience on a magical journey to discover that real beauty was not to be found in the superficial exterior of outward appearance, but in the attitude of the heart and the character that one possesses. Beauty is determined by our perspective of life and other people, and it is much deeper than what is seen in the mirror that reflects ourselves and others.

Allow the beauty of God to emanate from you and to be sought out as you relate to others. Life takes on an entirely new meaning when we behold it with our hearts and not just our eyes.

Prayer to Ignite Action:

God, please cultivate in me the ability to see others as You see them. Forgive me for being critical of others because of what my eyes have seen and my ears have heard. Help me not to quickly judge based on appearances, but to be sensitive enough to hear and understand the hearts and to respond to the needs of those You send my way today. In Jesus' name. Amen.

DAY 41

Inspiration:

"These things I have spoken to you, that My joy may remain in you, and [that] your joy may be full." ~ John 15:11, New King James Version

Insight:

There is a stark difference between happiness and joy. Happiness is dependent upon our reaction to what is happening around us, whereas joy is contingent upon our response to the source within us from whence joy comes. Joy is a constant state of mind, spirit, and being that exists even in the midst of changing circumstances. Therefore, we can be joyful when unexpected and unexplainable difficulties arise because we choose to trust God although we may not fully understand what He allows to occur. To maintain internal joy, we must focus on opportunities to view life with gratitude, have a positive attitude, and intentionally express actions that spread joy from ourselves to others. External happiness does not have the same effect, for it is short-lived and only lasts as long as the circumstance or event which caused it. Joy is more potent because the power to possess and profess it is literally within our grasp all the time, irrespective of our outward environment. It is no wonder that Jesus' desire for us is that His joy would remain in us in full measure. Our level of joy and our decision to keep it full, determines how fully we will live in and give to the world.

Prayer to Ignite Action:

Dear Lord, I boldly declare that the joy of the Lord is my strength. I choose to be joyful in my relationships, within the walls of my home, at work, and wherever else I must go today. I will not allow the perceptions, words, and actions of others to detract from or to deter me from experiencing joy--a state of mind, spirit and being that You have given me as a gift. Fill me up, Lord, so that my joy will overflow into the lives of people who desperately need it. In Jesus' name. Amen.

DAY 42

Inspiration:
With all this going for us, my dear, dear friends, stand your ground. And don't hold back. Throw yourselves into the work of the Master, confident that nothing you do for him is a waste of time or effort." ~ 1 Corinthians 15:58, The Message Bible

Insight:
I remember a quote from the movie, "The Great Debaters," which has depth and truth embedded within its words: "We must do what we have to do now so that we can do what we want to do later." I have found that statement to have both spiritual and practical implications when pondering the path my life has taken. I began training for ministry, education and administration, and writing during my pre-teen and adolescent years, with the fulfillment of my future in all of these areas and more unbeknownst to me at the time.

Suffice it to say, I did what I had to do and most importantly, was called to do. Now, because of the preparation forged on my path toward my purpose, I can do what I want to do and enjoy the immense blessings that come with being thankful for what has transpired, and even more excited for what is yet unfolding. I love writing and have the time to do more of it now than ever before. Opportunities to mentor young girls and adult-aged women along the way, give back to worthwhile charities that are making a difference in the lives of children and women, and speak across the country and around the world without sacrificing quality time with family and dear friends, are invaluable, priceless moments that continually fill my heart with inexpressible joy.

What is the lesson in all of this? Simply put, "Doing what has to be done now will afford you the privilege of doing what you want to do later."

Prayer to Ignite Action:
Father, I humbly ask that You will show me what must be completed now in my life. I am sorry for starting and not finishing the assignments

that You sent that were tailor-made just for me. I desire to be faithful in the stewardship of every task and resource that You give me with a grateful heart, knowing that the quality of my future is determined by the decisions and progress I choose to make today. In Jesus' name. Amen.

DAY 43

Inspiration:

The thief does not come except to steal, and to kill, and to destroy. I have come that they may have life, and that they may have [it] more abundantly." ~ John 10:10, New King James Version

Insight:

Jesus came that we may live an abundant life. That doesn't mean that life will be without problems. It does mean, however, that as Christians we have access to the One who possesses all wisdom, strength, and favor to aid us in overcoming challenges that come our way in order to cope, maintain hope, and move beyond the scope of what is seen by keeping our eyes on that which is to come. The attitude of one who overcomes is always positive in the midst of difficult decisions that have to be made and deeds that must be done. This unrelenting mental focus and unmitigated fortitude pushes past problems because of the purpose that drives us forward to experience bigger, better, and brighter horizons ahead.

Today, keep your mind focused upon the promise of your future rather than the problems of your present. Every challenge is an opportunity for you to release creativity, innovation, and the essence of who you are and what you are capable of contributing to the world. Besides, you won't find out what really lies within you until opportunity meets preparation, and when that happens, purpose will always prevail over problems!

Prayer to Ignite Action:

Dear Heavenly Father, I am awed by the fact that Your Son, Jesus, came to earth to show and give to us an abundant life both now and in eternity. Thank You that this life cannot be stolen because it is hidden and secure in You. I cherish my relationship with You, and I will focus on Your promises toward me rather than the problems around me. I accept abundance in every area of my life today and always. In Jesus' name. Amen.

DAY 44

Inspiration:

"But be doers of the word, and not hearers only, deceiving yourselves."
~ James 1:22, New King James Version

Insight:

The sports conglomerate, Nike, successfully branded a phrase that can be applied to all that we dream of endeavoring to accomplish in life--"Just do it!" This simple, yet profound admonition when heeded, puts an end to procrastination, fear, anxiety, lethargy, complacency, intimidation, and limitations. We hold the key to unlocking the mystery of the added value that we can offer to people, places, and predicaments around us when we follow through with what we alone can do. No one can leave an indelible mark upon the world like we can with the unique character, personality, talents, skills, and savvy that we inherently possess. The mere fact that our fingerprints and DNA are individually identifiable attest to the distinguishing difference we each are capable of making to touch the lives of others in ways that no one else can.

Don't wait for others to do what you were born to do. Take Nike's advice and "Just do it!" You will discover the joy in unleashing the latent potential within and the passion of fulfilling purpose that was encoded in your DNA to benefit you and bless those closest to you.

Prayer to Ignite Action:

Father, today I make a commitment to become a doer of Your Word and will for my life and not a hearer only. I will put away all excuses and put forth the necessary effort to do not just what comes easily and naturally to me, but to also stretch myself in ways that push me beyond my comfort zone and into my destiny. No one else can do what I can do like me, but me. With that knowledge, I submit myself totally to You so that the uniqueness of who You created me to be will be an example to others. In Jesus' name. Amen.

DAY 45

Inspiration:

So here's what I want you to do, God helping you: Take your everyday, ordinary life--your sleeping, eating, going-to-work, and walking-around life--and place it before God as an offering. Embracing what God does for you is the best thing you can do for him." ~ Romans 12:1, The Message Bible

Insight:

It is so wonderful to be able to experience life by living it to the fullest until it overflows onto others. We have the opportunity to view and participate in life positively and with intentionality right now. As long as we have breath and the capacity to think and act, then we can choose to live with authenticity, curiosity, and generosity by being who we were created to be, seeking to learn from life, and purposefully giving the best of what we have to offer to God and others to add value to the world around us.

Prayer to Ignite Action:

Dear Lord, I offer my life in its entirety to You today. Everything I am and all that I possess is a result of Your lovingkindness towards me. In return, the least I can do is to give myself and all that I have to You--the best that I can offer. Live in and work through me as only You can. In Jesus' name. Amen.

DAY 46

Inspiration:

"Finally, brothers, whatever is true, whatever is noble, whatever is right, whatever is pure, whatever is lovely, whatever is admirable--if anything is excellent or praiseworthy--think about such things." ~ Philippians 4:8, New International Version

Insight:

Today is a day to think about the goodness of God that overflows in our lives in ways too numerous to name. Thoughts of love, peace, mercy, and thanksgiving should permeate our minds and hearts, causing us to acknowledge and appreciate the greatness of God and the precious gift of people in our lives that we hold dear. When we allow our minds to dwell upon all that is good, there will be no room for entertaining thoughts of doom, depression or despair. We have the power to choose what we should think upon, which will ultimately determine the kind of life we live and the expressions of gratitude that we give.

Prayer to Ignite Action:

Father, too often my mind desires to wander to places and to think about things that are not beneficial to me and others. Forgive me for the times I've allowed my mind to dwell on unhealthy, unholy thoughts. Cleanse my thoughts and purify my heart so that wrong thoughts and motives are replaced by what is pure and praiseworthy today. In Jesus' name. Amen.

DAY 47

Inspiration:

"I returned, and saw under the sun, that the race [is] not to the swift, nor the battle to the strong, neither yet bread to the wise, nor yet riches to men of understanding, nor yet favor to men of skill; but time and chance happeneth to them all." ~ Ecclesiastes 9:11, King James Version

Insight:

Don't depend upon others to do what only you are responsible for accomplishing. Each person is given time and chance, and it is up to you to take advantage of the opportunities that come your way. Choices and concerted effort determine whether you will be living in poverty or prosperity, destitution, or destiny. The embodiment of success or failure is determined by the mindset and what it produces or prevents. There is no one formula for success, but a sure way to embrace a life of significance is to consistently follow principles of faith while putting time and chance to good use daily.

Prayer to Ignite Action:

Heavenly Father, I do not want to take time or chance for granted by wasting them. Open my eyes and ears so that I am aware of divine opportunities that are sent my way today. My desire is to have a life that is significant in its contribution, and I realize that my choices throughout the day will determine the kind of impact I have upon others and my corner of the world. Let the works I do speak for me today. In Jesus' name. Amen

DAY 48

Inspiration:

"For which of you, intending to build a tower, does not sit down first and count the cost, whether he has [enough] to finish [it]." ~ Luke 14:28, New King James Version

Insight:

There's a colloquialism that says, "Put your money where your mouth is." Now, I'm not condoning the act of gambling, but the statement does imply that whatever we say should be backed up by how much we're willing to pay to denote the value or worth of what is desired. Are we willing to back up what we really want with the payment of investing our unique skills and resources so that we can receive what we dream and talk about? Is it worth giving the best of who we are and all we are capable of doing in order to achieve the noteworthy goals that will add immense value to the world around us? If the answer is, yes, then we must rise to the challenge and begin to pay our way forward. In other words, we should be willing to invest in our future by paying with the currency of our time, talents, and treasures. The payoff or reward will be well worth the investment in life for us on earth as well as in Heaven.

Prayer to Ignite Action:

God, I pray for administrative and executive ability today so that I can be astute in my finances as well as in managing the rest of my life's affairs. Help me not to be hasty in making decisions and launching out into the deep without first counting the cost and knowing for sure that I am following where You lead. I choose to respond with faith and forethought with anticipation and expectation of receiving a harvest as I invest into my future. In Jesus' name. Amen.

DAY 49

Inspiration:

Therefore let us, as many as are mature, have this mind; and if in anything you think otherwise, God will reveal even this to you. Nevertheless, to [the degree] that we have already attained, let us walk by the same rule, let us be of the same mind. Brethren, join in following my example, and note those who so walk, as you have us for a pattern." ~ Philippians 3:15-17, New King James Version

Insight:

Before making major decisions of any kind, we must consider the possible implications and consequences of our choices. If a decisions will positively affect us and those closest to us, then we should move full steam ahead with God's guidance. However, if the choices we are about to make will negatively infect our lives and/or the lives of others, then the adverse consequences that could possibly occur should deter us from making wrong, impetuous decisions. Thinking before we act will create a habit of choosing to respond appropriately to life as opposed to reacting inappropriately and suffering the results of wrong choices. Someone else is always watching and listening who may choose to follow our example.

Prayer to Ignite Action:

Father God, I pray that I my thoughts and decisions today will be pleasing in Your sight. The choices I make today are connected to those who are closest to me. I need clarity of thought from You so that I can make decisions that reflect the values that I hold dear to benefit those who I hold near. In Jesus' name. Amen.

DAY 50

Inspiration:

"Then Abraham lifted his eyes and looked, and there behind [him was] a ram caught in a thicket by its horns. So Abraham went and took the ram, and offered it up for a burnt offering instead of his son. And Abraham called the name of the place, The-LORD-Will-Provide; as it is said [to] this day, "In the Mount of the LORD it shall be provided." ~ Genesis 22:13-14, New King James Version

Insight:

"Where there's a will, there's a way." All things are possible if we only believe and do what is necessary to achieve what we expect to receive. When our ideas, intents and the implementation of our plans are inspired by God, then we can rest assured that there will be provision for our vision. I have discovered that God always equips us to do all that He has assigned to our stewardship. Not even the pessimism of the media, the economic indicators of the stock market, or the critical cynicism of would-be dream-killers, can thwart the purpose of God for our lives. What God ordains, He sustains. He anoints whom He appoints and protects whom He selects. That's news that's good enough to celebrate right now! God is with us and for us, particularly as we choose to surrender our dreams and plans to Him so that His purpose for us can prevail.

Prayer to Ignite Action:

Father, You are Jehovah Jireh--God My Provider. Not only are You the God of provision who supplies all my needs, but You are the God of prevision who sees and knows what I need even before I ask. Since You already know what I, my family and others around me need, I thank You, in advance, that we already are provided for and equipped with everything that we should have today. In Jesus' name. Amen.

DAY 51

Inspiration:

"For God has not given us a spirit of fear, but of power and of love and of a sound mind." ~ 2 Timothy 1:7

Insight:

The Bible tells us that the righteous are as bold as a lion (Proverbs 28:1), but does that mean that we as Christians are and never will encounter fear? Of course not! There are instances throughout both the Old and the New Testament alike when God reminds us of just how frail, faulty, and fickle human beings can be--men and women--the strong and the weak, in terms of spiritual and physical growth and development. However, when we decide against using fear as an excuse not to move forward in faith (even when we're afraid), God will show Himself strong on our behalf and cause courage and confidence in Him to conquer F.E.A.R. (False Evidence Appearing Real). I have learned from the lives of men and women in the Bible such as Moses, Joshua, Deborah, Jael, Gideon, David, Priscilla, Lydia, and many other historical and contemporary men and women, that the distinguishing difference between those who are average and ordinary and those who are excellent and extraordinary is the choice made to exercise power, love, and soundness of mind in order to break the bondage of fear and move ahead with the drive to courageously accomplish during the day what others only dare to dream about during the night.

Discouragement is only the willful denial and dismissal of the courage that we already possess within to be who and do what God has already predestined. Don't allow F.E.A.R. to paralyze your potential and purpose, cripple your creativity, or deter your destiny. Today, you have the threefold cord of power, love and a sound mind to defeat the weapons of discouragement and fear. Do all that is in your heart and watch God honor your faith and works in due time!

Prayer to Ignite Action:

Father, You are awesome in all Your works and ways. I am grateful for the courageous spirit You have given me that calms all my fears; love that covers a multitude of sins; and soundness of mind that keeps me in perfect peace as I turn my attention towards You today. There is nothing that I cannot conquer because of Your power at work in me. In Jesus' name. Amen.

DAY 52

Inspiration:

"Don't be misled: No one makes a fool of God. What a person plants, he will harvest. The person who plants selfishness, ignoring the needs of others - ignoring God! - harvests a crop of weeds. All he'll have to show for his life is weeds! But the one who plants in response to God, letting God's Spirit do the growth work in him, harvests a crop of real life, eternal life. So let's not allow ourselves to get fatigued doing good. At the right time we will harvest a good crop if we don't give up, or quit." ~ Galatians 6:7-9, The Message Bible

Insight:

Birthdays are honored occasions in our household because they are earmarks of time that we intentionally set-aside to acknowledge, admire and appreciate each other in celebration of the invaluable contribution of the person whose life God has extended to make an irreplaceable impact upon us. We strive to invest our time, talents and treasures not only on birthdays, but every day to show how much we value one another.

I was reminded of the value of time as our family saw the movie, "In Time." It was a sobering cinematic saga depicting the difference between the haves and the have nots, the prosperous and the poor. All of them had to decide what they would do with the time they had and how much they really valued it, for it was to be exchanged as currency for anything they truly desired. We all must do the same in determining the value of our time, ourselves, as well as that of others while assessing not how much we can get, but how much we are truly willing to give. The principle of "Sowing and Reaping" (also known as "The Law of Reciprocity") will ensure that we will ultimately benefit from making the right choices regarding who and what we value most.

Prayer to Ignite Action:

Dear God, today I will give the best of who I am and what I have as a seed sown in fertile ground. I pray that I may see a tangible harvest from seeds I've sown in words spoken, deeds done, and resources given. As I result, I give my time, talents, and treasures cheerfully. In Jesus' name. Amen.

DAY 53

Inspiration:

"For a dream comes through much activity, And a fool's voice [is known] by [his] many words." ~ Ecclesiastes 5:3, New King James Version

Insight:

Today is given to us by the mercy and divine providence of God to stand up, step up and follow up with what we are capable of doing to determine the quality of life that we will have beyond today. There are many well-intentioned people who dream and talk big, but the distinguishing factor between the big dreamer and talker and the one who actually lives his or her dreams is what is done each day to make what the mind meditates upon and the mouth mutters come true. Now is our opportunity to activate our dreams and words with actions so that we become the miracles we dream and talk about and look for unapologetically. Let's not wait for something to happen tomorrow that can be realized and materialized by exerting extraordinary effort today. Short-term pain now for long-term gain later is well worth the sacrifice of making hard but necessary decisions, persistently pursuing after purpose, and acting upon the passions that God places within our hearts.

Prayer to Ignite Action:

Heavenly Father, I appreciate that You still allow me to dream. I pray that the dreams that I do have will be inspired by You, and that they will be large enough to include You and to benefit many people so that I cannot accomplish it with my ability alone. Today, please help my mind and mouth to work together synergistically so that my dreams are fulfilled in my future because of what I choose to pursue today. In Jesus' name. Amen.

DAY 54

Inspiration:
Create in me a clean heart, O God, And renew a steadfast spirit within me." ~ Psalm 51:10

Insight:
Have you ever asked yourself the question, "What is the motivation behind what I am doing?" If not, this is an important question to both ask and answer for reflection and self-evaluation to determine whether your ideas and actions are for personal gain alone or inspired by God for the good of others.

I have served on many church and community boards, and the work can range anywhere from tiresome to tedious, to tangibly rewarding once I remind myself of the reason or purpose that compelled me to become involved in the beginning. Asking and answering that question gives you the fuel to finish what you've started in your personal and professional life as you discover the motivation for your life's mission. I encourage you to also find the value in examining why you do what you do, and if there is none to your satisfaction, reinvent yourself by rediscovering your purpose and intentionally seeking to add value to those in your sphere of influence with the unique distinctiveness of your character and capabilities. The return will be well worth the investment.

Prayer to Ignite Action:
Heavenly Father, teach me how to be content and complete in the arenas and with the assignments You've given me. Please help me to develop the areas where improvement and refinement are most needed in and around me while maintaining motives that are pure and purposeful. When the seasons in my life change, lead me in recognizing and responding to those changes in ways that will bring out the best in me and others. In Jesus' name. Amen.

DAY 55

Inspiration:

Then the King will say to those on His right hand, 'Come, you blessed of My Father, inherit the kingdom prepared for you from the foundation of the world: for I was hungry and you gave Me food; I was thirsty and you gave Me drink; I was a stranger and you took Me in; I [was] naked and you clothed Me; I was sick and you visited Me; I was in prison and you came to Me....Assuredly I say to you, inasmuch as you did [it] to one of the least of these My brethren, you did [it] to Me.'" ~ Matthew 25:34-36, 40b

Insight:

I read a profound quote by philosopher, William James, years ago while taking a spiritual leadership course in seminary. He stated that, "The best use of one's life is to spend it for something that will outlast it. Life's value is not in its duration but its donation--not in how long we live, but how fully and how well." I shall never forget that, because it left an indelible mark upon my mind and heart to heighten the awareness of who I am in Christ and what He has invested in me so that I, in turn, can be motivated to invest what I have into the lives of others. Offering the best of who we are can only be done as a result of acknowledging who we are in light of God's Word and what our purpose is according to His predestined plan for our lives. To be filled ourselves so that we can fulfill our purpose requires staying connected to God through personal prayer, meditation and worship; attending and actively participating in our local church; and intentionally reaching out to others with compassion, concern, and more importantly, the light of Christ. We can offer our best when we determine to be our best at all times. Opportunities to do so are as endless as the possibilities that exist within us to unleash our latent potential, which reminds us to give our best by living fully and well daily.

Prayer to Ignite Action:

Father, please give me a heart that beats like Yours so that I may nourish and nurture those who hunger in thirst physically and spiritually in my presence, today. Make me aware of those who need to be healed, clothed and set free from bondages and brokenness. Use me as a channel through which Your blessings can flow as I become Your hands and feet today. In Jesus' name. Amen.

DAY 56

Inspiration:

"Words kill, words give life; they're either poison or fruit--you choose."
~ Proverbs 18:21, The Message Bible

Insight:

One Sunday, my husband preached a sermon to remind us of "The Law of Choice"--a power that is within each of us given by God to determine our own destiny. We can choose to live a blessed life of abundance in every area, or a mundane life of meager existence which is really beneath our inheritance as heirs of God and joint heirs with Jesus Christ. We can choose life or death, blessings or curses by the words that proceed from our mouths which are a direct result of what we choose to meditate upon and therefore, speak and follow through with our actions. This is the only life we get on earth before we inherit our eternal life, so we must be good stewards of it. Here are two powerful quotes to motivate us to make the most out of the life that God has entrusted to us by making quality choices:

"We make a living by what we get; we make a life by what we give."
~ Winston Churchill

"We manage the most valuable asset that God has, and that is life."
~ Bishop L. W. Francisco III

Prayer to Ignite Action:

Dear Lord, today I desire to become more mindful of the words that escape from my mouth. I ask for wisdom in choosing to speak positively to edify those closest to me. Let my words be kind and my ears attentive to listen with care so that I may respond with compassion. I choose life and blessings, and declare that they will abound in abundance in my conversation, conduct and even in the company I keep today. In Jesus' name. Amen.

DAY 57

Inspiration:

"Work from the heart for your real Master, for God, confident that you'll get paid in full when you come into your inheritance. Keep in mind always that the ultimate Master you're serving is Christ." ~ Colossians 3:23-24, The Message Bible

Insight:

Colossians 3:23-24 gives us wise advice regarding how we are to approach life each day: These verses remind us that all of life's efforts at home, work, church, in our community, and abroad for others and ourselves, should be done not to please people, but to please our audience of One -- the Lord Jesus Christ. Because we are called to serve Him with our efforts, we are to harness our energy to accomplish all that is assigned to us in a manner that is excellent, efficient and effective in every area of our lives. The choice to do so will have both earthly and eternal rewards.

Prayer to Ignite Action:

Father, I appreciate the opportunities given me to serve people in a variety of ways each day. Although serving people is a noble undertaking, it is to and for You that my service is devoted and committed. My desire is to please You with the life that I live and deeds that I give. Today, empower me to remain focused upon You--my Creator, Owner and Lord. In Jesus' name. Amen.

DAY 58

Inspiration:
"Before I formed you in the womb I knew you; Before you were born I sanctified you; I ordained you a prophet to the nations." ~ Jeremiah 1:5, New King James Version

Insight:
God reiterates to Jeremiah in this verse that He knows him, which implies both present and ongoing thought and deliberation about everything that concerns Jeremiah's purpose and well being. His best interest was on the mind and heart of God, and so is ours. We need to accept that God both knows and wants what is best for us, and that is why it is imperative that we take time to know God and His plans for us (rather than just our own). The events and experiences of our past, present, and future can be used by God as a mirror reflection of our life to promote peace, health, wholeness, and hope for ourselves and others for a greater purpose.

Allow God to reflect the best in you onto the world so that His purpose for your life can prevail. Living your life intentionally and fully with a heart of thanksgiving may also help to propel others toward their purpose as a result of your enthusiastic willingness to fulfill your life's mission.

Prayer to Ignite Action:
God, I give You praise for using my life to prepare me to fulfill my purpose. You knew me before I was placed in the womb of my mother, and I know that Your thoughts and plans for me are for my good. Today, I will listen for Your direction that I may follow it and lead others to You in all that I do. In Jesus' name. Amen.

DAY 59

Inspiration:

"You serve me a six-course dinner right in front of my enemies. You revive my drooping head; my cup brims with blessing. Your beauty and love chase after me every day of my life. I'm back home in the house of GOD for the rest of my life." ~ Psalm 23:5-6, The Message Bible

Insight:

We have the power to imagine the best or the worst for our lives by employing excellent thoughts or entertaining an excuse-laden mindset. The choice is ours to make to either wake up and get going with gusto (which is "hearty or keen enjoyment in action or speech"), or to wake up and give in to the gauntlet of fear, frustration, apathy and mediocrity-- characteristic traits of those who refuse to become fully involved in life because they'd rather sit on the sidelines while watching and criticizing others.

God's beauty and love only follow those who adequately prepare themselves to receive His blessings as a result of giving themselves wholly to knowing and obeying Him even in the midst of life's difficulties. That's what David discerned in the latter portion of the Psalm 23 passage. We are revived by God to seize opportunities and overcome obstacles that confront us daily. God has already prepared a table for us beforehand to equip us with all we need to serve Him and to do good towards others, and that includes loving, praying for and doing good towards our enemies. When we are serious about accomplishing all that we are capable of doing with a spirit of excellence, then God will ensure that beauty and love continue to follow us as our reward.

Prayer to Ignite Action:

Heavenly Father, to You I run when I feel overwhelmed and powerless, for I know that You will revive me in Your presence. With renewed strength, I will face all that this day brings my way. Nothing will separate me from Your love and beauty, for it is in me, all around me and following me all the days of my life. In Jesus' name. Amen.

DAY 60

Inspiration:

"In everything give thanks; for this is the will of God in Christ Jesus for you." ~ 1 Thessalonians 5:18, New King James Version

Insight:

I often think of how grateful I am for all the opportunities God has given me to share who He is with others through my life wherever, whenever, and however He opens the door and leads me to walk through it. As we surrender our mind, heart, and will to God, He will in turn direct us to do what He desires, which will cause us to be fulfilled as well. I've heard it said that "the safest place to be is in the will of God" and I couldn't agree more. There is so much peace and joy when we are in the center of God's will and the expression of being in such a place is simply a heart of gratitude, hands that are willing to serve, and feet that are ready to go and share the gospel in our sphere of influence. This kind of generous living causes us to respond with thoughts and actions of thanksgiving.

Prayer to Ignite Action:

Dear God, I am so thankful for all You've done for me. I have been blessed with family, relationships, and opportunities to represent You in so many ways. Most of all, I thank You for revealing Your will and ways to me so that I may know You more. I want to be found in the center of Your will, for that is where I find safety, security, joy, and peace. In Jesus' name. Amen.

DAY 61

Inspiration:

Give to every man that asketh of thee; and of him that taketh away thy goods ask [them] not again." ~ Luke 6:30, King James Version

Insight:

We are given the opportunity each day to make our lives count by giving ourselves away in the sense of sharing our natural gifts, developed skills, words of wisdom and encouragement, acts of kindness and/or tangible resources when, where and with whom God leads us. As we take the time to focus on making a difference in the world by being the difference we desire to see, we'll find that our efforts will extraordinarily impact those around us and ultimately leave a legacy of love and good works which will provoke others to do the same. The only way to change our home, community, nation and world is to start with ourselves by becoming excellent stewards of the inner and outer resources that God has given us. Then, our efforts will matter not only in our lifetime, but well into eternity.

Prayer to Ignite Action:

Father, my gifts, skills and abilities are a blessing from You. Teach me how to maximize what You've given me to please You and to bless the lives of others today. I will live in such a way that my life will make a difference to create a legacy for generations to come. In Jesus' name. Amen.

DAY 62

Inspiration:

"So go ahead. Eat your food with joy, and drink your wine with a happy heart, for God approves of this!...Whatever you do, do well. For when you go to the grave, there will be no work or planning or knowledge or wisdom."
Ecclesiastes 9:7 & 10, New Living Translation

Insight:

Life should not be a drudgery to live, or taken for granted and as a result, misused and abused. Life is simply time gift-wrapped daily to be opened, appreciated and enjoyed in the present. In fact, we should think of our individual life as an appreciating asset that becomes better, wiser and more valuable each day, regardless of our age. We have the incredible opportunity to live in such a way as to gain the maximum benefit out of life based on what we give to add meaning not only to our lives but to others who are impacted and influenced by our decisions and deeds. We've heard it said, "When life deals you lemons, make lemonade." That simply means that circumstances do not dictate to us whether or not we will enjoy life. We choose by our own approach and response, not to be dissuaded or deterred from living abundantly because we have the right and the responsibility to get out of life exactly what we put into it, and to enjoy the journey along the way.

Prayer to Ignite Action:

Heavenly Father, You have given me this day to enjoy and to live to its fullest. I pray that my desire to honor You in all I do causes me to appreciate my time and existence here on earth while striving to make the best use of every relationship and resource I have. I will cheerfully live, work and even set aside time to have fun today. In Jesus' name. Amen.

DAY 63

Inspiration:

"'Look!' he said. 'The people are united, and they all speak the same language. After this, nothing they set out to do will be impossible for them!'" ~ Genesis 11:6, New Living Translation

Insight:

Robert Schuller once made a profound statement regarding anything we desire out of life or from ourselves: "If it is to be, it is up to me." This is a prolific, profound statement that places the responsibility for our dreams and goals into our hands. No one else has the responsibility to make our life joyful or miserable for that matter. It is solely up to us to determine what we will do with the time and talents that we have. With God's help, there is nothing we cannot achieve or receive if we only believe and do the work necessary to fulfill our deepest desires (with the right motives, of course). I can do it and so can you if we only imagine what is possible. Once we set our minds to it, we must do it!

Prayer to Ignite Action:

God, I am so grateful for the opportunity to think critically and plan strategically. But more important than both of these is the motive and intent of my heart. Today, please give me purity of heart, clarity of mind and continuity of purpose so that the things that I do for You, others and myself are done for the right reason. I will be glad today, knowing that Your are guiding me in all my ways. In Jesus' name. Amen.

DAY 64

Inspiration:
"A man [that hath] friends must shew himself friendly: and there is a friend [that] sticketh closer than a brother." ~ Proverbs 18:24, King James Version

Insight:
The kind of friends we surround ourselves with as well as the choices we make regarding what we think about, will influence what we say and do and therefore, either positively or negatively impact our daily living. We do not have what we necessarily want, but we have in life the sum of what we choose to think about moment by moment.

Corrie ten Boom, a Dutch Christian who survived the horrors of Hitler's concentration camps during World War II, often said, "Look within and be depressed. Look without and be distressed. Look at Jesus and be at rest."

We have the power to use Jesus as our Prince of Peace to model our lives after in order to be at peace. The Bible rightly states for us to "let this mind be in [us] which was also in Christ Jesus" (Philippians 2:5) who despite the trials and persecutions of life, determined to endure and persevere in order to fulfill His purpose--all because He harnessed the power to make the right choices. We can do the same.

Prayer to Ignite Action:
Dear Lord, I pray for discernment in cultivating the relationships and friendships in my life that are meant to be. I also ask You for the courage to recognize and reevaluate the associations in my life that are detrimental to my spiritual and emotional growth and development. Strengthen me to follow the example of Jesus who chose His associations wisely so that He could fulfill His purpose. I trust You for the wisdom and insight to make the right decisions for the sake of those You have assigned to me as well as my own destiny. In Jesus' name. Amen.

DAY 65

Inspiration:

"Do not lay up for yourselves treasures on earth, where moth and rust destroy and where thieves break in and steal; but lay up for yourselves treasures in heaven, where neither moth nor rust destroys and where thieves do not break in and steal. For where your treasure is, there your heart will be also." ~ Matthew 6:19-21, New King James Version

Insight:

The pursuit of outward prosperity and possessions should not be the litmus test of what makes one rich. True wealth does not come from seeking to be rich financially or materially, but it is found when we choose to serve and obey God with a pure heart by following after His will rather than money. We are truly rich when we give of ourselves to enrich the lives of others and the world. Matthew 6:19-21 reminds us that the abundance of riches does not come from what we heap up for ourselves. Rather, the richness we are to experience should emanate from within as a result of what we inwardly hold dear in our hearts. That is where our real treasure should be, and that is what we should share with others.

Prayer to Ignite Action:

Father, remind me today of who and what truly matters. I thank You for the importance and value of the people placed in my life, especially those closest to me. Today, please help me to focus on finding time to appreciate them and to help those who are less fortunate by giving of myself to invest in them. Although I am grateful for what I possess here on earth, I am even more grateful for the treasures I will have in Heaven as a result of serving You. In Jesus' name. Amen.

DAY 66

Inspiration:

"A good life gets passed on to the grandchildren; ill-gotten wealth ends up with good people." ~ Proverbs 13:22, The Message Bible

Insight:

Where we choose to place our focus will determine the level of effort, enthusiasm and effectiveness we have regarding what matters most to us. We give the best of ourselves to that which gives meaning and adds value to our lives. Given this premise, we must examine, and if necessary, reevaluate our relationships, core values, and life's work. Our choices and the actions that follow them will be either positive and therefore productive, or negative and therefore, nonproductive. Today, make your choices count not just for you, but for those who will follow behind you.

Prayer to Ignite Action:

Father, open my spiritual eyes so that I can understand fully that life is about much more than I can physically see right now. I desire for my life to count so that I can leave an inheritance (both spiritually and materially) to those who will follow in my footsteps. May the trajectory of my life and that of generations to follow move onward and upward for the sake of expanding Your kingdom in the earth. In Jesus' name. Amen.

DAY 67

Inspiration:

"I, wisdom, dwell with prudence, and find out knowledge [and] discretion." ~ Proverbs 8:12, New King James Version

Insight:

There is an age-old adage that says, "Necessity is the mother of invention." When I think about the creative energy that has been birthed out of necessity in my own life as a result of experiencing difficult times, I know for sure that this adage is a truism. Many entrepreneurs initiate their ideas and brand their businesses in the midst of challenging environments. Difficulties and disappointments oftentimes serve as the driving force for those who are persistent and perseverant to achieve more than they would have otherwise if circumstances were ideal. Besides, true leadership is tested not when times are good, but when times are not so good.

Wisdom is defined as skill, shrewdness, and ethics which is to live alongside prudence. Possessing this pair of twins (wisdom and prudence) allows us to cautiously manage the practical matters and resources in our lives with discretion and care, not just for our own interests, but also for the interests of others.

Prayer to Ignite Action:

God, You are Omniscient in knowing and discerning all things. Your manifold wisdom is unfathomable to me, which is why I know I need it to make sense of the affairs in my life. Grant me wisdom to make ethical decisions that reflect my core beliefs, financial decisions that will yield prosperity, and discernment so that I can balance my life and relationships with wisdom and prudence. In Jesus' name. Amen.

DAY 68

Inspiration:

"And do this, understanding the present time. The hour has come for you to wake up from your slumber, because our salvation is nearer now than when we first believed." ~ Romans 13:11, New International Version

Insight:

No matter what happened in our past or what grandiose dreams we have for our future, we must not neglect the nearsightedness of now. Properly meditating upon and managing the myopic perspective of this moment in time will cause us to make full use of every opportunity that comes our way with the knowledge that how we view today and what we do with it is paramount. I have heard it stated that "Yesterday is history and tomorrow is a mystery; today is a gift which is why it is called the present." When we focus on the opportunity of now as being a gift that can only be opened with an emphasis on the present, then we won't spend an inordinate amount of time pondering the past or fretting about the future. The word now is mentioned 1,356 times in 1,321 verses in the King James Version of the Bible to remind us of the importance of capturing and treasuring the moment of time that is measured to us. With the gift of now presently in focus, let us live and learn from each moment faithfully and fully.

Prayer to Ignite Action:

Lord, I find joy in knowing that salvation is a gift from You to be treasured and that time is also a gift from You to be measured. Help me to enjoy my life and to employ my time so that both are managed wisely. Keep me focused on my present so that I do not wallow in my past or become anxious about my future. Today is the day that You have made, and I will rejoice and make full use of it now. In Jesus' name. Amen.

DAY 69

Inspiration:

"As it is written: 'I have made you a father of many nations.' He is our father in the sight of God, in whom he believed--the God who gives life to the dead and calls things that are not as though they were." ~ Romans 4:17, New International View

Insight:

The mind is a marvelous montage of information extracted from our experiences and images inspired by our imagination. It is completely up to us to use this information and these images to ignite us to pursue a quality of life and lifestyle that brings God pleasure and fulfills our purpose. We will not change our belief system unless what we believe fails to produce the results intended. Therefore, if the information and images etched upon the canvas of our minds are not producing the desired outcome, we must use the power of imagination to see what will be and allow our faith, conversation and actions to move us from the state of meditation to the stage of manifestation. Simply put, we must adopt the mindset of Abraham who was also known as the father of faith, who "called those things that be not as though they were." Abraham was able to align his words and actions with what he first imagined in his mind to see before it ever came into being. The imagination is strong enough to attract what is believed so that what we see as a mental image is what will eventually be seen in physical form. The imagination is a powerful tool for us to use.

Prayer to Ignite Action:

Heavenly Father, our faith is what moves You to act on behalf of Your people. Today, I will use my faith to imagine life as You originally designed it to be--superior in quality and superabundant in quantity. I refuse to settle for less than Your best for me and I will not tolerate mediocrity. Let my level of faith increase and my response to bring out the best in others increase as well. In Jesus' name. Amen.

DAY 70

Inspiration:

"And they overcame him by the blood of the Lamb, and by the word of their testimony; and they loved not their lives unto the death." ~ Revelation 12:11, King James Version

Insight:

I remember watching episodes of The Flip Wilson Show as a little girl. Before the days of Tyler Perry's Madea, comedian Flip Wilson would dress up in a costume with the persona of a character by the name of Geraldine who would often blame her poor choices, bad attitudes and misfortunes on the devil. Her infamous phrase was, "The devil made me do it." It was comical at the time, but as I've grown older, I've witnessed the same excuse used by several to justify wrong patterns of thinking, bad behavior and what befalls them in life. When that happens, it is not at all comical, but counterproductive for those who fall prey to such negativity.

Rather than having an excuse-laden mentality of blame and accusation against the devil, other people, or circumstances, we must focus on the time, opportunities, resources, and the people God places in our lives for a reason, a season or a lifetime to help bring the best out of us and vice versa. Adapting this kind of positive attitude and sharpening our focus by living life fully, intentionally and purposefully, does not allow time for erroneous excuses, pity parties or doldrums of depression. The devil may come to tempt us to succumb to such negativity, but he can't make us do anything (contrary to Geraldine's statement) unless we choose to give him the power that belongs to us to overcome by the blood of Jesus and our testimony. Positivity alone is not the answer, but the power we possess in praying, professing, praising and purposeful living gives us the victory!

Prayer to Ignite Action:

God, today I have the victory to overcome any situation in my life because of Jesus Christ's sacrifice on Calvary's Cross and the confession of my faith. I thank You for being Lord of my life and for the strength that I possess because of Christ living in me. I praise You and profess that this is a great day to share my testimony with others. In Jesus' name. Amen.

DAY 71

Inspiration:

"Do you not know? Have you not heard? The Everlasting God, the LORD, the Creator of the ends of the earth does not become weary or tired. His understanding is inscrutable." ~ Isaiah 40:28, New American Standard Bible

Insight:

God created all things by His wisdom. Since we are made in His image and likeness, surely we possess creative power that can be put to good use to make the world a better place in which to live. We can create the kind of life we desire to live by following God's Master plan. The Bible gives us detailed instructions regarding our relationship with God and people as well as the art of abundant living and creative thinking.

Allow creative ideas to flow through you today as you determine to live abundantly. What may have been viewed as obstacles are really opportunities that will bring out the brilliance in you for the sake of building character, confidence, and creativity in yourself and others.

Prayer to Ignite Action:

Lord, You are my Creator and my God. You know all about me and my capabilities because You originally designed me. I ask for Your creative Spirit--the same Spirit that spoke the heavens and the earth and all that is in them into existence--to think through, speak to and work in me. Please give me new ideas and methods that will prove to be useful and productive to me and the people I serve today. I thank You that creativity dwells in me now. In Jesus' name. Amen.

DAY 72

Inspiration:
"For the Son of Man came to seek and save those who are lost." ~ Luke 19:10, New Living Translation

Insight:
When Jesus lived on earth, He revealed His mission statement to His disciples so that they would know who He was and why His Father sent Him. This statement succinctly shared why Jesus was able to put up with people who either misunderstood Him or stood with Him during His earthly ministry, crucifixion, death, burial and resurrection, without losing focus. How powerful!

Corporate and nonprofit entities often have mission statements consisting of core values or principles that guide business practices and the service that its target audience of owners and customers expect. In like manner, we should have a personal mission statement that guides our behavior and delivers a promise of serving those in our sphere of influence. That mission becomes our life's charge or work not just because we've chosen to do it, but because we sense that it is what we are called and equipped by God to accomplish for the sake of pleasing Him and being a blessing to other people.

Prayer to Ignite Action:
Father, I thank you for the example Jesus gave in identifying and declaring His own mission statement--"to seek and to save those who are lost." Lead me in identifying the mission statement upon which my life is founded and my purpose is grounded. I pray that I will be led to unashamedly declare my mission and to live it with intensity and intentionality today. In Jesus' name. Amen.

DAY 73

Inspiration:

"God's kingdom isn't a matter of what you put in your stomach, for goodness' sake. It's what God does with your life as he sets it right, puts it together, and completes it with joy." ~ Romans 14:17, The Message Bible

Insight:

We are responsible for our own thoughts, decisions and actions which will either contribute to or collide with our joy. When we determine to live in such a way as to focus upon that which draws upon the essence of who we are, provoking us to push beyond our comfort zones to add value to the world around us through our living and giving, then we'll find that we fill our sphere of influence and ourselves with inexpressible joy. That is because the moment we discover the essence of who we are and what we are called to do, is the exact moment when our God-given personality, potential, purpose and passion meet with opportunities that are as original as God created us to be...and only we are able to seize those opportunities that come our way to fulfill our joy.

Prayer to Ignite Action:

Father, teach me to be alert and watchful in my choices so that my life reflects the collective wisdom of the choices I've made. I pray for opportunities that coincide with my interests, talents and skill set to come my way. Let me take full advantage of each opportunity because of the preparation process I have experienced. I have joy and God's favor today. In Jesus' name. Amen.

DAY 74

Inspiration:

"But thanks be to God, who in Christ always leads us in triumph, and through us spreads the fragrance of the knowledge of him everywhere."
~ 2 Corinthians 2:14, Revised Standard Version

Insight:

We have the final victory because of the finished work of Jesus Christ who died and rose again. Our ability to be triumphant is not predicated upon the predicaments that befall us from day to day. Rather, our choice to rejoice comes as a result of our personal relationship with God and the assurance of knowing that we can have joy in spite of the juxtapositions of our life's journey. Joy differs from happiness in that it comes from the inner resource of our spirit which is connected to the inexhaustible Well of Joy, Jesus Christ, who lives within us. Happiness, on the other hand, is dependent upon "what is happening." Instead of focusing on what is happening and letting that determine whether or not we will be happy, let us keep our minds firmly fixed on the fact that we are already victorious in every situation because of Christ who lives in us.

Prayer to Ignite Action:

God, I give You thanksgiving for every encounter that I will face today, knowing in advance that because of Christ I am already triumphant. Let my words be filled with faith and victory as an expression of what is also in my heart. There is nothing too difficult for You, and therefore, there is nothing too difficult for me and those I intercede for in prayer today. In Jesus' name. Amen.

DAY 75

Inspiration:

"See then that ye walk circumspectly, not as fools, but as wise, Redeeming the time, because the days are evil." ~ Ephesians 5:15-16, King James Version

Insight:

Now is the time to take advantage of the precious commodity of time that God gives to us each day. Ephesians 5:16 admonishes us to make full use of each moment by "redeeming the time." The Greek word for redeeming in this verse according to Strong's Concordance is "exagorazo," which means: (1) to redeem by payment of a price to recover from the power of another, to ransom, buy off (metaphorically of Christ freeing the elect from the dominion of the Mosaic Law at the price of his vicarious death); (2) to buy up, to buy up for one's self, for one's use; to make wise and sacred use of every opportunity for doing good, so that zeal and well doing are as it were the purchase money by which we make the time our own.

Suffice it to say, the only way to refute the evil of the day in which we live is to redeem the time we have been given, knowing that the ransom of Jesus' sacrificial death and glorious resurrection has recovered us from the power of the enemy, restored our fellowship with God the Father, and renewed our purpose and passion for using the commodity of time wisely to do good. We've been given each minute to put ourselves in it to win it!

Prayer to Ignite Action:

Lord, You are the originator and progenitor of time, and you measure it out so that each of us has exactly the same amount. Please teach me how to properly prioritize and organize the activities of my day so that I can use my time wisely to do good works. I thank You for trusting me with the wonderful resource of time and I will respect it as a precious commodity to be guarded and guided accordingly. In Jesus' name. Amen.

DAY 76

Inspiration:

"And everyone who competes [for the prize] is temperate in all things. Now they [do it] to obtain a perishable crown, but we [for] an imperishable [crown]." 1 Corinthians 9:25, New King James Version

Insight:

We need not wait for perfect conditions to exist to follow and live our dreams. The sooner we realize that perfect conditions and people do not exist, the closer we will be to setting and accomplishing our goals. We live beneath our privileges when we settle for mediocrity and surrender to procrastination which will only lead to stagnation. Simplistic advice to motivate us to move from dreaming to doing is found in this imperative command: "Get it done!" Don't wait...initiate and activate!

Prayer to Ignite Action:

Heavenly Father, You are a God of excellence who does all things well. I desire to represent You by being a good steward of the assignments that I am to complete today. I will not compare myself with others, for no one has the exact personality and abilities that You have given me to pursue my distinct purpose. Help me to focus on the race You have set for me to run and to stay in my own lane. My eyes are focused on the eternal rewards that I will receive for serving You with excellence. In Jesus' name. Amen.

DAY 77

Inspiration:

"They shall still bear fruit in old age; They shall be fresh and flourishing, To declare that the LORD is upright; [He is] my rock, and [there is] no unrighteousness in Him." ~ Psalm 92:14-15, New King James Version

"Let no one despise your youth, but be an example to the believers in word, in conduct, in love, in spirit, in faith, in purity." ~ 1 Timothy 4:12, New King James Version

Insight:

We're never too old to learn. Likewise, we're never too young to teach. No matter what our age, we have something to give and to gain when we place ourselves in a position both to sharpen and to be sharpened by others. To do so requires that we move beyond our comfort zones in a quest to receive wisdom, knowledge and understanding of life and how to master it by first seeking to master ourselves. The mere accumulation of information is useless unless we discern how to appropriately apply it in our lives and areas of influence in ways that intentionally expand our thoughts and therefore, our actions. Life is only lived without limitations when we decide to become our best, brightest, and most brilliant selves.

Prayer to Ignite Action:

Father, I will not complain about my age, but I will be thankful for the years I have lived and the lessons I have learned. I know I have so much more to learn so that I can share wisdom with others who need it. Strengthen me today to be fruitful and faithful with what I have so that I may become resourceful and relevant in this generation. Stretch me by moving me out of my comfort zone so that I can learn from and teach those who do not look or act like me so that I and those I meet may become spiritually mature. In Jesus' name. Amen.

DAY 78

Inspiration:

"O LORD, you have examined my heart and know everything about me. You know when I sit down or stand up. You know my thoughts even when I'm far away. You see me when I travel and when I rest at home. You know everything I do. You know what I am going to say even before I say it, LORD. You go before me and follow me. You place your hand of blessing on my head. Such knowledge is too wonderful for me, too great for me to understand!" ~ Psalm 139:1-6, New Living Translation

Insight:

My husband (L. W. Francisco III) makes this emphatic statement often in his sermons: "No one can do what you can do like you, but you." The reason why this is obvious, of course, is because although others may try to imitate or emulate, they can never duplicate you or the purpose for which you were created. You are as unique as your fingerprints, DNA, personality, innate gifts, developed skills and abilities. It is totally up to you as to how well you choose to express your distinct individuality to the world, for in so doing, you will add tremendous value to the people and world around you like no one else can in ways that will glorify God, edify others, and satisfy your pursuit of purpose. There is greatness inside of you, so be sure to unleash it for all to see!

Prayer to Ignite Action:

God, I am in awe of the fact that there is nothing about me or that concerns me that takes You by surprise. Your Spirit is always with me to lead me in the path that You have chosen for me. Today, I willingly submit to Your guidance so that I can be who You created me to be. Because You are great, I realize that there is greatness in me to be shared with the world. In Jesus' name. Amen.

DAY 79

Inspiration:

"But I have pleaded in prayer for you, Simon, that your faith should not fail. So when you have repented and turned to me again, strengthen your brothers." ~ Luke 22:32, New Living Translation

Insight:

None of us is perfect, and because of that we may make wrong choices, mistakes, and therefore, experience failure just like Simon Peter. However, there is a perfect God living within us when our lives are totally surrendered to Him who, even in our human frailty of failure, loves us unconditionally and offers mercy and grace to help us in our deepest times of need. I have learned that failure is not the end, and it may serve as the catalyst to catapult us towards a closer relationship with God and unlock the door of creativity as we learn to fail (and sometimes, even fall) forward instead of backwards. The goal is to keep moving in the direction of destiny and not to falter because of failure or detour due to defeat. So here's the lesson: even when we fail, we must learn how to fail forward. God is still with us as long as we stay on His winning team.

Prayer to Ignite Action:

Father, I ask for You to forgive me for my shortcomings and failures. Thank You for believing in me and thinking the best about me. Undergird my faith today so that it will not fail, but flourish. You are my strength when I am weak as I lean and depend upon You. In Jesus' name. Amen.

DAY 80

Inspiration:

"As I arrived on the outskirts of Damascus about noon, a blinding light blazed out of the skies and I fell to the ground, dazed. I heard a voice: 'Saul, Saul, why are you out to get me?' 'Who are you, Master?' I asked. He said, 'I am Jesus the Nazarene, the One you're hunting down.' My companions saw the light, but they didn't hear the conversation. Then I said, 'What do I do now, Master?'...You are to be a key witness to everyone you meet of what you've seen and heard. So what are you waiting for? Get up and get yourself baptized, scrubbed clean of those sins and personally acquainted with God.'" Acts 22:6-10a, 15-16, The Message Bible

Insight:

A prime example of a person who was converted from the legalism of religion to the liberty found in having a relationship with Christ was Saul of Tarsus, who after his Damascus Road experience with Jesus, became Paul. Before he was converted, Saul thought he was justified in persecuting Christians and consenting to the death of Stephen in the book of Acts. Paul's belief system was staunch and his behavior was stalwart in his "self-justified wrongdoing" until Jesus got His attention by speaking directly to Him while he traveled on the road to Damascus. That was when Paul, after experiencing the reality of Jesus who pursued him for the purpose of having a relationship with him, was converted immediately. Soon, Paul began to see, think, and therefore, act differently with his newfound relationship with Christ. His name change represented a change in his behavior and assignment. Instead of persecuting and consenting to the killing of Christians, he would now pursue a relationship with them and seek to relate to sinners to share with them what it meant to have a relationship with God through Jesus Christ--one that was possible no matter how horrendous one's past was.

Real conversion carries with it the evidence of real change in our creed, conduct, conversation, and companions. The past has no hold on our present or our future when we allow Christ to convert us from the inside out. Thus, the difference in having religion versus having a relationship with Christ can be seen in the fruit or evidence of real conversion.

Prayer to Ignite Action:

God, I thank You for the transforming power of Your Holy Spirit that has converted me and still convicts me of my sins. I draw closer to You so that I can know You more and serve You better. I believe that there are others who, like me, desire a real relationship with You, God, and not just another religious experience. Help me to tell others about the change that has occurred in my life when given the opportunity, today. In Jesus' name. Amen.

DAY 81

Inspiration:

"Surely He has borne our griefs and carried our sorrows; Yet we esteemed Him stricken, Smitten by God, and afflicted. But He [was] wounded for our transgressions. [He was] bruised for our iniquities; The chastisement for our peace [was] upon Him, and by His stripes we are healed." ~ Isaiah 53:4-5, New King James Version

Insight:

Jesus pushed Himself forward to fulfill His mission as prophesied by Isaiah and other biblical patriarchs. Because He pushed forward to fulfill prophecy and destiny, we now have access to salvation for our soul, healing for our body, freedom from religious legalism, and reconciliation with God our Father. Now, we like Jesus, can push ourselves forward to fulfill our distinct purpose despite the challenges that come our way. We can do all that we were predestined to do, and become all that we were foreordained to become, and we owe it all to our suffering Savior who is now sitting at the right hand of God interceding on our behalf. You and I can make it, because Jesus showed us the way!

Prayer to Ignite Action:

Dear God, Your love for the world was vividly shown when You allowed Your only begotten Son to be crucified for us. Because of the obedience of Jesus and His resurrection, all who confess their sins and accept Jesus as Savior and Lord can be saved. I thank You for loving and saving me and those who will come to know You as Lord today. I also thank You for real relationship, healing, and freedom that is found in Your presence. In Jesus' name. Amen.

DAY 82

Inspiration:

"And we know that all things work together for good to those who love God, to those who are the called according to [His] purpose." ~ Romans 8:28, New King James Version

Insight:

No matter what comes our way, it is our perspective and attitude that will gauge how we choose to respond. There is no guarantee that everything in life will be perfect or pristine, but we can be confident that God will use everything that is allowed to cross our path to refine us when we respond as a student willing to be taught in order to mentor others with the lessons that we have mastered. Approaching life in this way helps us to accept what God allows for a greater purpose while living joyfully not because of circumstances but despite them. It is our Perfect God, not perfect conditions, that strengthens us in the midst of an imperfect world and gives us grace to respond to life in ways that please Him.

Prayer to Ignite Action:

Heavenly Father, today I accept the fact that all things in my life—good, bad and indifferent—will be used by You to work in my best interest because I love you and am called according to Your purpose. Character is being formed in me as my faith is deepened and my spirit is renewed. I know that what You have in store for me is greater than any plan I could possibly imagine. I trust You to work in, through and around me as Your plan for my life unfolds. In Jesus' name. Amen.

DAY 83

Inspiration:
"I can do all things through Christ who strengthens me." ~ Philippians 4:13, New King James Version

Insight:
Doing what others said or thought couldn't be done (including ourselves) is an exhilarating feeling, especially because of the satisfaction that is gained not only from the accomplishment itself, but also from the sheer joy that comes from knowing that perseverance pushed past pessimism, courage conquered critics and action annihilated our own anxieties. God's power working in and through us to accomplish His purpose will be evident to all when we surrender our ways and will to His and choose to follow His lead. However, in order to hear and obey, we must place ourselves in a position of spending quality time with God and fine-tuning our spiritual ear to hear His voice as He speaks to us in various ways.

Prayer to Ignite Action:
God, my strength is found in You, and because of that, I have a surplus of power to accomplish everything I need to do today. I will be effective and efficient in managing and completing all that is assigned to my hands without being distracted because I am full of faith and sharpened in my focus. In Jesus' name. Amen.

DAY 84

Inspiration:

For you were called to freedom, brethren; only do not turn your freedom into an opportunity for the flesh, but through love serve one another." ~ Galatians 5:13, New American Standard Bible

Insight:

Life has no meaning until we discover our purpose and determine to utilize our gifts, talents, abilities and skills to add meaning to life. Doing so creates the value-added benefit of impacting the lives of others while leaving an indelible mark on our assigned sphere in the world. The value we create by being authentically ourselves and participating fully in life by bringing the best of who we are and what we can do to the table, so to speak, opens up a smorgasbord of opportunities to be useful, resourceful, and influential as we dare to make a difference by the life we live and the service we give.

Prayer to Ignite Action:

Father, there is so much more to life than what I have experienced thus far. Lead me in the way that You have prepared for me as I continue to discover deeper meaning of a life that is rich and full enough to serve many people for Your glory. In Jesus' name. Amen.

DAY 85

Inspiration:

"You have heard that it was said, 'You shall love your neighbor and hate your enemy. But I say to you, love your enemies, bless those who curse you, do good to those who hate you, and pray for those who spitefully use you and persecute you, that you may be sons of your Father in heaven; for He makes His sun rise on the evil and on the good, and sends rain on the just and on the unjust.'" ~ Matthew 5:43-45, New King James Version

Insight:

Life has built within it contradictions and complexities that are sometimes beyond our comprehension, but yet it is to be lived with the assurance of knowing that God can and will use all of it--the polarities of the good and bad--to test our faith, strengthen our resolve and cultivate our character. It is utterly impossible and improbable to encounter only mountaintop experiences, for if God only allowed us to live in this ubiquitous state of euphoria, we would fail to rely upon Him fully and thus miss learning the many lessons of wisdom and value to be grasped not only for our sakes but also for the sake of sharing our tests and testimonies with those in search of His love, light and liberation. Our lives are to be living epistles of the embodiment of ups and downs to show that there is a Shelter in Whom we can find solace, stability, and strength in the midst of life's vicissitudes and victories.

Prayer to Ignite Action:

Father, life is unpredictable and full of uncertainties at times, but You remain the same. You love me unconditionally, provide for me consistently, and protect me faithfully. Although circumstances and situations may change, I find stability in You and in the promises of Your Holy Word. I know that You rain on the just and the unjust and that everyone experiences good and not so good times. Still, I rest in the assurance that You care for your own, and that Your grace for me today is sufficient. In Jesus' name. Amen.

DAY 86

Inspiration:

"But be doers of the word, and not hearers only, deceiving yourselves."
~ James 1:22, New King James Version

Insight:

I have learned a myriad of valuable lessons in life, one of which has helped me to release fears, inhibitions and the opinions of others in order to hear and follow God's call. That lesson is encapsulated in a phrase that I have often taught others: Action cures fear; do it now! We often shrink back from daring to fulfill our dreams because we over-analyze or talk ourselves out of what God has prompted us to do (or, we may offer to God our short list of names that He could choose to complete a task that He has assigned to us). Our purpose is precious to God, and in order to regard it as such to us, we must follow the path He has predestined for us which does not always equate to the path of least resistance. It may not be easy to put forth the necessary effort when called upon to do so, but the earthly blessings and most importantly, the eternal reward will be well worth it when we hear the words, "Well done My good and faithful servant; you were faithful over a few things, I will make you ruler over many things. Enter into the joy of your lord" (Matthew 25:21 NKJV).

Prayer to Ignite Action:

Dear Lord, please grant unto me the fortitude to be a doer of Your word and not a hearer only. My desire is to be found in the center of Your will. Today, I will follow Your direction without fear or hesitation. Let my actions be pleasing in Your sight. In Jesus' name. Amen.

DAY 87

Inspiration:

"None of this fazes us because Jesus loves us. I'm absolutely convinced that nothing--nothing living or dead, angelic or demonic, today or tomorrow, high or low, thinkable or unthinkable--absolutely nothing can get between us and God's love because of the way that Jesus our Master has embraced us." ~ Romans 8:37-39, The Message Bible

Insight:

Love and persistence are admirable traits to possess because they drive us on despite discouragement or difficulties that may arise. When the love of God motivates us, we can tenaciously tackle any challenge that befalls us. The nature of love and persistence will compel us to continue forward, determined not just to endure but to outlast and overtake the opposition and obstacles in our way. We are more than conquerors through Christ who strengthens us. Nothing will faze us because Jesus is our ultimate example of love and persistence in action.

Prayer to Ignite Action:

Father, Your love for me is incomprehensible. I will tell of Your love and show it to others in my persistence to keep moving forward in the direction that You lead, even in the midst of opposition. You have given me the power to conquer and triumph over the tactics of the enemy. Today, I am a winner! In Jesus' name. Amen.

DAY 88

Inspiration:

"For now we see in a mirror, dimly, but then face to face. Now I know in part, but then I shall know just as I also am known. And now abide faith, hope, love, these three; but the greatest of these [is] love." ~ 1 Corinthians 13:12-13, New King James Version

Insight:

Have you ever taken the time to think of what you would do in life if money were no object? What is it that you would do for free even if you never received a dime for it? Once you discover that, you have uncovered your true purpose and released the potential of what you do best. Whatever that passion is, it remains easier for you to do and more difficult for others to take on because God has already equipped you with the desire to accomplish what brings Him, others, and you joy. That desire begins as a seed planted in your heart to serve as a clue to what you really were created to do. Don't neglect that seed of desire, but rather, nurture it by watering it with faith, hope, love and the willingness to act upon those virtues through meaningful service. After all, faith is useless without works, hope unused defers and diminishes desire, and love underdeveloped does not express the true nature of God or compassion for others. If the truth be told, the only way to become our best is by cultivating faith, hope, and love. Developing these virtues in our lives daily--with more emphasis on the virtue of love--will cause us to mature in our Christian walk and motivate us to do good works that will follow us into eternity.

Prayer to Ignite Action:

God, You are the embodiment of love in perfection. I worship You as the Lord and love of my life. I pray that Your unconditional, unending love will flow through me today and that its evidence will be seen and sensed by my compassion, empathy, and service to others in my home, church, workplace, community, and wherever else You may lead me. My faith, hope, and love are in You. Thank You for increasing these virtues, especially love, in my life. In Jesus' name. Amen.

DAY 89

Inspiration:

"Give, and it will be given to you. A good measure, pressed down, shaken together and running over, will be poured into your lap. For with the measure you use, it will be measured to you." ~ Luke 6:38, New International Version

"Do not be deceived: God cannot be mocked. A man reaps what he sows. The one who sows to please his sinful nature, from that nature will reap destruction; the one who sows to please the Spirit, from the Spirit will reap eternal life. Let us not become weary in doing good, for at the proper time we will reap a harvest if we do not give up. Therefore, as we have opportunity, let us do good to all people, especially to those who belong to the family of believers." ~ Galatians 6:7-10, New International Version

Insight:

I have learned that the more I give of my time, talents, and treasures to God and others, the more I receive in return. In other words, as we continue to give the best of ourselves in abundant supply, our inner and outer resources receive constant replenishment. This is good news, and proves that the principle of "Sowing and Reaping" which is also known as "The Law of Reciprocity" really works. To some, this may not make sense, but God's Word (which has been tested throughout the ages and found to be true) supersedes our own thoughts. God is honored and others are blessed through our giving, and the added benefit is that we will reap a harvest in return that never runs out.

Prayer to Ignite Action:

Father, I am blessed by the fact that You chose to use me as a channel through which resources can flow to add to Your kingdom and bless others. The more that I give, the more You continue to give back to me. I thank You for trusting me with the stewardship of resources so that I can be generous in my giving while reaping what was sown in my living. In Jesus' name. Amen.

DAY 90

Inspiration:

"For all have sinned and come short of the glory of God, being justified freely by His grace though the redemption that is in Christ Jesus, whom God set forth [as] a propitiation by His righteousness, because in His forbearance God had passed over the sins that were previously committed, to demonstrate at the present time His righteousness, that He might be just and the justifier of the one who has faith in Jesus." ~ Romans 3:23-26, New King James Version

Insight:

Despite the fact that all have sinned (Romans 3:23), the price was paid by Jesus on Calvary's cross to cover our sins and unrighteousness. Because of our Savior's sacrifice, we need not settle for an excuse-ladened, mundane or mediocre life--nor should we return to old habits, patterns, and sins that once held us captive. We are now made righteous, blameless, holy, and worthy of receiving the shed blood of Jesus as atonement (amends, satisfaction or reparation) for our wrongdoing. We have a higher standard and purpose in life to pursue because of what Christ accomplished through His life, suffering, death, and resurrection.

Our sins were put to death when Christ was nailed to the cross, along with low-level thinking and living beneath our heritage as sons and daughters of God. Rather than raising our sins up again, we should choose to let our standards rise to the level of our integrity, righteousness, and standing in Christ.

Prayer to Ignite Action:

Heavenly Father, my heart overflows with gladness because You choose to forgive me of sin and to cleanse me from everything I've ever thought, said and done that was contrary to Your Word and will for my life. Today, I thank You that as I confess my sins, I believe that they are not only forgiven, but forgotten by You. Help me to also forgive myself and those who sin against me, and to take the high road in choosing not to let what is in the past haunt my present or hold hostage my future. In Jesus' name. Amen.

DAY 91

Inspiration:

"Come to me, all you who are weary and burdened, and I will give you rest. Take my yoke upon you and learn from me, for I am gentle and humble in heart, and you will find rest for your souls. For my yoke is easy and my burden is light." ~ Matthew 11:28-30, New International Version

Insight:

Jesus taught us to give our cares and concerns to Him, which includes the weight of the baggage we carry from others that are too heavy for our shoulders. Once we take upon ourselves the yoke of Christ, we learn this valuable lesson: we are only responsible for our own choices. What others think, say and do is based upon their own decisions apart from us. It is a fact that some people make wrong choices, and then try to blame others for the wrong choices they have made instead of taking responsibility for those choices themselves. The best thing that we can do is to decide to take responsibility for our own lives and to let go of the temptation to carry guilt, condemnation, shame, or blame that never belonged to us anyway. Refusing to be overloaded with the weight of others' choices and accepting responsibility only for our own, frees us to fully explore and enjoy our lives so that we can equip others with the lessons we've learned from the triumphs and tragedies that God allows to come our way.

Prayer to Ignite Action:

Dear Lord, I come to You with humility of heart, releasing all worry, anxiety, shame, blame, condemnation, and guilt. I release myself from the responsibility of carrying burdens that my shoulders are not equipped to handle. Please give me the wisdom and willpower to cast upon You all of my cares and concerns while accepting responsibility for my own choices. I realize that I am ultimately accountable to You, and I thank You for leading me in the way that is right today. In Jesus' name. Amen.

DAY 92

Inspiration:

Watch the way you talk. Let nothing foul or dirty come out of your mouth. Say only what helps, each word a gift. Don't grieve God. Don't break his heart. His Holy Spirit, moving and breathing in you, is the most intimate part of your life, making you fit for himself. Don't take such a gift for granted." ~ Ephesians 4:29-30, The Message Bible

Insight:

There's an old adage that says, "When life hands you lemons, make lemonade!" It may sound comical to some, but it is actually a strategy that, if used, allows us to make the best of any situation that comes our way. Choosing to respond appropriately to life by thinking critically and following through with words and actions that create value, lessens the likelihood of reacting emotionally to problems or people that rub us the wrong way. Nothing and no one has the power to annoy, irritate or aggravate us unless we willingly give away that power. Instead, it is much more advantageous to expend that power in positive ways by directing it towards the greater good--such as a goal or vision to be achieved or a cause that is larger than any individual--which will, in turn, serve the needs of others as well as fulfill our own dreams.

Prayer to Ignite Action:

Heavenly Father, today I need Your power to work in me so that I do not allow other people or predicaments to pull me in the wrong direction or away from reflecting godly character. By Your strength, I will make the best of every situation that comes my way. Use me in ways I never thought possible as I yield my will to You while being keenly aware of and focused on my life's purpose. I thank You that my purpose also involves finding a great need and filling it today for the good of others. In Jesus' name. Amen.

DAY 93

Inspiration:

After looking at the way things are on this earth, here's what I've decided is the best way to live: Take care of yourself, have a good time, and make the most of whatever job you have for as long as God gives you life. And that's about it. That's the human lot. Yes, we should make the most of what God gives, both the bounty and the capacity to enjoy it, accepting what's given and delighting in the work. It's God's gift! God deals out joy in the present, the now. It's useless to brood over how long we might live." ~ Ecclesiastes 5:18-20, The Message Bible

Insight:

We've heard it said that tomorrow is not promised. I believe such a statement was made as a reminder to focus on what we have and can do today. That is not to say that we should not plan for the future or set goals in order to accomplish and therefore, live out our dreams. In essence, it is wise to plan for the future, but not at the expense of neglecting the possibilities and opportunities that are afforded to us in this present time. Time does not wait for anyone, so we must be good stewards of every minute and not take the challenges, joys, or the people in our lives for granted. All we have right now is this moment in time, which comes and goes quicker than we can blink an eye. Making the most of each moment requires focus, strategic thinking, flexibility, and the ability to follow through with the actions that will back up our words by putting feet to our God-inspired ideas so that life will not pass us by without us making full use of all that it has to offer.

Philosopher, William James, made a profound statement regarding his perspective of life--one that we would all do well to consider and adopt: "Life's value is not in its duration but its donation--not in how long we live, but how fully and how well."

Prayer to Ignite Action:

Dear God, I praise You for who You are and for all the bountiful blessings I and others have--blessings of a sound mind, peace, joy, health, ability,

118

the capacity to love and be loved, and to give and receive. With each moment, help me not only to be thankful, but to become intentional about how fully and well I live as determined by how generously and cheerfully I give. What matters most is who and what I choose to value in my life. Today, I will make a conscious effort to demonstrate that value in my actions. In Jesus' name. Amen.

DAY 94

Inspiration:

"Before I formed you in the womb I knew you, and before you were born I consecrated you; I appointed you a prophet to the nations." ~ Jeremiah 1:5, English Standard Version

"If I say, 'I will not mention him, or speak any more in his name,' there is in my heart as it were a burning fire shut up in my bones, and I am weary with holding it in, and I cannot." ~ Jeremiah 20:9, English Standard Version

Insight:

To live with intention is to live with focused attention directed towards fulfilling our life's mission. Our mission or reason for living is what drives us to accomplish a predetermined purpose that was planted as a seed in us before we became an embryo in our mother's womb. According to Jeremiah 1:5, God had a conversation with the prophet Jeremiah to tell him what He had predestined for Jeremiah to become before he was born. As a result, Jeremiah was able to live out his purpose of becoming a prophet to the nations, and he intentionally did so against all opposition and in the midst of difficult times. Even when faced with the temptation to quit, Jeremiah's purpose became like fire in his bones to rekindle his passion so that he refused to give up. Living with intention will allow us to be passionate about who God has created us to be and what He has predestined us to do. Consistently communing with God keeps us connected to Him and in sync with His plans for us so that we can intentionally respond to His leading in our daily living.

Prayer to Ignite Action:

Father, You have known my life's plan and purpose even before I was born. Today, I desire to intentionally pursue with passion the path upon which I was predestined to trod. I will not allow opposition to deter me from my destiny. Show me clearly the ways in which I should walk and ignite me with zeal and fervor to follow where You lead with joy. When times are difficult, I will remember that You have already spoken to my heart and shown me the way. I will not give in or quit because my passion is the fire that fuels my purpose. In Jesus' name. Amen.

DAY 95

Inspiration:

One night Joseph had a dream, and when he told his brothers about it, they hated him more than ever." ~ Genesis 37:5, New Living Translation

Then his brothers came and threw themselves down before Joseph. 'Look, we are your slaves!' they said. But Joseph replied, 'Don't be afraid of me. Am I God, that I can punish you? You intended to harm me, but God intended it all for good. He brought me to this position so I could save the lives of many people." ~ Genesis 50:18-20, New Living Translation

Insight:

What do you love? Whatever it is that you are truly passionate about should serve as the driving force that consumes the best portion of your time, energy, and money--even when others do not believe in or support it. If what you give the majority of your attention, effort, and resources to is not what is truly your heart's desire, then it is best to reevaluate where you are and what you are doing. A self-assessment of your gifts as well as where and how you can use them for maximum effectiveness, will help to redirect and reinvent your life if necessary so that you actually love living, learning, and letting the best of who you are and all that you are able to offer add value to the people and the world around you. Don't let your destiny lie dormant. Awaken the dreamer within and begin to live the life you dream about every day.

Prayer to Ignite Action:

Father, I thank You, today, that I am still able to dream about and envision Your plan for my life. Continue to speak to my heart with precision and clarity so that my mind will become laser-focused on using my God-given gifts, talents and abilities to offer value to the people and world around me. I offer myself to You to be molded and shaped like clay in the hand of a potter so that the dreams You inspire and implant within me will become reality. In Jesus' name. Amen.

DAY 96

Inspiration:

The thief comes only in order to steal and kill and destroy. I came that they may have and enjoy life, and have it in abundance (to the full, till it overflows)." ~ John 10:10, Amplified Bible

Insight:

Jesus told us that He came to earth to live, die, and rise again so that we can experience abundant living. A life of abundance denotes an extremely plentiful, over-sufficient quality, quantity, and supply that is overflowing, holistically wealthy and therefore, able to be fully enjoyed by ourselves with enough left over to flow onto someone else. Knowing that God sent His Son, Jesus, so that we can have (not just think about or wish for) that kind of life keeps us focused and on fire to experience it daily without reservation or hesitation.

You have countless opportunities afforded to you, today, to experience an abundant life--a life that is rich, rewarding, and yes, fulfilling to the nth degree! Seize those opportunities by focusing on your predestined purpose with a desire to live in such a way that the fire of your passion ignites others to live abundantly just like you.

Prayer to Ignite Action:

Lord, I am extremely thankful for the abundant life that You sacrificed Your life for so that we may obtain it. I know that You know and want what is best for Your children, just as a parent does. I receive abundance in my life today as an inheritance from my Heavenly Father, and I will allow it to flow in me fully until it overflows into the lives of others. I boldly proclaim that I have more than enough of what I need and that I am blessed to be a blessing today. In Jesus' name. Amen.

DAY 97

Inspiration:
If you are willing and obedient, You shall eat the good of the land." ~ Isaiah 1:19, New King James Version

Insight:
It really is possible to live life on our own terms, which simply means that we choose to obey God while taking control of our own decisions and actions without delegating them to others and subsequently blaming them for the outcome. After all, we are responsible for the choices we make daily and the consequences of those choices. Procrastination, lack of motivation, intimidation, and stagnation are thieves that come to rob us of our time, energy, confidence, and progress. They are merely excuses for not moving forward and allowing the brilliance of God's light to shine through us. When we reject and eject the excuse-laden mentality that points the finger at others for what we should take responsibility for ourselves, we'll find that excellence will make its abode with us and the results will be incredible. Now, that is what it means to truly live life on our own terms!

Prayer to Ignite Action:
Father God, my obedience to You is better and more valuable than any other sacrifice I could offer. Today, I set my heart and will in agreement to obey and serve You. The promise of Isaiah 1:19 declares that I will be prosperous if I willingly obey You. Forgive me for the times when my own stubbornness and disobedience kept me from realizing the benefit of Your promises towards me. Cultivate humility and integrity of heart in me so that my thoughts and deeds are motivated by my desire to honor and obey You. In Jesus' name. Amen.

DAY 98

Inspiration:

For as he thinks in his heart, so is he." ~ Proverbs 23:7a, Amplified Bible

The upright (honorable, intrinsically good) man out of the good treasure [stored] in his heart produces what is upright (honorable and intrinsically good), and the evil man out of the evil storehouse brings forth that which is depraved (wicked and intrinsically evil); for out of the abundance (overflow) of the heart his mouth speaks." ~ Luke 6:45, Amplified Bible

Insight:

What we perceive is what we believe, and what we believe is in essence what we are destined to receive. These scriptural passages remind us that what we think upon will travel from our head to our heart, and from our heart to our tongue. Therefore, the power of our thoughts will influence our heart (which is the seat of our emotions and feelings). The heart is powerful enough to make a correlation between that which we choose to feel and consequently speak into the atmosphere. These three powerful components of thought, heart, and tongue affect one another, and the proper or improper use of all three will determine our destiny or hasten our demise.

You have the power to hone in on or to halt your destiny with your head, heart, and tongue. Choose to use the power of these three forces wisely.

Prayer to Ignite Action:

Father, I commit and submit the thoughts of my mind, the meditation of my heart, and the words of my mouth to You afresh today. I ask for the wisdom of the Holy Spirit to be with me so that my perceptions and beliefs are based upon the truth of Your Word and not false or circumstantial evidence. Let my thoughts, conversation, and conduct be critically constructive so that I can follow in pursuit of my destiny and help others to do the same. In Jesus' name. Amen.

DAY 99

Inspiration:
...And God saw that [it was] good." ~ Genesis 1:10b, 12b, 18b, 21b, 25b, New King James Version

Then God saw everything that He had made, and indeed [it was] very good. So the evening and the morning were the sixth day." ~ Genesis 1:31, New King James Version

Insight:
We are responsible for creating the kind of life that we desire--one that is rewarding and fulfilling. Such a responsibility can never be delegated to someone else, for the right and will to create has been bestowed upon us by our Creator. God, in His Sovereignty, created the heavens and the earth and all that dwells therein, and as if that were not enough, He stood back and admired His own handiwork by stating that what He had done was indeed good! The mere fact that God saw and said that all that He created was good implies that He found pleasure and delight in what He had accomplished as recorded throughout the first chapter of the book of Genesis...and then, He rested.

We, too, will gain a sense of fulfillment when we utilize the creative power of God within to bring into fruition the vision that we see and speak each day. Whatever we deem as valuable, meaningful, and good in our eyes will demand the very best of our time, talent, and treasures. Taking this kind of ownership and pleasure in a God-given vision is what allows true purpose to be revealed and untapped potential to be released.

Prayer to Ignite Action:
God, I desire to follow Your example by knowing that all that I imagine and create, and therefore do, is good. As I conduct the business at hand in my home, workplace, church, community and elsewhere, please help me to be mindful that what I produce should reflect my core beliefs and values as a Christian. When I complete my daily tasks, I want to rest in the assurance of knowing that You can look at what I've done and also say, "It was good." In Jesus' name. Amen.

DAY 100

Inspiration:
"Commit your way to the LORD, Trust also in Him, And He shall bring [it] to pass." ~ Psalm 37:5, New King James Version

Insight:
Everything that we need to do on a daily basis may not be pleasant, but if it is to be accomplished, it is possible when we commit our ways to God and make what we need to do a matter of priority. By making up our minds to complete the task, we eliminate all excuses and are motivated to move forward with decisive action. Any task can be undertaken and any ambition achieved when we adopt this attitude and follow through with simply doing what needs to be done. The outcome will be well worth the commitment and at the end of the day, we'll thank God, and yes, ourselves, for being decisive enough to act in the best interest of keeping the bigger picture in mind as we pursue our dreams.

Prayer to Ignite Action:
Lord, I need wisdom and guidance in the goals I set for today, as well as in the strategy needed to accomplish each goal. I commit all that I am to do today into Your hands, trusting You to lead me in all my ways. I am empowered to be efficient and effective in all my endeavors. In Jesus' name. Amen.

DAY 101

Inspiration:

Until the time came to fulfill his dreams, the LORD tested Joseph's character." ~ Psalm 105:19, New Living Translation

May you always be filled with the fruit of your salvation--the righteous character produced in your life by Jesus Christ--for this will bring much glory and praise to God." ~ Philippians 1:11, New Living Translation

Insight:

Although what we do should be strategically defined, we are not solely defined by what we do. It is important that we give proper attention to the goals that we choose to pursue and accomplish, for goals should be driven by the results we desire to achieve. However, how we conduct ourselves along the way as well as the methods we choose to use stem from a deeper place within us. It is our character that shapes and forms us, and thus becomes the very nature of who we are. True identity comes from within and therefore defines us. That is why it is paramount that we understand who we really are based on the One who created us and the Word that He has spoken to us. When we are confident in whose and who we are, then all that we think and do emanates from that place of assurance and excellence is sure to follow.

Prayer to Ignite Action:

God, I thank You for forming righteous character in me by placing people and orchestrating events in my life to strengthen and bring out the best in me. I know that my character has been and will be tested along the way. My desire is to pass each test with excellence and learn the lesson from it so that I can share it with others. In Jesus' name. Amen.

DAY 102

Inspiration:

The master said, 'Well done, my good and faithful servant. You have been faithful in handling this small amount, so now I will give you many more responsibilities. Let's celebrate together!' ~ Matthew 25:23, New Living Translation

Insight:

The best part of waking up is not "Folger's in your cup" but the opportunity to celebrate and live life to the fullest in all its richness. There are so many ways in which to express the love of God, the value of service and the purpose for which we were created. What is truly important to us will become the impetus that motivates us to live each day with a mission that keeps us faith-filled, focused and fueled with the fire of a passion that cannot be quenched. That mission becomes our life's charge or work, not just because we've chosen to do it, but because we sense that it is what we are called and equipped by God to accomplish for the sake of pleasing Him, blessing other people, and thus, living a rich and rewarding life.

Do you have a personal mission statement? If not, take the time to seek God for His wisdom and direction so that you will discern, know and live out what is truly important to you. You cannot help but celebrate once you discover just how rich and full your life can be.

Prayer to Ignite Action:

Father, my life is meant to be celebrated, not tolerated. Open my eyes so that I can see and appreciate the beauty of life within and around me as I become more cognizant of the reason for my existence. Reveal to me my personal mission so that all my efforts will be energized by it today. Help me to be faithful with and thankful for the responsibilities I now have. I will be content in my place of purpose today, knowing that You will expand my capacity to handle more responsibilities as a result of being a good steward of what You have already placed in my hands. In Jesus' name. Amen.

DAY 103

Inspiration:

"Train up a child in the way he should go, And when he is old he will not depart from it." ~ Proverbs 22:6, New Living Translation

"Hope deferred makes the heart sick, but when the desire is fulfilled, it is a tree of life." ~ Proverbs 13:12, Amplified Bible

Insight:

The earliest recollection I have of who God is came as a result of my mother and father taking me to church, Sunday School and Vacation Bible School. I was amazed at the way the choir sung and the musicians played, and at five years old, I asked my mother if I could learn how to play the piano. The desire to do so was very strong to the point where it spilled over into my childhood dreams. The manifestation of my dream of playing the piano was realized several years later, and many other desires were launched from that dream as well.

Looking back, I believed I learned two very important lessons:
1) Purpose often unfolds as a result of our childhood dreams.
2) God-given purpose is attached to the thing we desire to do. Although what we desire to do may be delayed, it shall come to pass.

An African Proverb says, "The danger of this generation is that they want to eat their dinner in the morning." In an age where the invention of the microwave oven allows us to prepare and eat food quickly, we tend to think that the rest of life--including the fulfillment of our goals and dreams--should manifest just as quickly. However, waiting for the divine timing and season for us to reap what we have sown will allow wisdom to be awakened and patience to be perfected in us.

Prayer to Ignite Action:

Dear Lord, I thank You that Your blessings have followed me from childhood to adulthood. Please grant me the courage to resist the fear that may have held me back from pushing myself toward the fulfillment of the dreams You've placed in my heart. A delay is not the same as a denial. My predetermined purpose will be realized in the time and season that is meant just for me. In Jesus' name. Amen.

DAY 104

Inspiration:

"Roll your works upon the Lord [commit and trust them wholly to Him; He will cause your thoughts to become agreeable to His will, and] so shall your plans be established and succeed." ~ Proverbs 16:3, Amplified Bible

Insight:

Our Omnipotent (All Powerful) God created the heavens and the earth as well as man with the wisdom and creativity that flowed from the Godhead Trinity. That same power, wisdom, and creativity are available to us when we allow God to direct our thoughts and works. We are afforded opportunities each day to display the boundless creativity and capability of our minds when we commit all that we desire to accomplish to God and ask Him to establish our thoughts. In so doing, we invite God's presence, power and purpose to permeate our mind, body, and spirit, and the results are evident, excellent and effective for others to see.

Prayer to Ignite Action:

Dear God, I commit and trust into Your care everything that I need to accomplish today. You are the One who knows how my day will go, so allow me to think, speak, and act in agreement with Your will. I invite Your presence, power and purpose to direct my path, believing that everything I do will yield results that will please You. Thank You for working in and through me for Your glory. In Jesus' name. Amen.

DAY 105

Inspiration:

"Among those who belong to Christ, everything connected with getting our own way and mindlessly responding to what everyone else calls necessities is killed off for good--crucified. Since this is the kind of life we have chosen, the life of the Spirit, let us make sure that we do not just hold it as an idea in our heads or a sentiment in our hearts, but work out its implications in every detail of our lives." ~ Galatians 5:24-25, The Message Bible

Insight:

Today, God has set before us the ability to choose for ourselves...a power that should not be delegated to others while we have full, capable faculty of mind and will. We can choose to be better or bitter, to live abundantly or accursed, to love lavishly or with limits, to speak with conviction or complaint, to move forward in faith or to grovel in fear and failure. The choice is always ours to make, and deciding to follow the right choice will influence and impact not only our lives, but leave an impression and a lasting legacy upon those who are watching, listening to, and following us, particularly our children.

Prayer to Ignite Action:

Father, I am so grateful that all of my past, present and future sins were nailed to the cross when Jesus was crucified. Help me not to resurrect wrong thoughts and actions as I allow the Holy Spirit to guide my every decision today. God, I give You permission to invade every area in my life and to fill me afresh with the Spirit so that I am energized and empowered to make a difference in the world. In Jesus' name. Amen.

DAY 106

Inspiration:

Now Daniel so distinguished himself among the administrators and the satraps by his exceptional qualities that the king planned to set him over the whole kingdom. At this, the administrators and the satraps tried to find grounds for charges against Daniel in his conduct of government affairs, but they were unable to do so. They could find no corruption in him, because he was trustworthy and neither corrupt nor negligent." ~ Daniel 6:3-4, New International Version

Insight:

There are many who choose to follow the way of the crowd rather than to pursue the road less traveled. It is much easier to do what has already been done and to go where others have gone than it is to forge a path as a trailblazer. Consequently, being the first or the only person to tackle what others dare not think about or attempt to do requires unwavering fortitude, untapped creativity, unyielding resolve and unmitigated nerve. It takes courage to resist the voices of the masses who favor what is popular and familiar, to follow the orchestral arrangement of a purpose that resounds in the deepest recesses of your soul where God is the Master Conductor and you are the featured musician poised to perform according to His interpretation of music that only you can hear. It is much easier to blend in with the average and status quo than it is to stand out because of a spirit of excellence that drives you to be better, wiser, stronger, healthier and happier. Choosing the way of excellence as opposed to the way of ease, albeit difficult, is well worth the effort.

Prayer to Ignite Action:

Dear Lord, I choose the narrow easement to excellence rather than the broad road to mediocrity today. I thank You for creating me to be unique, distinct and peculiar on purpose so that I can stand out and stand up for what is right. Give me the courage to minister to, rather than blend in with the masses. My aim is to represent You in all I say and do. Let my life be an example so that others are led to follow You, I pray. In Jesus' name. Amen.

DAY 107

Inspiration:

"But if you refuse to serve the LORD, then choose today whom you will serve. Would you prefer the gods your ancestors served beyond the Euphrates? Or will it be the gods of the Amorites in whose land you now live? But as for me and my family, we will serve the LORD." ~ Joshua 24:15, New Living Translation

Insight:

Have you ever thought about how powerful we are? God has given you and me the authority to determine the course of our destiny and to do what is necessary to make it so. It is totally up to each of us to discover, discern, and determine to do what is most expedient not just for ourselves, but also for those closest to us. We have the power to formulate the right thoughts and to eliminate the wrong ones--to choose blessings rather than to accept curses--to add value and order to the world instead of chaos and disorder--to use our innate gifts and abilities and not to take them for granted by misusing or abusing them. Oh, yes--we are powerful indeed!

Prayer to Ignite Action:

Father, all dominion and power are Yours. Your ways are majestic and Your name alone is mighty. Today, I pray that Your power will work in and through me so that the choices I make will positively influence my family, friends, and others who cross my path whose lives are to be intertwined with mine. Let all that I am and possess be used for Your glory and the good of others. In Jesus' name. Amen.

DAY 108

Inspiration:

"And now, dear brothers and sisters, one final thing. Fix your thoughts on what is true, and honorable, and right, and pure, and lovely, and admirable. Think about things that are excellent and worthy of praise." ~ Philippians 4:8, New Living Translation

Insight:

It is a wonderful thing to channel our energy and effort into the direction of what resonates most with our purpose and deepest passions. It does not serve us well to concentrate on negative, unproductive thought patterns, plans or people. If what we are thinking upon and doing at this present time does not serve us well, then it is obvious that our focus needs to be redirected. Only then will we experience different results and find ourselves in the center of God's will which is the best and safest place to be.

Prayer to Ignite Action:

God, I desire to be found in the center of Your will, and that begins by centering my thoughts upon You. I pray for razor sharp focus today so that the best of my energies and efforts are directed towards the purpose that I am to fulfill. Help me to dismantle any thoughts that would deter me from concentrating on what truly matters throughout the day. I submit my thoughts and plans to You, and in so doing, I believe that You will guide me in all my ways. In Jesus' name. Amen.

DAY 109

Inspiration:

"But I do more than thank. I ask--ask the God of our Master, Jesus Christ, the God of glory--to make you intelligent and discerning in knowing him personally, your eyes focused and clear, so that you can see exactly what it is he is calling you to do, grasp the immensity of this glorious way of life he has for Christians, oh, the utter extravagance of his work in us who trust him--endless energy, boundless strength!" ~ Ephesians 1:17-19, The Message Bible

Insight:

There is a vast difference between an occupation and a vocation in life. An occupation is the employment that serves the purpose of meeting financial obligations by using a skill set and/or abilities to perform the work for which compensation is received. A vocation is the calling that God has placed upon one's life to pursue and yield to His purpose using natural gifts and talents as well as skills that are honed to accomplish that which God has ordained to glorify Him, bless others and fulfill the desire of one's heart in the process.

The ideal situation would be for our occupation and vocation to intersect so that we actually do what we love to do (that which brings us joy) while making an impact upon others for the sake of expanding God's kingdom...and the additional icing on the cake would be to receive compensation for it. Here are questions to ask concerning our occupation and vocation when desiring to discover the pathway to fulfillment:

1. Am I currently pleased and at peace with where I am and what I am doing right now?
2. Does my present place of employment place a demand on my potential causing me to excel in the utilization of my gifts and talents?
3. Am I able to serve as an example in my lifestyle and work ethic in pointing others to Christ?
4. Would I want to continue doing what I am doing now even if I never received compensation for it, and would I be fulfilled?

5. What can I realistically do (and when) to ensure that my occupation and vocation intersect?

Take the time to answer these questions honestly and put yourself on the pathway to fulfilling your heart's desires as God leads.

Prayer to Ignite Action:

Lord, I cannot thank You enough for loving, caring and providing for me in ways that are beyond comprehending. I need Your unending mercy and unfailing grace extended to me again as I accept and walk in the divine calling upon my life today. I say, yes, to all that I am to pursue and complete in this season of my life, and I trust You fully to direct me as I push forward to fulfill my destiny with decisive action, peace of mind, and joy in my spirit. In Jesus' name. Amen.

DAY 110

Inspiration:

"Blessed [is] that servant whom his master, when he comes, will find so doing." ~ Matthew 24:46, New King James Version

Insight:

There is a marked difference between the effort of trying and the effort of doing. Merely trying often does not require as much effort, visionary insight, and forethought as does the attitude of doing what is necessary to achieve anticipated and expected results. Focusing on accomplishing something worthwhile and meaningful adds value not only to the task itself, but also to the doer of the task and others who are impacted in some way by what has been done. There is no greater fulfillment than knowing that our life has touched another by what we decided to actually do in a day's work.

I read a poem by Edger A. Guest years ago that I included in my book, Parenting and Partnering with Purpose, to remind myself and others of the attitude we should have in accomplishing feats even in the face of ridicule or doubt. May it ignite a spark of action towards whatever it is that others say you can't do, but God declared that you can!

Somebody Said It Couldn't Be Done
by Edger A. Guest

Somebody said it couldn't be done,
but he with a chuckle replied
That maybe it couldn't, but he would be one
who wouldn't say so till he'd tried
He waded right in with a trace of a grin
on his face; if he worried, he did it.
He started to sing as he tackled the thing
that couldn't be done--and he did it.
Somebody said, "Oh, you'll never do that,
at least no one ever has done it."

But he took off his coat and he took off his hat;
and the first thing we know, he'd begun it.
With a lift of the chin and a bit of a grin,
without any doubting or "quit it,"
He started to sing as he tacked the thing
that couldn't be done--and he did it.
There are thousands to tell you it cannot be done,
there are thousands to prophesy failure.
There are thousands to point out to you, one by one,
the dangers that wait to assail you.
But just buckle in with a lift of the chin,
take off your coat and do it.
Starting to sing as you tackle the thing
that cannot be done--and you'll do it.

Prayer to Ignite Action:

Father God, I want to be both a hearer and a doer of Your Word and will. Trying may be a good attempt for some, but I desire to take it a step further by letting consistent effort lead to the accomplishment of what should be placed on my list of priorities today. Grant the stamina to stay focused and to stick to what I need to complete by Your grace. Quitting is not an option for me. I WILL finish what I have started. In Jesus' name. Amen.

DAY 111

Inspiration:

"You will show me the path of life; in Your presence is fullness of joy, at Your right hand there are pleasures forevermore." ~ Psalm 16:11, Amplified Bible

Insight:

We are only responsible for our own decisions and actions, and not those of others. In like manner, we are also responsible for our own fulfillment and joy in life which can and should not be delegated to others. Whereas family and friends are important and valuable relationships to have, they are not to be depended upon to make us happy or whole. Others should not be expected to fill the void that was created to be filled by having a healthy and whole relationship with God and ourselves. Once we accept the fact that God sent His Son, Jesus, so that we can enjoy a full life on earth as well as in eternity, we then realize that true joy and fulfillment comes from within rather than from without based on circumstances or people.

Prayer to Ignite Action:

Lord God, I praise You for who You are in my life--my Provider, Counselor, Teacher, Guide, Protector and Friend. In You I find the pathway to life that is healthy, whole, joyful, and fulfilling. Thank You for leading me in the right way. I will follow You all the days of my life, from earth to eternity. In Jesus' name. Amen.

DAY 112

Inspiration:

"When Jesus saw him lying there and learned that he had been in this condition for a long time, he asked him, "Do you want to get well?" ~ John 5:6, New International Version

Insight:

The remedy for boredom, stagnation, lethargy or apathy is deciding to change the condition and therefore, the position. The condition has to do with an existing state of being--that upon which something else is contingent. Therefore, if the condition one is in is not satisfactory or productive, it can only be altered by changing the position of one's conscious thoughts, conversation and conduct. A position, according to the dictionary, is merely a "condition with reference to place, location and/or situation; bodily posture or mental attitude; stand." A better condition is the result of thinking, speaking and acting from a better place or position. The position of the mind determines the condition of one's life. Selah! (Pause, and think about it. Then take a stand if necessary to change the position of your posture and mental attitude and therefore, your condition.)

Prayer to Ignite Action:

Father, You have given us the power and authority to change the condition of our minds so that we can transform our position in life. I ask for the strength to be resolute in right thinking so that it can manifest right living. Today, I will meditate on thoughts that will produce hope, healing, peace and prosperity for me and the specific people I am interceding for in prayer. Thank You for answering my prayer. In Jesus' name. Amen.

DAY 113

Inspiration:

"God is keeping careful watch over us and the future. The Day is coming when you'll have it all--life healed and whole. I know how great this makes you feel, even though you have to put up with every kind of aggravation in the meantime. Pure gold put in the fire comes out of it proved pure; genuine faith put through this suffering comes out proved genuine. When Jesus wraps this all up, it's your faith, not your gold, that God will have on display as evidence of his victory." ~ 1 Peter 1:5-7, The Message Bible

Insight:

Past hurts, disappointments, mistakes and misunderstandings have a way of trying to encroach upon our present endeavors. However, instead of allowing them to cause us to fear or fail to move forward, we can use them as combustible fuel to ignite and inspire us to passionately pursue today's tasks. There is value in past experiences when we extract lessons from what transpired and use them to propel us into our purpose as God directs. Each new day is a reminder that we are still here to fulfill God's plan and our dreams, and that is only possible when we focus on the value of today and all we can learn from and contribute to it.

Prayer to Ignite Action:

Father, I commit to you all my past hurts, fears, and disappointments. I thank You for a healthy and whole life that glorifies You by turning the trials and tests of my past into a testimony in my present and future. Help me to learn the lessons from what I have experienced so that I can share them with those who need them most as I continue pursuing my purpose. In Jesus' name. Amen.

DAY 114

Inspiration:

"No, dear brothers and sisters, I have not achieved it, but I focus on this one thing: Forgetting the past and looking forward to what lies ahead." ~ Philippians 3:13, New Living Translation

Insight:

My husband and I had the privilege of being asked to co-officiate the wedding of one of our church members in Frederick, MD. It was a joy to watch them focus on one another during the ceremony, and to remind them that focusing on their love relationship even in the midst of challenging times that were sure to come, would help them to weather the worst of storms.

Focus is a powerful tool to keep us single-mindedly attentive and attuned to what matters the most at any given time in our lives. We need focus to stay on track in our relationship with God, loved ones, work, church and other responsibilities that require our effort and energy. Maintaining mental vigilance, spiritual victory and physical vitality will allow all of our dreams to become a reality.

Prayer to Ignite Action:

Father, sharpen my focus so that my attention is fixed foremost upon my relationship with You. Help me to be single-minded in vision while remaining vigilant in mind, victorious in spirit and valuable in the service that I willingly give to my family, friends, church and broader community. In Jesus' name. Amen.

DAY 115

Inspiration:

"And David was greatly distressed, for the people spake of stoning him, because the soul of all the people were grieved, every man for his sons and for his daughters: but David encouraged himself in the LORD his God." ~ 1 Samuel 30:6, King James Version

Insight:

We can only impart to others what we have first received. Scripture reminds us of this when we read about how David, after having experienced obstacles and opposition from his enemies and fellow Israelites at Ziklag, encouraged himself in the Lord. He wasn't dependent on others for encouragement. Instead, he realized that motivation to move forward came from within, and that is what empowered him to fulfill his purpose as Israel's king, leader and warrior.

Today, allow your inner spirit to motivate and empower you to become who God predestined you to be and to reach others for maximum kingdom impact. You will discover that there is no greater joy than to know that your life is making a difference for the cause of Christ and for the sake of being a blessing to others.

Prayer to Ignite Action:

Dear Lord, life has a way of presenting twists and turns that are unexpected and unwarranted. In the midst of the unknown events that will occur today, remind me of the power You've given me to encourage myself in You, in spite of what I see, hear or feel. I choose to be motivated by my life's mission and inspired by the principles of Your Word so that I can be relatable to whomever I meet and relevant wherever I go. In Jesus' name. Amen.

DAY 116

Inspiration:

"Give your entire attention to what God is doing right now, and don't get worked up about what may or may not happen tomorrow. God will help you deal with whatever hard things come up when the time comes." ~ Matthew 6:34, The Message Bible

Insight:

What we decide to do today will directly determine what will unfold for us tomorrow. In other words, the effort we put into what is most important to us or the lack thereof will either yield dividends for us or depreciate the value of what we desire for our future. Whatever and with whomever we spend the majority of our time and effort ultimately determines what and whom we value most. When God directs us in assuring that our priorities are in the right place today, then our targeted efforts will pay off in greater ways than we could possibly imagine tomorrow.

Prayer to Ignite Action:

Father, thank You for emphasizing the importance of who and what I should value most in my life today. I pray that I will not be distracted or deterred by anything that would cause me to have misplaced or displaced priorities. I appreciate that this is the day that You have made so that I can make the choice to focus on what needs to be done today without being anxious about what may or may not happen tomorrow. You know what tomorrow holds, and I trust You to handle what unfolds in my future while I concentrate on what I am directed to do now. In Jesus' name. Amen.

DAY 117

Inspiration:

"Then the LORD said to me, 'Write my answer plainly on tablets, so that a runner can carry the correct message to others." ~ Habakkuk 2:2, New Living Translation

Insight:

Brian Tracy said, "People with clear, written goals, accomplish far more in a shorter period of time than people without them could ever imagine." I have found this to be quite true. When I take the time to heed the words of the prophet Habakkuk and write down my vision in clear, concise steps that are both believable and achievable, then I can (as the visionary and writer) read and allow others to run with what I have been given while holding myself accountable.

Any goal can be accomplished if it has the anatomy of what it takes to be worthwhile. The anatomy of a goal consists of the goal itself (to answer the "What" question), the benefits (the "Why" that motivates us to follow through), and the strategy (the "How" which gives details to include the plan and specific dates/times as measurement metrics). The end result will not be realized without adopting and assessing the anatomy of our goals along the way which will in turn establish direction for our lives and challenge us to continue to develop and grow while remaining relevant and on the cutting edge. This builds confidence, reduces stress and helps us to focus on our God-given vision while making full use of our abilities and resources to achieve intended results that will be well worth the effort.

Prayer to Ignite Action:

Dear God, I thank You for renewed vision and vitality today so that I can write down clear and concise goals and follow through with the energy needed to accomplish them. I pray that You would ignite a fire in me so that the flame within will keep my passion burning as I and others run in hot pursuit of fulfilling God-inspired vision and sharpening our spiritual and professional edge along the way. In Jesus' name. Amen.

DAY 118

Inspiration:

"Whoever pursues righteousness and unfailing love will find life, righteousness, and honor." ~ Proverbs 21:21, New Living Translation

Insight:

On July 27, 2011, my husband and I celebrated 28 years of marriage. Our anniversary gift to ourselves was a trip to San Juan, Puerto Rico. We spent the week enjoying time with each other in a way that we often cannot at home because of our daily schedules and commitments. It is good to take time away to reflect, renew, restore, relax and re-prioritize so that what is truly important is valued and nurtured. Relationships are more important than routines, and our commitments to God and family should always supersede the tasks that demand our attention on a daily basis.

The beauty of sharing life with those we love and not taking our relationships for granted is what truly makes everything else that we do richer and more rewarding. As my husband and I enjoyed each other's company over food, fun and frolicking in the San Juan sun as we zip-lined from mountain peak to mountain peak across the rain forest, valleys and rivers 1,500 feet below, we were reminded of the gift of loving each other and life--a truly adventurous journey that has stood the test of time. What is even more exciting is that there is so much more waiting for us to explore as we continue to learn and grow together, and the same is true for you. That's the abundant life that we all have access to for our enjoyment, fulfillment and God's glory.

Prayer to Ignite Action:

Father, I realize that life is a gift given to us so that we can enjoy our time and existence on earth. I want to follow after righteousness so that I can live by an internal moral compass that leads me in choosing Your ways over my own. Let unconditional love and compassion for others brighten the day as Your light shines in and through me for the world to see as my life takes on new meaning and significance to honor You and yield an abundant harvest. In Jesus' name. Amen.

DAY 119

Inspiration:

"Now Jabez was more honorable than his brothers, and his mother called his name Jabez, saying, 'Becaue I bore [him] in pain.' And Jabez called on the God of Israel saying, 'Oh that You would bless me indeed, and enlarge my territory, that Your hand would be with me, and that You would keep [me] from evil, that I may not cause pain!' So God granted him what he requested." ~ 1 Chronicles 4:9-10, New King James Version

Insight:

I love the song "No Limits" by Israel Houghton. The lyrics refer to a prayer by Jabez (meaning pain or sorrow) whose mother named him such because she bore him in pain. Yet, Jabez did not allow his name or present surroundings to dictate his destiny. In 1 Chronicles 4:9-10, we are told that he was still more honorable than the rest of his brothers and family, and that Jabez asked God to bless him as well as to enlarge his coast or territory. In other words, he wanted God to release his hidden potential and to allow him to see and accomplish more than Jabez or his family could ever imagine. And God did indeed grant his request!

Like Jabez, we can pray and expect God to do what others perhaps think is impossible once we remove all limitations, whether they are self-imposed or otherwise. Israel Houghton's lyrics are powerful, for they remind us not to settle for less than God's best in and for our lives: "No limits; no boundaries. I see increase all around me. Stretch forth; break forth. Release me. Enlarge my territory...Say what you heard [from God] so you can see what you said. Take the limits off...No limits!"

Prayer to Ignite Action:

Father, I do not take for granted the many blessings that You have bestowed upon me. Thank you for Your goodness and faithfulness towards me. Help me not to settle for less than Your best in my life, and to see beyond my present in anticipation of what You have in store for my future. Like Jabez, I pray that You would enlarge my territory by stretching me in ways that will increase my faith, sharpen my intellect, develop my skills and expand my circle of influence. In Jesus' name. Amen.

DAY 120

Inspiration:

"The Spirit of God has made me, And the breath of the Almighty gives me life." ~ Job 33:4, New King James Version

"What man is he who desires life and longs for many days, that he may see good? Keep your tongue from evil and your lips from speaking deceit. Depart from evil and do good; seek, inquire for, and crave peace and pursue (go after) it!" ~ Psalm 34:12-14, Amplified Bible

Insight:

Some people refer to life as a game to be played, and if so, they consider themselves symbolically as actors on a metaphoric stage. Well if that were true, authenticity would be exchanged for the angst of trying to figure out what role to play for whom at any given time depending on the audience who is watching. Life is not a game, but rather, it is a gift that is to be lavishly loved and lived in such a way that the genuineness of who we really are and all the wondrous capabilities of our mind, spirit and body are explored and employed to add distinct value to the world from our own unique perspective.

My husband says it this way: "No one can do what you can do like you, but you." So here's the challenge for you and me. I'll be me to the best of my ability while you do the same with God's wisdom and grace, and together we'll anticipate unlimited possibilities to unfold as our untapped potential is unleashed because we choose to be authentic from the inside out.

Prayer to Ignite Action:

Father, I treasure the life You've given me as a gift to be received, enjoyed and shared with others. I express my gratitude to you for the grace to operate in my area of expertise with a spirit of excellence, doing what no one else can do quite like me because of the potential You placed within me that only I can release to the world. God, You are awesome in all Your ways and wondrous in all Your works, and I thank You for continuing to work on, in and through me so that my authenticity and transparency will draw others closer to You. In Jesus' name. Amen.

DAY 121

Inspiration:

"Dear friend, if bad companions tempt you, don't go along with them. If they say--'Let's go out and raise some hell. Let's beat up some old man, mug some old woman. Let's pick them clean and get them ready for their funerals. We'll load up on top-quality loot. We'll haul it home by the truckload. Join us for the time of your life! With us, it's share and share alike!' Oh, friend, don't give them a second look; don't listen to them for a minute. They're racing to a very bad end, hurrying to ruin everything they lay hands on." ~ Proverbs 1:10-16, The Message Bible

Insight:

We are only responsible for our own decisions and actions, and should not take on the responsibility of others' choices and behaviors. Once we discern and discover the necessity of taking personal responsibility for our own life rather than someone else's (excluding the stewardship and guardianship of our own children), we free ourselves to embrace destiny and to release the people pleaser personality. There is one simple word that must become a regular part of our vocabulary in order to avoid the people pleaser personality, which can easily cause us to become overburdened with tasks and responsibilities that perhaps our neighbor should carry, and that simple word is "no." Others will be able to tell if we are serious when we respond to them based on how this simple word is communicated, and whether or not we back up our response with our intended display of tough love. Remember that our goal is not to please people, but to please our audience of one--God.

Bill Cosby made a profound, prolific statement when he retorted, "I don't know the key to success, but the key to failure is trying to please everyone."

Today, decide to only take on the responsibilities that belong to you, and to let everything else go without feeling guilty or condemned. You'll notice that you'll begin to breathe a little easier, walk a little straighter and that your own load of responsibilities will become a little lighter.

Prayer to Ignite Action:

Dear Lord, You created me with the ability to think and choose for myself. Although there are many voices and influences around me, I desire to make choices that are healthy for my mind, body and spirit. Please grant me the courage needed to ensure that my personal relationships, friendships and associations as well as the rest of my life's affairs and actions reflect wise choices. I also pray for discernment in knowing when to say no and to whom so that I do not find myself in compromising situations. My desire is to please You, God--my audience of one--rather than people today. In Jesus' name. Amen.

DAY 122

Inspiration:

"I have taught you in the way of wisdom; I have led you in right paths. When you walk, your steps will not be hindered, And when you run, you will not stumble. Take firm hold of instruction, do not let go; Keep her, for she [is] your life." ~ Proverbs 4:11-13, New King James Version

Insight:

No one has the right to live our life or to dictate how it should be lived. However, there is wisdom available from God and biblical principles that when applied, can help us to design the kind of life that will bring us pleasure while serving a cause greater than ourselves. Although challenges may come and go along the way, they serve as a reminder that they can be overcome by our tenacious, indomitable will that is empowered by God. When we decide to become fully engaged in life and enthralled by all that we have to offer, we can make an indelible mark upon the world that will not be easily forgotten.

Prayer to Ignite Action:

Father, I need Your wisdom to direct and correct me today. I am so blessed to know that You are with me everywhere I go. Speak to my mind and heart so that I may apply the wisdom of Your Holy Word in every area of my life. There is nothing too difficult for You, and because You are living in me, I can overcome every obstacle and conquer ever challenge that may come my way. I will be strong and bold enough to stand up for what is right and good even in the midst of what is wrong and evil. With Your help, my life will make a difference today. In Jesus' name. Amen.

DAY 123

Inspiration:

"Now go, write it before them on a tablet, And note it on a scroll, That it may be for time to come, Forever and ever." ~ Isaiah 30:8, New King James Version

"And then God answered: 'Write this. Write what you see. Write it out in big block letters so that it can be read on the run. This vision-message is a witness pointing to what's coming. It aches for the coming--it can hardly wait! And it doesn't lie. If it seems slow in coming, wait. It's on its way. It will come right on time." ~ Habakkuk 2:2-3, The Message Bible

Insight:

It is imperative to keep a dream or vision before our eyes--not just in our imagination--but in black and white such as recorded in a journal, notebook, business plan or on a vision board. A visual reminder of what we desire to accomplish or achieve will give us the motivation and inspiration to awaken each morning with a renewed sense of purpose to pursue a passion that is worth the effort, energy, service and sacrifice expended each day. In Habakkuk 2:2 of the Message Bible translation, God told the prophet (and he admonishes us as well) to "write what you see. Write it out in big block letters so that it can be read on the run." That scripture implies that we are to be moving, progressing and running towards the fulfillment of the vision that God gives us -- a vision with a mission that motivates the writer and reader to continue pressing forward positively and persistently in both action and attitude. We determine our own destiny once we decide to devise a strategy in visual form to keep us focused on our future, one day at a time.

Prayer to Ignite Action:

God, inspire me to dream again--to dream big and large enough so that the accomplishment of the vision requires Your intervention and power as well as the strength of others. Help me to do my part as I seek You for clarity and a strategy with specific goals to be written down, met and measured along the way. Let Your creative and persevering Spirit breathe and brilliantly work through me today as I focus on doing what needs to be done while I also keep my eyes on the visual image of what will unfold in the future. In Jesus' name. Amen.

DAY 124

Inspiration:

"Yes indeed, it is good when you obey the royal law as found in the Scriptures: 'Love your neighbor as yourself.'" ~ James 2:8, New Living Translation

Insight:

Have you ever created a "things to do list" to accomplish projects and tasks at home, work and/or church, and later discovered that everyone and everything had been included on your list except yourself? It is important to care for and meet the needs of others as we are led by God and are equipped to do so, but we must also remember to make decisions regarding our own health and wellness in the process. The choices we make today concerning ourselves as well as others will determine the kind of life we will have both now and in the future. Every action invites a reaction just as every choice invites a consequence. If we desire better consequences, then we must give full attention to making quality decisions that will produce a quality life for ourselves and those we love.

Prayer to Ignite Action:

God, it is good for me to love and care for my family, friends and neighbors as needed, but please help me not to neglect myself in the process. I make a commitment to love others in direct proportion to the love I provide for my spirit, mind and body. In all the tasks that I am to complete and the needs of others that I am compelled to meet, I will remember to set aside time for practicing self-care today. In Jesus' name. Amen.

DAY 125

Inspiration:

"To the Chief Musician. On a stringed instrument. [A Psalm] of David. Hear my cry, O God; Attend to my prayer. From the end of the earth I will cry to You, When my heart is overwhelmed; Lead me to the rock that is higher than I. For You have been a shelter for me, A strong tower from the enemy. I will abide in Your tabernacle forever; I will trust in the shelter of Your wings. Selah. For You, O God, have heard my vows; You have given [me] the heritage of those who fear Your name. You will prolong the king's life, His years as many generations. He shall abide before God forever. Oh, prepare mercy and truth, [which] may preserve him! So I will sing praise to Your name forever, That I may daily perform my vows." ~ Psalm 61:1-8, New King James Version

Insight:

I have often learned the most valuable lessons in my life as a result of disappointment and painful circumstances. No one wants to willingly walk through the valley of disappointment, and often there is very little rejoicing while enduring the valley experience. Yet, as a result of having gone through it, there are opportunities to learn more about ourselves and others while our character and resolve are strengthened. In addition, the disappointment or painful circumstance may serve as the catalyst to catapult us toward discovering and utilizing creativity, ingenuity and talents that would have otherwise remained dormant.

King David of Israel wrote about every emotion he experienced from one end of the spectrum to the other. Even in the midst of a whirlwind of disappointment, discouragement, disillusionment and despair, his heart remained fixed on who God was and how He had been with him in and through every circumstance. The valley experiences that David encountered and so openly penned in his poetic prose, allowed him to appreciate the mountaintop experiences in his life all the more because of the lessons he learned along the way.

One of the valuable lessons that we can learn from Psalm 61 is that we can surrender all our anxieties, emotions, concerns and fears to God with full assurance in His ability to hear and answer our prayers.

Prayer to Ignite Action:

Dear Lord, I stand in need of prayer today. I confess that I sometimes feel disheartened by disappointments, but yet I refuse to be in despair. Strengthen me from the inside out as I release all my anxiety, fear and disappointments to You. Please grant me the ability to see obstacles as opportunities. Today, I will not be overwhelmed because I am an overcomer empowered by Your might. In Jesus' name. Amen.

DAY 126

Inspiration:

"Do not let your heart envy sinners, But [be zealous] for the fear of the LORD all the day long." ~ Proverbs 23:17, New King James Version

"A sound heart [is] to the body, But envy [is] rottenness to the bones." ~ Proverbs 14:30, New King James Version

Insight:

Envy is a feeling of discontent or covetousness with regard to another person's advantages, success or possessions. It has been referred to by some as "the green-eyed monster" because it has such an ugly connotation and disposition on its bearer and wearer. Envy, according to Proverbs 14:30, manifests itself as "rottenness in the bones." However, the antithesis of envy is joy and gratitude which result in "a sound heart [which gives] life to the body." Envying others regardless of who they are, what they have or what they have achieved, is unhealthy and harmful, and produces nothing good. Exchanging envy for enthusiasm is a sure way to channel energy positively so that we are motivated to be excited about and thankful for the plan that God has for us while we celebrate others along the journey. In fact, rejoicing when others succeed may very well push us closer to manifesting the success desired in our own lives.

Prayer to Ignite Action:

Father, forgive me for the spirit of envy whenever it has reared its ugly head in my heart. Help me not to be complacent, but to be content with what You have blessed me with and who I am. I know that I cannot be who I am not, but I can become all that You desire me to be as I focus on my purpose without comparing myself with other people. Today, I choose to celebrate life as well as the blessings of others. In Jesus' name. Amen.

DAY 127

Inspiration:

"Thou art worthy, O Lord, to receive glory and honor and power: for thou hast created all things, and for thy pleasure they are and were created." ~ Revelation 4:11, King James Version

Insight:

Revelation 4:11 reminds us that we were and are created for the purpose of glorifying God as we give the best of ourselves away as an act of worship. That means that all that we think, say and do should reflect the glory of God, thereby giving Him pleasure. The beautiful thing about living our lives in this way is that God allows the overflow of His glory and pleasure to rest upon us so that we are blessed and can continue to be a blessing to those around us. Just think ... whenever we strive to be and do our personal best, then we are instrumental in inspiring and pleasing our Creator, and in so doing, our joy becomes full as well.

Prayer to Ignite Action:

Father God, I am awestruck by the fact that You created all things and all people to show forth Your glory. Everything that exists is to exude the excellence of Your creative purpose. Use my life by extracting out of it all that You originally planned to please You and to serve others. I live to love and worship You today. In Jesus' name. Amen.

DAY 128

Inspiration:

"Examine me, O LORD, and prove me; Try my mind and heart." ~ Psalm 26:2, New King James Version

Insight:

We often have expectations regarding whether others are producing desired results, but do we have the same stringent requirements for ourselves? Although we may have leadership responsibilities that influence others, the greatest influence we can make is by evaluating ourselves and determining to achieve results conducive for our own spiritual growth and professional development. People respond more to our actual actions than our words as we set the bar in our example of excellence and exemplary service. After all, if real results are to ever be, it is essentially is up to you and me.

Prayer to Ignite Action:

Father, search my mind and heart today and remove anything that is contrary to producing growth in my personal and professional life. I pray for discernment to see my own shortcomings rather than those of others, courage to acknowledge weak areas and wisdom to correct what is wrong while building upon the foundation of what is right. I thank You for allowing my actions to agree with my words as I evaluate myself and strive for excellence. In Jesus' name. Amen.

DAY 129

Inspiration:

"Therefore, whether you eat or drink, or whatever you do, do all to the glory of God." ~ 1 Corinthians 10:31, New King James Version

"Let every detail in your lives--words, actions, whatever--be done in the name of the Master, Jesus, thanking God the Father every step of the way." ~ Colossians 3:17, The Message Bible

Insight:

There is an old saying that tells us that, "if at first we don't succeed, then try, try again." To try means to attempt or to put forth some effort toward accomplishing a goal or task. Trying is not as strong of a word as doing. Doing is synonymous with other words such as performing, executing, accomplishing, exerting, completing and finishing. When we adopt this mindset, the old adage that we are familiar with will change because we'll find ourselves literally succeeding as a result of following through with Nike's simple but profound slogan: "JUST DO IT!"

Prayer to Ignite Action:

Lord, today I make a commitment not to try, but to do all that is within the scope of my responsibilities to accomplish. Help me to persevere and to complete and see to the end each task that I begin. I desire not just to finish what has been assigned to my stewardship, but to finish well. Enable me to have a work ethic that represents Your nature living within me, and to pass it on to others so that they may be motivated to do the same. In Jesus' name. Amen.

DAY 130

Inspiration:

"Is there a thing of which it may be said, See, this is new? It has already been, in the vast ages of time [recorded or unrecorded] which were before us." ~ Ecclesiastes 1:10, Amplified Bible

"To EVERYTHING there is a season, and a time for every matter or purpose under heaven." ~ Ecclesiastes 3:1, Amplified Bible

Insight:

Time waits for no one! So why is it that we procrastinate and put off for tomorrow what desperately needs our attention today, as if we have a monopoly on dispensing time to arrive and depart at our pleasure? Time is a gift that is to be valued and managed well as we use it efficiently and effectively to prioritize and manage all of life's daily affairs. Now is the time to take time seriously, and to spend it wisely.

Prayer to Ignite Action:

Lord, please forgive me for not valuing the precious commodity of time as I should. You graciously give to each of us the same amount of time each day in which to accomplish everything that matters. You have dispensed my time, but I must deploy it so that it accomplishes the very purpose for which You sent it in my life. Today, I commit my time to You so that I can spend it wisely by alleviating procrastination, attaining specific goals, and achieving purpose-driven results. In Jesus' name. Amen.

DAY 131

Inspiration:

"But Peter and John replied, 'Judge for yourselves whether it is right in God's sight to obey you rather than God.'" ~ Acts 4:19, New International Version

"We are witnesses of these things, and so is the Holy Spirit, whom God has given to those who obey him." ~ Acts 5:32, New International Version

Insight:

Regardless of the thoughts, opinions and albeit well intentioned wishes of others, there is a wellspring of wisdom inside of us from which we must ultimately take our own counsel. Within each of us is the capacity to access the Source of all wisdom who knows the plans predestined for our lives better than any other person, including ourselves. Once we seek God for direction regarding the path of our purpose each day, we must diligently follow that path trusting that we will follow the leading of the inner voice that speaks to us when we take the time to intentionally listen. We must never allow the dissenting voices of others to dissuade or deter us from doing what we know is right. Whenever given the choice, we must choose to obey God rather than men.

Prayer to Ignite Action:

Father, I thank you for the inner voice of the Holy Spirit within me that speaks wisdom so that I may follow the path that has been predestined for my life. Although there are many voices that chatter, my desire is to hone in on the certainty and clarity of what I should think, say and do today. By an act of my will, I choose to obey Your Word and to follow Your ways. In Jesus' name. Amen.

DAY 132

Inspiration:

"I do not consider, brethren, that I have captured and made it my own [yet]; but one thing I do [it is my one aspiration]; forgetting what lies behind and straining forward to what lies ahead, I press on toward the goal to win the [supreme and heavenly] prize to which God in Christ Jesus is calling us upward. So let those [of us] who are spiritually mature and full-grown have this mind and hold these convictions; and if in any respect you have a different attitude of mind, God will make that clear to you also." ~ Philippians 3:13-15, Amplified Bible

Insight:

Determining to achieve what we dare to believe is the catalyst to guarantee what we will receive. We will only accomplish and enjoy the rewards of what we have mentally fixed our attention upon and focused our efforts towards. Inspiration (whether it is a good idea or a God-idea) alone will not produce the results that we desire. Inspiration must give way to the application of action steps necessary to achieve not just what we can fathom, but what we will discipline ourselves to literally do. Don't just talk about it; decide to be about it!"

Prayer to Ignite Action:

Father, thank You for giving me the ability to leave my past behind me and to fine-tune my focus upon what is to be accomplished today. I am grateful for the inspiration You've given me, and will show my appreciation by appropriating the necessary discipline and effort to achieve my destiny while helping others to do the same. Words spoken have power, but deeds done have the power to influence my present and to procure my future. Let my words and actions honor Your purpose for my life today and for all eternity. In Jesus' name. Amen.

DAY 133

Inspiration:

"So Daniel was called in. The king asked him, 'Are you the Daniel who was one of the Jewish exiles my father brought here from Judah? I've heard about you--that you're full of the Holy Spirit, that you've got a brilliant mind, that you are incredibly wise. The wise men and enchanters were brought in here to read this writing on the wall and interpret it for me. They could't figure it out--not a word, not a syllable. But I've heard that you interpret dreams and solve mysteries. So--if you can read the writing and interpret it for me, you'll be rich and famous--a purple robe, the great gold chain around your neck--and third-in-command in the kingdom.' Daniel answered the king, 'You can keep your gifts, or give them to someone else. But I will read the writing for the king and tell him what it means.'" ~ Daniel 5:13-17, The Message Bible

"But Daniel, brimming with spirit and intelligence, so completely outclassed the other vice-regents and governors that the king decided to put him in charge of the whole kingdom." ~ Daniel 6:3, The Message Bible

Insight:

Perfection is unattainable in this life, and striving for it will only produce overwhelming frustration for ourselves and others. However, attaining excellence is not only possible, but believable and achievable in areas of our personal and professional lives where we focus our attention and time. The areas that we neglect will not exemplify excellence unless we value and prioritize those areas enough to give ourselves fully to them in purposeful thought and action. Excellence requires attention to detail and performance that produces a desired result to honor our time, effort, integrity and character.

Today, let's follow the example of Daniel whose commitment to God was demonstrated in his pursuit of excellence. Serving God and striving for excellence will cause great men and women to recognize, appreciate and call upon the gifts that are within us.

Prayer to Ignite Action:

Gracious God, I am humbled that Your Spirit lives in me. I pray that wisdom, knowledge, understanding, counsel and might from Your Spirit would emanate from me and manifest in excellence as I represent You today. I am thankful that my commitment to serve You and other people with the gifts I have will advance Your kingdom on earth and yield benefits beyond what I can imagine. In Jesus' name. Amen.

DAY 134

Inspiration:

"An excellent wife, who can find? For her worth is far above jewels. The heart of her husband trusts in her, And he will have no lack of gain. She does him good and not evil All the days of her life...She rises also while it is still night And gives food to her household And portions to her maidens. She considers a field and buys it; From her earnings she plants a vineyard. She girds herself with strength And makes her arms strong...Strength and dignity are her clothing, And she smiles at the future. She opens her mouth in wisdom, And the teaching of kindness is on her tongue. She looks well to the ways of her household, And does not eat the bread of idleness. Her children rise up and bless her; Her husband also, and he praises her, saying: 'Many daughters have done nobly, But you excel them all.'" ~ Proverbs 31:10-12,15-17, 25-29, New American Standard Bible

Insight:

Proverbs 31 gives us a pictorial view of the woman who seamlessly balances everything with grace upon her life, pep in her step, kindness on her tongue, a smile on her face, and commendations from her family and community. This lady evidently could do it all, but I am convinced that she didn't accomplish everything at the same time. She had to have a prioritized plan that was realistically doable...and let's not forget that she had some maidens to help her as indicated in verse 15!

Having a prioritized plan which lists anything that is important to us along with the order in which tasks are to be accomplished and the specific day and time frame for each task (preferably listed in the calendar format of a cell phone or something small that can be carried) helps to alleviate undue stress and keeps us from overly committing or doubly booking ourselves. It is true that whatever we devote the majority of our time, energy and effort to is our true priority. Actions still speak much louder than words.

It is also important to establish boundaries, not just for us so that we know when to say no, but also for others so that everyone involved in our lives can respect the boundaries that we have set and help to establish relationships of accountability.

Prayer to Ignite Action:

Father, I know that superman and superwoman are fictitious characters that do not exist. Help me to set realistic, believable and achievable goals for today and my future and to realize that I am not called to be all things to all people simultaneously. My desire is to please You by being and doing my best, for by doing so, others who matter in my life will admire and appreciate my efforts. Most of all, I thank You for power to say, 'yes,' to what I capable of doing and to say, 'no,' to what should be done by someone else as I prioritize and organize my responsibilities. In Jesus' name. Amen.

DAY 135

Inspiration:

"Give, and [gifts] will be given to you; good measure, pressed down, shaken together, and running over, will they pour into [the pouch formed by] the bosom [of your robe and used as a bag]. For with the measure you deal out [with the measure you use when you confer benefits on others], it will be measured back to you." ~ Luke 6:38, Amplified Bible

Insight:

We weren't born with a silver spoon in our mouths so to speak, so there is no need to have a mentality of thinking that the world owes us something. Quite simply, we will get out of life what we are willing and determined to put into it. It is a biblical principle that what we give will be given back to us again, not only in good measure (according to what we have given), but with a greater return than we ever could have imagined. If we give of our time to those who are dearest and most important to us, than they will do the same to show that they value the investment that was made in their lives. If we give of our talents to help those less fortunate than ourselves, as well as to help others who are levels above us in order to fulfill their dream/vision, we will be rewarded in return by our Father in heaven as well as by others on earth. Some call this The Law of Reciprocity, meaning that we will indeed reap whatever we have sown, either sparingly or generously. Life doesn't owe us a thing, but we do owe it to God and ourselves to give our best so that we can live our best and most blessed lives.

Prayer to Ignite Action:

Heavenly Father, cultivate the spirit of generosity in me so that I may ask, 'What can I give?' rather than 'What can I receive?' Today, I will look for opportunities to be a blessing to those in need by offering the gift of my time, talent or treasured resources. Although I am to give without expecting anything in return from those in need, I am motivated by the fact that You will reward me in ways that are abundantly rich and fulfilling beyond comparison. In Jesus' name. Amen.

DAY 136

Inspiration:

"But we will not boast beyond our measure, but within the measure of the sphere which God apportioned to us as a measure, to reach even as far as you. For we are not overextending ourselves, as if we did not reach to you, for we were the first to come even as far as you in the gospel of Christ; not boasting beyond our measure, that is, in other men's labors, but with the hope that as your faith grows we will be within our sphere, enlarged even more by you, so as to preach the gospel even to the regions beyond you, and not to boast in what has been accomplished in the sphere of another." ~ 2 Corinthians 10:13-16, New American Standard Bible

Insight:

Having a dream and taking the time to set goals to accomplish it is admirable, but in order for our dream to become a reality we must endeavor to follow through with the necessary effort so that our goals are achieved. The word W-O-R-K, as difficult as it may be to hear, harness and hone, is well worth the effort and energy. Our success depends on the preparation, pursuit and persistence of the work (exertion or effort directed to produce or accomplish something) that we are willing to wield. According to a dictionary reference, the word wield means to exercise power, authority and influence as in ruling or dominating; to use effectively, to handle or employ actively; to govern and manage.

We only have the power and authority to have dominion and rule over what has been assigned to us--that is, our own thoughts, words and actions as well as the sphere of influence that God has given us. Paul reminds us that we are only called to operate within the sphere that belongs to us rather than in another person's sphere of accomplishment in 2 Corinthians 10:13-16. Within that sphere, the possibilities are as limitless as our dreams and desires. However, we must seize every possible opportunity to work our plans in believable and achievable action steps if we want to enjoy the fulfillment that will surely follow as we begin to launch and live our dream.

Prayer to Ignite Action:

Dear Lord, I praise You for being the God who sees, knows and works in and through me to accomplish great things. I know that You assign to each person a sphere of influence, and that we will only be effective when we recognize and stay within that sphere. Thank You for trusting me with the ability to do what comes naturally by employing my best gifts and exerting my best energy to accept, appreciate and operate in my calling. May my life have maximum impact as I exercise dominion over my (rather than someone else's) assignment with joy. In Jesus' name. Amen.

DAY 137

Inspiration:

"I know what I'm doing. I have it all planned out--plans to take care of you, not abandon you, plans to give you the future you hope for." ~ Jeremiah 29:11, The Message Bible

Insight:

No one knows what is best for us better than God and ourselves. Although those in our circle of influence may offer counsel to take and mistakes to avoid, we must seek God and follow His direction as well as our own gut instincts or intuition. Some people call the latter a "sixth sense" of sorts. I believe it is the work of the Holy Spirit tugging at our conscience to follow the right path and to avoid the wrong one with each decision that must be made. No one is responsible for making the decisions that will govern our lives but us, and we should not give away that God-ordained power of choice -- for in doing so, we become pawns or puppets for others to play with as they so chose. Instead, we must follow the plan that works best for us, and that plan becomes clearer each day as we spend time with God and submit our plans as well as our decisions to Him. After all, He is the true Expert and Mastermind.

Prayer to Ignite Action:

God, I believe You planned my life for me before I was born. You knew who my parents would be, when my birthday would be, where life would take me and with whom I would spend time and space to become the person I am today. More important, You know what the future holds for me. Help me to make choices that agree with what is to be my destiny. I trust the voice of Your Spirit tugging at my conscience so that I can aim for what is right and avoid what is wrong for me and those I care about today. I submit myself and my plans to You afresh, asking in return for the direction and determination to follow the path You planned for me. In Jesus' name. Amen.

DAY 138

Inspiration:

"The blessing of the LORD makes a person rich, and he adds no sorrow with it." ~ Proverbs 10:22, New Living Translation

"A faithful man will abound with blessings, But he who hastens to be rich will not go unpunished." ~ Proverbs 28:20, New King James Version

Insight:

Proverbs 10:22 lets us know that being rich has very little if anything to do with money or possessions. True wealth does not come from seeking to be rich financially or materially, but it is found when we choose to serve and obey God with a pure heart by following after His will rather than money.

I have learned that the blessing of the Lord that makes us rich carries with it favor from God which is priceless and supersedes the value of money. When we are faithful in and consistent with using the resources of our time, abilities and money wisely, we will abound with blessings. Pursue faithfulness in being authentically you from the inside out, and watch God's blessing chase away the sorrow in your life.

Prayer to Ignite Action:

God, You have made me rich in ways that far outweigh monetary value. I exalt You because of Your lovingkindness and faithfulness that never ends. Thank You for blessing me so abundantly, and for allowing me to understand that my relationship with You is to take precedence over everything and everyone else. Let me never be motivated by money. My desire is to be motivated by the mission You've given me to love and serve You so that I can be the conduit through which blessings flow to benefit others. In Jesus' name. Amen.

DAY 139

Inspiration:

"Be anxious for nothing, but in everything by prayer and supplication, with thanksgiving, let your requests be make known to God; and the peace of God, which surpasses all understanding, will guard your hearts and minds through Christ Jesus." ~ Philippians 4:6-7, New King James Version

Insight:

Philippians 4:6 is a scripture that has conditions that must be met and a promise that will be realized as a result. The conditions are as follows:
1. Decide not to be anxious.
2. Commit everything to God in prayer.
3. Pray with supplication (humble entreaty or petition).
4. Pray with thanksgiving unto God.

When we meet the fourfold condition of this passage, we can expect to receive the promise of embodying the peace of God which carries with it the fourfold benefit of replacing anxiety, surpassing our understanding, guarding (hence protecting) our hearts as well as our minds. Now that promise of peace is enough positive power to get us through, carry us over, and lift us above any situation that comes our way. Let's position ourselves to meet the fourfold conditions found in Philippians 4:6 so that we can receive the fourfold promise!

Prayer to Ignite Action:

Father, there are so many promises in Your Word with benefits. Today, I commit myself to meeting the conditions found in Philippians 4:6 so that I can receive the benefits found in Philippians 4:7. I consciously decide not to be anxious, but to instead commit all my concerns and requests to you right now. I pray not only for myself today, but also on behalf of specific people that need my prayers of supplication today in areas that require Your attention and provision and their accountability and obedience. Now, I humbly give You thanks for hearing and answering my requests. I receive Your peace to replace my anxiety, surpass my understanding, and guard my heart and mind today. In Jesus' name. Amen.

DAY 140

Inspiration:

"Any enterprise is built by wise planning, becomes strong through common sense, and profits wonderfully by keeping abreast of the facts." ~ Proverbs 24:3-4, The Living Bible

Insight:

Do you have a potential book, poem, song, creative idea or business inside of you? Your dream will remain dormant unless you decide to unleash your potential by turning your formulated, creative thoughts into firm, concrete action steps. Start today to realize your potential by doing what is necessary to research your idea. Discover what you need to do to get started and seek out and surround yourself with those who can mentor you who have accomplished or achieved success in your area of interest. Solicit their help to devise a strategy to assist in the development stages of launching your dream, but decide to take responsibility for doing the work of working your own plan, step by step, with all the creativity, energy, diligence and determination you can muster. Before long, you'll find that the reality of the principles shared in Proverbs 24:3-4 have unlocked your potential by bringing your dream to life. Then, you can mentor others by sharing the same wisdom that you have learned and put into action.

Prayer to Ignite Action:

Dear Lord, I know there is much more to me than eyes can see. You have placed vast and unlimited potential within me that is waiting to be released. Stir up my dreams so that they will not lie dormant. Lead me in the direction needed to find and be surrounded by dream-builders instead of dream-killers. As I seek out mentors who possess the expertise that will cause me to grow, help me to listen intently to them and to internalize their counsel by choosing to use wise planning and common sense while keeping abreast of and staying on the cutting edge in my own area of interest and expertise. Today, I am determined and empowered to make a demand on my potential. In Jesus' name. Amen.

DAY 141

Inspiration:

"Have you not known? Have you not heard? The everlasting God, the LORD, The Creator of the ends of the earth, Neither faints nor is weary. His understanding is unsearchable." ~ Isaiah 40:28, New King James Version

"And let us not grow weary while doing good, for in due season we shall reap if we do not lose heart." ~ Galatians 6:9, New King James Version

Insight:

How we decide to live today is the determining factor of what we can expect to receive tomorrow. The choices we make, the deeds we do and the relationships we prioritize today will greatly impact and influence the path that is forged ahead of us. If we desire to attract valuable, meaningful and significant people and resources into our lives as we move forward, then we must give special attention to how we think, speak and act in the span of time that we have in this moment. Today is the day to live fully, faithfully and freely, for we will reap the fruit tomorrow and thereafter of what we strategically sow today.

Prayer to Ignite Action:

Everlasting God, You are always the same. Your nature is unchangeable and Your understanding is unsearchable. Although I cannot fathom Your work of creation, I am grateful for Your faithfulness towards me even when I didn't deserve it. You never tire or grow weary in loving and caring for all that You created, including me. Strengthen and enable me not to grow weary in what You've called me to do, for You promised that I would reap a harvest if I do not faint or give up along the way. I thank You for answering my prayer. In Jesus' name. Amen.

DAY 142

Inspiration:

"But the time is coming--it has, in fact, come--when what you're called will not matter and where you go to worship will not matter. It's who you are and the way you live that count before God. Your worship must engage your spirit in the pursuit of truth. That's the kind of people the Father is out looking for: those who are simply and honestly themselves before him in their worship. God is sheer being itself--Spirit. Those who worship him must do it out of their very being, their spirits, their true selves, in adoration." ~ John 4:23-24, The Message Bible

Insight:

John J. Murphy disclosed a powerful yet profound pearl of great price by stating "when we are in harmony and balance with our core essence, our authentic self, we act with power, strength, confidence, and grace." Our core essence is the real us--the spirit or nature of who we really are without the shell of our outer body or other influences to cover us up. We can and should not change who we are to please people or to pretend to be someone else. When we discover our true selves, we then unlock the passion and pursuit of purpose and the ability to follow through with the God-inspired plans that we are to accomplish, while being uniquely ourselves.

Today is filled with brand new opportunities to share our authenticity and uniqueness with the world. Let's give our best and trust God to handle the rest.

Prayer to Ignite Action:

Father, You provided an excellent example to us of what it means to live with authenticity, power and purpose. Jesus lived to please You while being true to who He was and what He believed in while on earth. The essence of God shone brightly through His words and works. God, allow the essence of who I was originally created to be shine through me today. Let me be genuinely sincere and authentic so that people will see my heart and spirit--the real me--as You created me to be. I pray that I would also become keenly aware of the true spirits of those around me today and that I will not lead or be led astray by wrong decisions and influences. I will confidently and passionately pursue my purpose as an offering of worship to You. In Jesus' name. Amen.

DAY 143

Inspiration:

"Let no foul or polluting language, nor evil word nor unwholesome or worthless talk [ever] come out of your mouth, but only such [speech] as is good and beneficial to the spiritual progress of others, as is fitting to the need and the occasion, that it may be a blessing and give grace (God's favor) to those who hear it." ~ Ephesians 4:29, Amplified Bible

Insight:

Too often, we take life's opportunities and the people closest to us for granted without even realizing it. To avoid such an oversight, we can intentionally focus our attention towards prioritizing the relationships and realities that are assigned to our stewardship with an attitude of appreciation expressed by our words. This shift alone will cause us to resist the temptation to complain and to sublimate that energy in a positive way by thinking and speaking positively and acting proactively. In so doing, we allow ourselves to appreciate the people and predicaments that are placed in our lives, realizing that they all work together for a greater purpose to glorify God, fortify our character and solidify what we value the most.

Prayer to Ignite Action:

Heavenly Father, forgive me for worthless words that should not have been spoken on my part. I ask for the wisdom to select wise words that are appropriate for every person and setting where You lead me today. Help me to use my energy positively as I relate to others without taking them or life itself for granted. I know that You will cause everything to work together for a greater purpose so that who and what is truly important will retain value and worth. In Jesus' name. Amen.

DAY 144

Inspiration:

"Only be careful, and watch yourselves closely so that you do not forget the things your eyes have seen or let them slip from your heart as long as you live. Teach them to your children and to their children after them." ~ Deuteronomy 4:9, New International Version

"And these words which I am commanding you this day shall be [first] in your [own] minds and hearts; [then] You shall whet and sharpen them so as to make them penetrate, and teach and impress them diligently upon the [minds and] hearts of your children, and shall talk of them when you sit in your house and when you walk by the way, and when you lie down and when you rise up." ~ Deuteronomy 6:6-7, Amplified Bible

Insight:

Although my children are now adults, I often reflect on times when they were much younger. God allowed me the honor of not only teaching them, but learning from them as well. One such lesson came as a result of my daughters interrupting me when I was having a personal time of prayer and bible study in my bedroom. They were very young and I used to long for the quiet times that I spent alone with God--so much so that I would become rather perturbed when they disrupted my devotional time--until God interrupted my so called disruption. He impressed upon my heart that each time my children entered my bedroom was not a disruption, but a divine interruption and opportunity for instruction. It hit me like a ton of bricks! From that moment on, I decided that I would view and use every opportunity as God had spoken to share my devotional time on an age appropriate level with my daughters whenever they divinely interrupted my personal time with God. I would read and explain the scriptures to them as well as give them the chance to read and ask questions to make sure they could understand and apply the lessons I taught them.

Today, as I see my adult daughters who love and serve God as a result of developing their own personal relationship with Him, I am thankful for disruptions in life, for I now perceive them as divine interruptions in our schedule and opportunities to learn lessons that can be taught to others.

Prayer to Ignite Action:

Father, thank You for writing Your word upon my heart so that I can recall it at the exact moment that I need it. I also thank you for teaching me the lesson that every disruption can be transformed into a divine opportunity from which to learn so that I may teach others. Let me become the mentor You created me to be not to influence my generation only, but to leave a legacy for the next generation to come. I take this responsibility seriously, and will do my part to pass on the wisdom of Your Word and my life's experiences to those who will also be able to teach others. In Jesus' name. Amen.

DAY 145

Inspiration:

"His master said to him, Well done, you upright (honorable, admirable) and faithful servant! You have been faithful and trustworthy over a little; I will put you in charge of much. Enter into and share the joy (the delight, the blessedness) which your master enjoys." ~ Matthew 25:21, Amplified Bible

Insight:

Although thoughts determine actions, and actions determine habits, our habits determine the character by which we become known and identified by others. Therefore, it is imperative that we make wise decisions to begin with so that our conduct and character represent who we decide and desire to be as well as every endeavor that we consequently set in motion. Patterns are first formulated in our minds before they are followed through with corresponding actions. If we want to accomplish any worthwhile task, then we must renew our minds by rejecting thoughts that are counterproductive and replacing them with a "can do" mentality and "will do" movement. Before we know it, the goals we originally set will be reached and we'll be able to change our "things to do" list to "things already done." Then we can move on to accomplishing bigger and greater endeavors.

Prayer to Ignite Action:

Dear God, I want to partner with You in all I think, say and do. My objective is to hear the words, "Well done, good and faithful servant," as I live today with an expectation of spending eternity with You. May the musing of my thoughts, the meditation of my heart, and motion of my hands determine what will please You and prosper as I begin each task and finish it well. In Jesus' name. Amen.

DAY 146

Inspiration:

"Therefore, if anyone [is] in Christ, he is a new creation; old things have passed away; behold, all things have become new." ~ 2 Corinthians 5:17, New King James Version

Insight:

Today is a sure thing. It has arrived to remind us that new possibilities exist and that potential is yet to be realized for the greater good of ourselves and others. Yesterday is behind us as is our past. We have brand new opportunities today to display Christ in us and to take full advantage of all that today offers.

A butterfly goes through a metamorphosis as it leaves the pupa, larva and caterpillar stage behind. Exiting from its previous form was necessary for the caterpillar to experience the true beauty of what it was meant to become. The same is true for those who are new in Christ. Accepting Jesus as Lord and Savior transforms us as the sins of our past are forgiven and the beauty of our new life begins.

Prayer to Ignite Action:

Dear Lord, what an awesome opportunity afforded to all who confess Jesus as Lord and believe in their hearts that He died and rose again to save us from our sins, and from ourselves. In exchange for our sins, You give us new life on earth as well as in eternity as we spend it with You. Thank You for forgiving my past sins and freeing me to pursue the purpose for which I was created. I am grateful to be a new creation, and I will intentionally share the same opportunity with others so that they can experience the beauty of a transformed life. In Jesus' name. Amen.

DAY 147

Inspiration:

"May He grant you according to your heart's desire and fulfill all your plans. We will [shout in] triumph at your salvation and victory, and in the name of our God we will set up our banners. may the Lord fulfill all your petitions." ~ Psalm 20:4-5, Amplified Bible

Insight:

Have you ever stopped to think about the impact you are making, or desire to make, upon others in your family, community, church, workplace, and world? What difference can you make by being authentically you and joyfully offering the best of who you are? When we discover our natural gifts and talents and hone our skills to become even more proficient by doing what we love, we'll find that our deepest passions are awakened and as a result, we will leave a legacy that is not only priceless, but proof that we have lived to fulfill our purpose and to positively impact the lives of others who crossed our path.

Prayer to Ignite Action:

Father, I thank You for another opportunity to awaken and fulfill purpose today--not just for my own fulfillment--but so that I can make a difference in the lives of others by loving what I do and doing what I love. I pray that every talent and ability that I have will be used to add value and worth to the people and places I go today. In Jesus' name. Amen.

DAY 148

Inspiration:

"Lot went out and warned the fiances of his daughters, 'Evacuate this place; GOD is about to destroy this city!' But his daughters' would-be husbands treated it as a joke. At break of day, the angels pushed Lot to get going, 'Hurry. Get your wife and two daughters out of here before it's too late and you're caught in the punishment of the city.' Lot was dragging his feet. The men grabbed Lot's arm, and the arms of his wife and daughters--GOD was so merciful to them!--and dragged them to safety outside the city. When they had them outside, Lot was told, 'Now run for your life! Don't look back! Don't stop anywhere on the plain--run for the hills or you'll be swept away.' ...But Lot's wife looked back and turned into a pillar of salt." ~ Genesis 19:14-17, 26, The Message Bible

"Remember Lot's wife." ~ Luke 17:32, New King James Version

Insight:

Our past has a way of trying to resurface when something or someone in our present pulls the same painful trigger. The challenge is to replace rather than to preserve that memory by transforming our thoughts with the principles and practice of God's Word and reinventing ourselves by determining what and with whom we choose to celebrate our present and future. Tolerating old thoughts and patterns of behavior that continue to minimize rather than maximize the quality of life that Jesus died and rose again to give us, diminishes and devalues the best of who we were meant to be as the original, handcrafted masterpiece of God. Choosing to discover and uncover all the wondrous capabilities of our mind, body and spirit as we partner with God in living a purpose-driven life, frees us to make choices that are in alignment with our destiny rather than our history. Today, let's make a conscious effort to reject anything in our past that prevents us from loving our present and living for our future. The choice is ours, starting now!

Prayer to Ignite Action:

Merciful God, how blessed I am to experience your goodness and grace.

You have forgiven my past and preserved my life from danger seen and unseen. Thank You for helping me to love the moment I am living in right now and to anticipate the wonderful future that lies ahead. I will not be held hostage by my past by looking back, but I will keep my eyes on You and what is in store for my life by applying the principles of Your Word. In Jesus' name. Amen.

DAY 149

Inspiration:

"The wise in hart will be called prudent, And sweetness of the lips increases learning. The heart of the wise teaches his mouth, And adds learning to his lips." ~ Proverbs 16:21, 23, New King James Version

Insight:

Our mind, heart and mouth are more powerful than we can possibly imagine. Whatever thoughts we choose to entertain, whether positive or negative, will be reflected in the emotions we encounter and the words we allow to proceed from our lips. As a result, what we attract toward or repel away from us is a reflection of what we think, feel and speak. We have the ability to determine the quality of our lives based on the quality of our decisions. Today, let's make every effort to attract what we desire by cultivating a positive mindset, a pure heart and a purpose-filled conversation that is in direct alignment with God's best for us. Expect to attract what your mind dwells upon, your heart desires, and your mouth declares!

Prayer to Ignite Action:

Father, teach my how to think, speak and act positively today as I represent You. I pray for the ability to manage my life responsibly while working towards maintaining balance within and around me. I thank You for empowering me to make prudent decisions today, and I look forward to the results that will follow. In Jesus' name. Amen.

DAY 150

Inspiration:
"Concentrate on doing your best for God, work you won't be ashamed of, laying out the truth plain and simple. Stay clear of pious talk that is only talk. Words are not mere words, you know. If they're not backed by a godly life, they accumulate as poison in the soul." ~ 2 Timothy 2:15-17a, The Message Bible

Insight:
No one else can or should make decisions on our behalf unless we are unable or unwilling to do so. You and I are responsible for our own choices, actions, goals, dreams, happiness and joy. Conversely, we are also responsible for our wrong choices and conduct, as well as the lack of fulfillment regarding personal desires and professional benchmarks. Whatever we aim for we will surely reach if we remain consistent, diligent and confident in who God is, whose we are, and what we are capable of accomplishing and possessing to honor God while being a blessing to others. Whatever we want is within our reach if we just require more of ourselves.

Prayer to Ignite Action:
Dear God, I will be diligent in the choices that I make and the actions that I take today. You approve of a life that is marked by godliness, and not just good works. Let me not be ashamed of my decisions and activities today as I concentrate on doing my best to please You--not with mere words--but with a servant's heart as I accomplish the goals set before me and help others to do the same. In Jesus' name. Amen.

DAY 151

Inspiration:

"For God did not give us a spirit of timidity but a spirit of power and love and self-control." ~ 2 Timothy 1:7, Revised Standard Version

Insight:

Our perspective of people, personal circumstances and our place in the world, stems from the kind of thoughts we allow ourselves to ponder. We will either respond appropriately or react inappropriately based on the picture painted on the canvas of our minds. For instance, we can choose to concentrate on thoughts of faith which will propel us forward, or fear which has the opposite effect and will paralyze our progress. The power to choose is ours to use daily, and choosing wisely will allow us to view obstacles as opportunities and to focus on being a conduit of blessing to others. Exercising this God-given right will lessen stress (an internal force brought on by mental, emotional or physical tension) and help us to maintain equilibrium and stability in life. Right thinking produces a healthy view of our ourselves, others and the world around us.

Prayer to Ignite Action:

Father, I release all timidity, intimidation and fear to You today in exchange for boldness, confidence and self-control. I realize that I have the power to maintain equilibrium and stability in my life because You are living in me. Help me to recognize indicators of stress in and around me, and to do what is necessary to alleviate it proactively. Then, I can be of greater service to others. In Jesus' name. Amen.

DAY 152

Inspiration:

"Now you've got my feet on the life path, all radiant from the shining of your face. Ever since you took my hand, I'm on the right way." ~ Psalm 16:11, The Message Bible

"Until now you have not asked for anything in my name. Ask and you will receive, and your joy will be complete." ~ John 16:24, New International Version

Insight:

When my 40th birthday arrived several years ago, I began to ask questions regarding how significant my relationships and accomplishments could and should be from that point forward. I was grateful to God for His goodness shown towards me and the work He had wrought in and through me up until that point, but all of a sudden I had an epiphany that reaching the milestone of 40 afforded me another opportunity to define significance and meaning for my present and future life. One of the challenges I faced was reinventing myself in such a way as to only pursue the plans and people that were congruous with the purpose God designed specifically for my life. I found that the persons who identified with and appreciated the passion that propelled me to do what I was created to do in that new season of my life, would be automatically assigned to me, and vice versa, because of our mutual desire to accomplish what mattered to God (and us) the most.

What is it that matters most to you? Are you satisfied with the life you are currently living and the contribution you are making to the world for God's glory? If not, you don't have to wait for a milestone birthday to arrive to reinvent yourself and to discover what is meaningful to you. Following after that which brings your spirit joy also perpetuates joy in others while adding richness and longevity to your life as well.

Prayer to Ignite Action:

Heavenly Father, You created me to joyfully pursue my destiny and to be aware of the seasons in my life when I am to be fruitful and productive. I am thankful that You desire to do great exploits through willing vessels regardless of age or past accomplishments. Set me on the path of life that is designed especially for me where I discover meaning, significance, richness and longevity that can be shared with others. In Jesus' name. Amen.

DAY 153

Inspiration:

"O LORD, you have examined my heart and know everything about me. You know when I sit down or stand up. You know my thoughts even when I'm far away. You see me when I travel and when I rest at home. You know everything I do. You know what I am going to say even before I say it, LORD. You go before me and follow me. You place your hand of blessing on my head...You saw me before I was born. Every day of my life was recorded in your book. Every moment was laid out before a single day had passed. How precious are your thoughts about me, O God. They cannot be numbered! I can't even count them; they outnumber the grains of sand! And when I wake up, you are still with me!" ~ Psalm 139:1-5, 16-18, New Living Translation

Insight:

I've heard it said that, "we are our own worst enemy." To some degree that is true because we are most critical of ourselves based on our sense of self worth and esteem. However, we can have a paradigm shift and adopt a mentality to declare the following: I am the sum total of my positive thoughts, gifts, abilities, desires and dreams. I am the epitome of God's masterpiece equipped with everything I need in order to fulfill the purpose for which I was created. I am a wellspring of wisdom and a reservoir of relevance to those assigned to my circle of influence. There is no limit to the wondrous world of possibilities that await my presence and participation once I give God permission to utilize my life fully for His glory and others' benefit.

Prayer to Ignite Action:

Dear Lord, thank you for making me so wonderfully complex. Your workmanship is beyond my comprehension, and I am humbled to know that Your thoughts about me are more than can be numbered. You created me with intrinsic worth so that I can appreciate the value in myself and others as a gift from You. Please fill me up so that I can pour out the best use of my life as an offering to those who assigned to my circle of influence. In Jesus' name. Amen.

DAY 154

Inspiration:

"You watched me as I was being formed in utter seclusion, as I was woven together in the dark of the womb." ~ Psalm 139:15, New Living Translation

"We are assured and know that [God being a partner in their labor] all things work together and are [fitting into a plan] for good to and for those who love God and are called according to [His} design and purpose." ~ Romans 8:28, Amplified Bible

Insight:

I was invited to attend the Swearing-in Ceremony of my friend, United States Ambassador-at-Large for International Religious Freedom, Dr. Suzan Johnson Cook, which was conducted by Secretary of State Hillary Rodham Clinton in the Benjamin Franklin Room of the Department of State Building in Washington, D.C. Afterward, Ambassador Sujay generously hosted a private reception for family and friends at B. Smith's Restaurant at Union Station. The entire afternoon and evening created savoring, surreal moments woven into the fabric of my life forever.

Albert Einsein once said, "There are two ways to live your life. One is as though nothing is a miracle. The other is though everything is a miracle." I choose the latter as the mantra by which my life is lived. Every relationship made, lesson learned, small or great deed done, and place visited, has been woven together as God's tapestry for me--a masterpiece of miracles coupled with a wealth of wisdom for which I am sincerely grateful beyond words.

When you think of your life, what miracles have served as threads woven together to create who you are? Take the time today, and in the future, to thank God for His divine providence in and purpose for your life. No need to look for a miracle because you are a miracle!

Prayer to Ignite Action:

Oh Lord, I love You with all my heart and soul. You have created me wondrously and woven every intricate detail of my life to fit into Your plan and purpose for me. Every relationship and experience whether good, bad or indifferent is working together for my good as a reminder to me and a testimony to others of Your miraculous power, mercy and grace. I am thankful for everything that You have allowed me to face, for it has increased my faith and trust in You. In Jesus' name. Amen.

DAY 155

Inspiration:

"Until the time came to fulfill his dreams, the LORD tested Joseph's character." ~ Psalm 105:19, New Living Translation

"We can rejoice, too, when we run int problems and trials, for we know that they help us develop endurance. And endurance develops strength of character, and character strengthens our confident hope of salvation. And this hope will not lead to disappointment. For we know how dearly God loves us, because he has given us the Holy Spirit to fill our hearts with his love." ~ Romans 5:3-5, New Living Translation

Insight:

The true essence of who we really are is not what or who we see in the mirror each day, nor is it found in the definition of what we do to earn a living. Who we are is rooted in the traits of our character--the very nature of the core of our being--which is often tested by God. Characteristics such as honesty, loyalty, integrity, kindness, mercy, faithfulness, dependability, trustworthiness and of course, an attitude of love and gratitude, should emanate from us to display the very nature of our relationship with God. When we stay connected to our true source of character, the byproduct or fruit of that relationship will be evident not just in who we are, but also in what we do.

Prayer to Ignite Action:

Father, I have come to know Your love for me because of the ways in which my character has been tested to bring out the best in me. I would never know the possibilities of my potential if it were not for the problems and pain of life. Yet, in the midst of trials and tests, You have proven to be faithful and the promises of Your Word are true. Today, I pray that the true nature of my character will be revealed as my life and lifestyle reflect my relationship with You. In Jesus' name. Amen.

DAY 156

Inspiration:

"[So let] each one [give] as he purposes in his heart, not grudgingly or of necessity; for God loves a cheerful giver. And God [is] able to make all grace abound toward you, that you, always having all sufficiency in all [things], may have an abundance for every good work. As it is written: 'He has dispersed abroad, he has given to the poor; His righteousness endures forever.' Now may He who supplies seed to the sower, and bread for food, supply and multiply the seed you have [sown] and increase the fruits of your righteousness, while [you are] enriched in everything for all liberality, which causes thanksgiving through us to God." ~ 2 Corinthians 9:7-11, New King James Version

Insight:

This passage of scripture is often referred to during offering times in many churches. We are encouraged to give not grudgingly, but willingly and cheerfully. This is a principle that can be applied to the giving not only of our finances, but also of our time, gifts and abilities. If we give of ourselves merely from a sense of duty or obligation, then the motive of our heart is not a cheerful one. Instead, when we give by God's providential grace and wisdom, it causes a sense of joy to resonate in us because we are willing and obedient to the prompting of God rather than men. When we offer ourselves and all that we have in this way, we are truly cheerful givers and therefore, pleasing to God in the process. As a benefit, God will multiply what we've given and increase opportunities for us to give more. We are blessed, therefore, to be a blessing to the kingdom of God.

Prayer to Ignite Action:

Father, You are the source of all my blessings. It is because of You that I am able to give cheerfully without complaining, knowing that my willingness to give is an attitude of the heart that makes You glad. Thank You for giving me the wherewithal to share my resources with the church as I participate in giving a tithe (10% of my income) and an offering to building the kingdom of God on earth. Let my heart remain pliable so that I can continue to be the channel through which more resources can flow to transform the lives of others in my church, community and around the globe. In Jesus' name. Amen.

DAY 157

Inspiration:

"It's news I'm most proud to proclaim, this extraordinary Message of God's powerful plan to rescue everyone who trusts him, starting with Jews and then right on to everyone else! God's way of putting people right shows up in the acts of faith, confirming what Scripture has said all along: The person in right standing before God by trusting him really lives." ~ Romans 1:16-17, The Message Bible

Insight:

I was reminded by a friend that many Christians do not take what it means to be a Christian seriously enough. Lifestyle evangelism mandates that we offer Christ to others by demonstrating the message of the Gospel of salvation through Jesus Christ by our everyday conduct and conversation. Sin and salvation from hell--a real place described in the scriptures just as heaven is--may not be preached about as often as it once was, but we can still be effective witnesses of God's Word and will to others by lovingly showing them the way to heaven to escape the reality of hell. In so doing, we will find that we are confidently and persistently living a life of purpose and expanding God's kingdom here on earth.

Prayer to Ignite Action:

God, forgive me for ignoring and missing opportunities to share my faith with those that I have met. Please give me a heart of compassion for the souls of those who do not know You as Lord of their lives. I thank You for wisdom, discernment and courage to speak up and to stand up for righteousness in the midst of an increasingly agnostic and hostile world. Today, I will not be ashamed to share my testimony with those whose hearts You will prepare in advance to receive what I say as the solution to whatever problem they may be facing. Speak through me with love and boldness so that I may lead someone to Christ. In Jesus' name. Amen.

DAY 158

Inspiration:

"For the LORD God [is] a sun and shield; The LORD will give grace and glory; No good [thing] will He withhold From those who walk uprightly."
~ Psalm 84:11, New King James Version

Insight:

Psalm 84:11 reiterates the fact that God will provide us with clarity of direction (sun), protection from harm and danger (shield), favor even when we don't deserve it (grace), recognition and promotion (glory), and the provision for every good thing to prevent us from experiencing lack. These precious promises are extended to us when we meet the condition explicitly expressed in the contingency clause of this verse--the admonition to "walk uprightly" before our God. As we strive to please God with our life and lifestyle, we'll discover that our needs will be met and we will be fulfilled as a result.

Prayer to Ignite Action:

Father, in You I find everything that I need to live abundantly and triumphantly no matter what comes my way. In the midst of life's uncertainties, You are with me to provide direction, protection, favor and provisions as I strive to walk upright in Your sight. Oh how I love Your Holy Word, for I find safety, stability and security in the surety of Your promises toward me. Keep my feet on the straight and narrow pathway of my purpose. All my hopes and expectations are in You. In Jesus' name. Amen.

DAY 159

Inspiration:

"In Him we also were made [God's] heritage (portion) and we obtained an inheritance; for we had been foreordained (chosen and appointed beforehand) in accordance with His purpose, Who works out everything in agreement with the counsel and design of His [own] will, So that we who first hoped in Christ [who first put our confidence in Him have been destined and appointed to] live for the praise of His glory!" ~ Ephesians 1:11-12, Amplified Bible

Insight:

Did you know that we have a personality, perspective, and purpose just as distinct as our DNA and fingerprints? I believe we are uniquely created by God to discover our destiny as He gently gives us clues along our journey of life. Some of those clues may include recurring dreams sent our way, natural gifts and talents, favor with people, resources that are attracted to us, and a compelling need to break out of the box of conformity and limitations in order to forge a new path that resonates with our innermost desires. It is up to us to remove the barriers and barricades that box us in so that our true potential can be pursued with unrelenting passion. No one else can give us the courage and fortitude that we alone must acknowledge and employ in order to leave an indelible mark and a lasting legacy that cannot be erased--a mark and a legacy that will be our unique contribution to our family, community and world.

Prayer to Ignite Action:

Lord God, Your purpose for me is as unique and distinct as my personality, fingerprints and DNA. I know that there is no one like me, and for that I am extremely grateful. You created me to be different and peculiar on purpose. Therefore, I do not need to compare myself to anyone else. You appointed and approved of me beforehand so that I do not have to seek approval and validation from others. As I set myself in agreement with the plans and purpose You have for me, I pray that my life will contribute greatly to the betterment of my family, community and world. In Jesus' name. Amen.

DAY 160

Inspiration

"Do nothing out of selfish ambition or vain conceit, but in humility consider others better than yourselves."
Philippians 2:3, New International Version

"But if you harbor bitter envy and selfish ambition in your hearts, do not boast about it or deny the truth."
James 3:14, New International Version

"For where your treasure is, there your heart will be also."
Luke 12:34, New International Version

Insight:

The Bible lets us know that our heart is in the same place as our treasure. Consequently, whatever we are most passionate about is where we will focus the majority of our time, energy and resources. Therefore, it is imperative that we make sure that our heart is in the right place, for the right purpose. Spending quality time with God through prayer, meditating on biblical principles, and setting ourselves in agreement with His plan for our lives rather than our own, ensures that the motives of our heart remain pure. As a result, our lives will be utilized to accomplish much more than we could ever imagine to please our Heavenly Father and to serve others for a purpose larger than ourselves or our own ambitions.

Prayer to Ignite Action:

Father, cleanse my heart of secret sins and selfish ambitions. Create in me a clean heart and renew within me a right spirit so that out of the abundance of my heart flows a passion to serve You for a purpose that is much larger than me--a purpose that is untainted by selfishness and unrestrained by the trappings of this world. A God-given vision is big enough to require insight from You and to include participation from others who will also bear, declare and share the vision along with me. I thank You for providing me with the natural and human resources needed to fulfill my purpose as I also help others to fulfill theirs. In Jesus' name. Amen.

DAY 161

Inspiration:

"Behave yourselves wisely [living prudently and with discretion] in your relations with those of the outside world (the non-Christians), making the very most of the time and seizing (buying up) the opportunity." ~ Colossians 4:5, Amplified Bible

Insight:

It has been said that "yesterday is history, tomorrow is a mystery and today is a gift, and that's why it's called the present." If we value each moment that we have as the gift from God that it is, then we'll make the most of every minute by filling it with what matters most. For some, that will mean prioritizing relationships and placing everything else in its proper order, while for others, different measures may be taken to pursue a dream or passion that has laid dormant for far too long. The fact of the matter is this: whatever we choose to do with the present time we now have will have far reaching implications as to what kind of future we can expect. Each second, minute and hour of this day is a gift. Let's open it with the same wide-eyed wonder we experienced on Christmas morning as a child and treasure it the same way.

Prayer to Ignite Action:

Heavenly Father, You are the Ancient of Days--the One who existed before creating time and throughout the ages while dwelling in the present and holding the future. I value the time that You have given as a gift to be treasured and measured wisely. Let me use wisdom in managing all my relationships and affairs well today as I make the best use of time and opportunities by valuing each moment, person and responsibility as a gift with Your help. In Jesus' name. Amen.

DAY 162

Inspiration:

"O Master, these are the conditions in which people live, and yes, in these very conditions my spirit is still alive--fully recovered with a fresh infusion of life! It seems it was good for me to go through troubles. Throughout them all you held tight to my lifeline. You never let me tumble over the edge into nothing. But my sins you let go of, threw them over your shoulder--good riddance!" ~ Isaiah 38:16-17, The Message Bible

Insight:

We have the incredible opportunity each day to decide what kind of life we will live for ourselves and give to others. We can choose to live beneath our potential, go along with the status quo of being average, or opt in for a life that is excellent, exceptional and extraordinary. Choosing the latter involves more energy and effort on our part, but the reward is well worth it as we seek to grow and develop spiritually, intellectually, physically and socially. Not only will we reap the benefits inwardly and outwardly, but we will leave a legacy that will continue to speak as we impart the best of who we are to serve God and those in our community, nation and world. Now that is the definition of living a life par excellence!

Prayer to Ignite Action:

Dear Lord, today I choose excellence over mediocrity in my life's work, purpose and relationships. Grant me the resolve to go the extra mile in serving You and others as well as in caring for my own spirit, mind and body. My heart's desire is to represent the quality of life that represents You well and attracts others so that they, too, may know and serve You. In Jesus' name. Amen.

DAY 163

Inspiration:

"Behold, thou desirest truth in the inward parts: and in the hidden
[part] thou shalt make me to know wisdom."
Psalm 51:6, King James Version

Insight:

I believe it was Shakespeare who said, "To thine own self be true."
However, the psalmist David stated it another way according to Psalm
51:6 to emphasize that truth and authenticity are what God requires.
God sees and knows the very intentions and motives of our hearts. We
cannot be pretentious with Him, nor should we be for the sake of pleasing
people. Our audience of One is God who desires for us to be truthful as
we represent His character and nature in our thoughts, words and
deeds. As we live openly and honestly before God and other people, we'll
find that our innate spiritual and natural gifts will resonate with who we
really are as well as with the vocation or calling that we choose to
fulfill. And once we accept our calling, the possibility of releasing our
full potential to realize our destiny becomes easier and our life becomes
richer.

Prayer to Ignite Action:

Father, because You are the True and Living God, truth lives in me. Help
me to be my true and authentic self without compromising what I stand
for and believe. I can hide nothing from You, for You know the thoughts
of my mind and the motives of my heart. I thank You for the ability to
love You and to love others enough to be truthful with them. I accept the
calling upon my life to use my spiritual gifts and natural talents while
remaining true to who I am. In Jesus' name. Amen.

DAY 164

Inspiration:

"Then He said, 'Go out, and stand on the mountain before the LORD.' And behold, the LORD passed by, and a great and strong wind tore into the mountains and broke the rocks in pieces before the LORD, [but] the LORD [was] not in the wind; and after the wind an earthquake, [but] the LORD [was] not in the earthquake; and after the earthquake a fire, [but] the LORD [was] not in the fire; and after the fire a still small voice." ~ 1 Kings 19:11-12, New King James Version

Insight:

The prophet Elijah in this passage of scripture was feeling abandoned, depressed and oppressed. He found himself in a polarized position and was on the brink of giving up on life after experiencing victory in the face of defeat just days before. Elijah needed to hear an encouraging word from God to say the least, and his desire was granted.

Much can be attained and gained as a result of our willingness to put forth the necessary effort in following the still, small voice of God. He speaks to us constantly through His Holy Word, the Holy Spirit, as well as through the people, places and predicaments in our lives. We must learn to be quiet and attentive enough to listen and then to obey as God gives us instruction and direction for our own benefit.

Prayer to Ignite Action:

God, You are with me when I am in the valley of hardship and when I am on the mountaintop of victory. I need You to walk with me and talk with me throughout the day and the rest of my life. Help me to be sensitive to the sound of Your voice and the ways in which You desire to speak to me today. I choose to listen more and to speak less so that I will not miss hearing the wisdom of Your instructions and following Your directions. In Jesus' name. Amen.

DAY 165

Inspiration:

"That is why I tell you not to worry about everyday life--whether you have enough food and drink, or enough clothes to wear. Is't life more than food, and your body more than clothing? Look at the birds. They don't plant or harvest or store food in barns, for your heavenly Father feeds them. And aren't you far more valuable to him than they are? Can all your worries add a single moment to your life? And why worry about your clothing? Look at the lilies of the field and how they grow. They don't work or make their clothing, yet Solomon in all his glory was not dressed as beautifully as they are." ~ Matthew 6:25-29, New Living Translation

Insight:

One of the best ways to get and keep joy in our lives is to acknowledge and then let go of worry and anxiety. There is no reason to worry about things, circumstances or people that we cannot change. Doing so is not only unproductive, but it is also unwise and unhealthy for our spiritual, mental, emotional and physical growth and wellbeing. Maintaining a high level of joy by being thankful and appreciative in our attitudes and actions will help us to focus our attention and energy in a positive way while keeping worry at bay.

Prayer to Ignite Action:

Heavenly Father, I know that You care for the birds of the air and the flowers of the field. Nothing that lives on the earth escapes Your all-seeing eye. By this, I know that there is no reason for me to worry, for You will provide everything I need that is essential for my life. I also pray for those who need Your healing and caring touch today. Use me as Your hands and feet as I find and fill the needs of those sent my way today. Cultivate a heart of thanksgiving within me as I learn to trust and depend on You more. In Jesus' name. Amen.

DAY 166

Inspiration:

"In the beginning God created the heaven and the earth. And the earth was without form, and void; and darkness [was] upon the face of the deep. And the Spirit of God moved upon the face of the waters. And God said, Let there be light: and there was light."
~ Genesis 1:1-3, King James Version

"Let all things be done decently and in order."
~ 1 Corinthians 14:40, King James Version

Insight:

Our thoughts determine our actions and habits, as well as how we will face whatever or whomever will confront us on a daily basis. If our thinking is disorganized, then our reaction to situations and people around us (including our surroundings) may be disorganized as well. In order to approach life in an orderly fashion and to have a clearer perspective in order to respond rather than react to life, we must address what I call our "P. O. Box" which reminds us to embrace prioritization and organization in areas where we need to most. Before we can prioritize and organize our day and the tasks on our to-do list, we must first prioritize and organize our thinking. Since all things should be done "decently and in order" as implied in I Corinthians 14:40, let us begin each day by asking God to help us to properly prioritize our thoughts so that divine order will lead us as we follow in its path. We have the example of God to follow, for light came into existence as well as the rest of creation as a result of His divine ability to organize and prioritize.

Prayer to Ignite Action:

God, You created the entire universe and caused order to replace chaos. Although the earth was without form and full of darkness, You saw the potential and possibilities of order that would appear before You spoke it into existence. Today, I pray for the ability to create order out of chaos in my thoughts first so that I can speak intelligently and act strategically in all that is entrusted to my stewardship. Sharpen my skills so that I can properly prioritize and organize my surroundings, activities and life's affairs. Thank You for showing me in Your Word how to do all things decently and in order. Let me live by that creed and by my lifestyle, teach it to others. In Jesus' name. Amen.

DAY 167

Inspiration:

"Since then, we do not have the excuse of ignorance, everything--and I do mean everything--connected with that old way of life has to go. It's rotten through and through. Get rid of it! And then take on an entirely new way of life--a God fashioned life, a life renewed from the inside and working itself into your conduct as God accurately reproduces his character in you." ~ Ephesians 4:22-24, The Message Bible

Insight:

There are many old habits that can cause us to cease to grow spiritually, personally and professionally if we do not let go of them completely and replace them with new habits that are conducive for growth and development. Some people think of sin when old habits and ways of life come to mind. However, there are some behaviors that may not be considered as sin, but the effects of these behaviors can also be detrimental and prohibitive to our progress.

A proverbial saying admonishes us not to put off for tomorrow what we can do today. That nugget of wisdom will alleviate the temptation of keeping old habits and behaviors such as procrastination as a way of life, if we heed its counsel. Whatever is on our plate of things to accomplish is waiting for us to start nibbling at it, one bite at a time. The entire plate of projects and tasks may seem overwhelming at first glance, but once we dig in and just do what needs to be done, the feeling of accomplishment will fill us and the evidence of seeing it through to completion will thrill us!

Prayer to Ignite Action:

Dear Lord, what a blessing it is to know that we can exchange our former habits and way of life for new life in You that transforms us. Today, I ask that You would help me to see the habitual patterns in my life that need to change for the sake of my own growth. I choose to let go of whatever might be preventing me from growing and progressing, and to work towards establishing new habits and behaviors for the good of myself and those closest to me. In Jesus' name. Amen.

DAY 168

Inspiration:
"I therefore, the prisoner for the Lord, appeal to and beg you to walk (lead a life) worthy of the [divine] calling to which you have been called [with behavior that is a credit to the summons to God's service.] [Living as becomes you] with complete lowliness of mind (humility and meekness (unselfishness, gentleness, mildness), with patience, bearing with one another and making allowances because you love one another." ~ Ephesians 4:1-2, Amplified Bible

Insight:
In chapter one of my first book, Wisdom for Women of Worth and Worship, I explain the difference between an occupation and a vocation (or calling) as indicated in the following excerpt:

"A vocation differs significantly from an occupation in that it carries with it a sense of urgency to fulfill a mandate or purpose predestined by God as opposed to a profession or employment needed merely for the sake of receiving a paycheck to satisfy financial obligations. There is something uniquely special about pursuing a life of purpose that allows one to be enlightened, empowered, and energized as natural and spiritual gifts, talents and abilities are passionately engaged daily, especially for a cause greater than oneself."

When we are motivated by our vocation (which can also be referred to as our purpose or calling), then we will find ourselves having fun and feeling fulfilled while blessing others along life's journey.

Prayer to Ignite Action:
Father, I thank You for the understanding I have regarding the difference between an occupation and a vocation. Give me the insight and the foresight to focus on the calling on my life that enables my gifts and abilities to be used to fulfill my unique purpose. I am passionate about the opportunity to be a blessing to others while doing what I love. The compensation for accepting my vocation far surpasses any monetary value as You bless me with the capacity to enjoy life fully. In Jesus' name. Amen.

DAY 169

Inspiration:

"Are not five sparrows sold for two pennies? And [yet] not one of them is forgotten or uncared for in the presence of God. But [even] the very hairs of your head are all numbered. Do not be struck with fear or seized with alarm; you are of greater worth than many [flocks] of sparrows." ~ Luke 12:6-7, Amplified Bible

Insight:

Some people define themselves by what they do or accomplish, which is unwise. We are not the sum of our daily deeds, chosen occupation or vocation, for if that were true, the moment we fail to follow through with accomplishing a goal or if our chosen occupation or vocation ceased, so would our sense of self-worth and value. Rather than being defined by what we do, let us anchor ourselves in the knowledge of who and whose we really are.

My daughters have learned from their dad and me that they are made in God's image and likeness first, and then in ours. Therefore, all that they are and can be is embodied in the infinite creativity and nature of God as well as in the lessons of life we have taught them as their parents. They have the best of God and us reflecting through them to undergird who they are individually. All of us have the same manual (the Bible) from which we govern our lives by to follow the path that best resonates with who we are. When we each take that road, results are sure to follow that point not to good deeds done alone, but to a life well lived.

Prayer to Ignite Action:

Dear God, how wonderful it is to know that I am Yours and You are mine. I am defined not by who others say I am or what I do, but by the fact that I am created in Your image and likeness. I pray that I am able to let my personality and character reflect who You are and the authenticity of who I am today. Thank You for Your love and care in molding me into a one-of-a-kind masterpiece. In Jesus' name. Amen.

DAY 170

Inspiration:
"For it is God who works in you to will and to act according to his good purpose." ~ Philippians 2:13, New International Version

Insight:
There is something that requires your attention -- an assignment that belongs to you because of your distinct capabilities and innate qualities that no one else can accomplish quite like you. The only obstacle between you and the completion of your assignment is the resolve to tackle it head on and to see it through to the end. Determine to begin the task at hand that is uniquely yours today and to put forth effort that exemplifies excellence beyond the call of duty to please God whose ability is working within you to do His good will and pleasure.

Prayer to Ignite Action:
Father, I celebrate who You are and the good purpose that You have in store for everyone who desires to pursue a life of meaning. I am so grateful for another day to live a life of purpose, on purpose. May my conversation and conduct add value to those around me for the common good of all. In Jesus' name. Amen.

Inspiration:

"Be not deceived; God is not mocked: for whatsoever a man soweth, that shall he also reap." ~ Galatians 6:7, King James Version

Insight:

Some people believe in good or bad luck while others believe in karma. I believe in what is known as The Law of Reciprocity. If we desire better thoughts, friends, opportunities, and therefore, a better quality of life, then we must require better of ourselves to acquire what we desire. Luck has nothing to do with it, but learning to unleash the power within us can will produce the changes that we want. All that we can possibly imagine rests in our own head, heart and hands. With God's wisdom and direction, we can reap the best when we sow the best of ourselves and our resources. It's a biblical principle that works, and I know it to be true from my own experiences.

Prayer to Ignite Action:

Dear Lord, the principles of Your Word have been tried and proven to be true. I hunger and thirst for more of You. Reveal who You are to me as I meditate on Your Word, and help me to rightly apply what I learn in my life. I know that I will reap what I sow, and that is why I desire to sow seeds of the right thoughts, words and actions so that I may reap the right harvest in my life, relationships and business. In Jesus' name. Amen.

DAY 172

Inspiration:

"'No weapon formed against you shall prosper, And every tongue [which] rises against you in judgment You shall condemn. This [is] the heritage of the servants of the LORD, And their righteousness [is] from Me,' Says the Lord." ~ Isaiah 54:17, New King James Version

"O God, [You are} more awesome than Your holy places. The God of Israel [is] He who gives strength and power to [His] people. Blessed [be] God!" ~ Psalm 66:35, New King James Version

Insight:

Robert Schuller made a profound and provocative statement years ago that was indelibly etched upon my mind and heart: "If it is to be, it is up to me." That expression alone removes an excuse-laden mentality and prevents us from the temptation of blaming others for a lack of success in any area of our lives. Acknowledging the fact that the kind of life we live is directly related to the choices we make and the consequences of those choices, empowers and enables us to move beyond feelings of frustration and to receive instead the reward of true fulfillment as we work towards envisioning and enlisting our own abilities in concert with God to attain our dreams and goals each day. Now is the time to live, love, laugh, learn and lay down any self-imposed limitations in exchange for liberation. We are free to be who God has predestined us to be at the very moment we decide to pursue and fulfill destiny.

Prayer to Ignite Action:

Omnipotent God, You are the source of all power. From You, I receive strength and might to overcome every obstacle and to defeat the odds that may come against me. Nothing is too difficult for me as long as my faith remains in You and I work diligently to attain the dreams and goals You've inspired. I am free to pursue and fulfill destiny, and You have blessed me with the ability to do just that. In Jesus' name. Amen.

DAY 173

Inspiration:

"Not that we venture to class or compare ourselves with some of those who commend themselves. But when they measure themselves by one another, and compare themselves with one another, they are without understanding." ~ 2 Corinthians 10:12, Revised Standard Version

Insight:

Isn't it wonderful to know that God deliberately designed a master plan to fit the framework of our distinct personalities, natural talents, spiritual gifts and individual abilities? There is a reason why we think, speak and act the way we do as opposed to the way others would. Each day, we have divine opportunities to share the essence of who we really are and what only we can accomplish for the sake of making the world a better place in which to live. In the midst of pessimistic indicators of media sources and the negativity of others, we have the power to decide to rise above the status quo in order to allow the Spirit of God to be seen as a light in a dark world as God's ambassadors of hope, love and healing. There is definitely something that we can give each day, for it is in our giving that we truly receive.

Prayer to Ignite Action:

Heavenly Father, I humbly acknowledge the fact that I am and can do nothing without You. Wisdom, knowledge and understanding come from You. I thank you for granting me a measure of each of these divine attributes for the call upon my life. I dare not compare myself with others, for each of us are distinctly different for a reason. Help me to give more of myself away today so that I can be refilled to do it all again. In Jesus' name. Amen.

DAY 174

Inspiration:

"And let us consider how to stir up one another to love and good works, not neglecting to meet together, as is the habit of some, but encouraging one another, and all the more as you see the Day drawing near." ~ Hebrews 10:24-25, English Standard Version

Insight:

God has indeed formed and fashioned us not to fit into anyone else's cookie cutter mold, nor to be a carbon copy of another person no matter how much we may admire him or her. The fact is that we are unique in every way to reveal the brilliance and beauty of who God has made us to be by sharing the best of who we are and what we can offer to influence, inspire, encourage and empower others to live their best lives as well. There is nothing greater than acknowledging the Greater One within us and accepting the mandate to provoke one another to love God, life, each other, and the calling of God to fulfill His purpose for our lives. That is why God gave us life. Let's honor Him, and the mentors in our lives who push us to be all that we were predestined to be.

Prayer to Ignite Action:

Father, You have given us a mandate not only to love one another, but to help to stir up the gifts in one another as an expression of our love. Today, I pray that You will lead me to those who are wondering about their purpose in life and how they can discover their own unique gifts. Help me to assist and encourage them to find their niche and to use their talents in their local church and community as opportunities are presented. Use me as Your mouthpiece to speak what is possible as they release their potential. In Jesus' name. Amen.

DAY 175

Inspiration:

"May the Lord answer you in the day of trouble! May the name of the God of Jacob set you up on high [and defend you]; Send you help from the sanctuary and support, refresh, and strengthen you from Zion;...Now I know that the Lord saves His anointed; He will answer him from His holy heaven with the saving strength of His right hand."
~ Psalm 20:1-2, 6

Insight:

Psalm 20 is a powerful passage of scripture to meditate on when seeking purpose, protection, healing, direction and prosperity. Rather than seeking a miracle, we are reminded that we are God's miraculous masterpiece. As we pursue our relationship with God, let us not forget to put forth the effort to pray, not just because God hears and answers our petitions, but because He is our passion and communing with Him guarantees His presence in and provisions for our lives.

Prayer to Ignite Action:

Heavenly Father, I don't have to wish for or look far to find a miracle. I now realize that I am a living, walking, breathing miracle. I am also aware of the miracles I see in the faces of other people. Today, I pray for others who need healing, direction and protection for their lives. I am grateful that You not only hear but answer the prayers of Your people. In Jesus' name. Amen.

DAY 176

Inspiration:

"Whatever you do, do well. For when you go to the grave, there will be no work or planning or knowledge or wisdom." ~ Ecclesiastes 9:10, New Living Translation

Insight:

Whatever we dare to believe and determine to achieve, is exactly what we can expect to receive. In order to move from a dreaming mentality to the manifestation of making our goals a reality, we must initiate a strategy of what it will take to achieve our dream to include the reason we desire it, how we will follow through to make it happen, and the benefits that will be afforded to others as well as ourselves which will motivate us to keep pressing towards the fulfillment of it. Anything worth having is truly worth working for.

Prayer to Ignite Action:

Dear God, I dare to believe that I can achieve anything, as long as what I believe is inspired by You and will improve the quality of life for others. While I am living, I desire to make a difference in the world by working diligently with excellence. By Your grace, I will do all things well today. In Jesus' name. Amen.

DAY 177

Inspiration:

"The LORD [is] good to all, And His tender mercies [are] over all His works." ~ Psalm 145:9, New King James Version

Insight:

No matter what challenges may confront us from day to day, there is always a promise greater than the problem that rests in the brand new mercies measured out to us by God that is to be extended not just to ourselves, but as a gift from us to others. Life carries with it ebbs and flows, ups and downs, triumphs and tragedies. Yet in the midst of it all there is something that we can focus on to give God thanks, and that attitude of gratitude will outweigh the negativity that may confront us.

Prayer to Ignite Action:

God, Your promises are greater than any problem and Your mercies are generously extended to all of Your creation. Oh how I worship You, my King, for Your love, goodness and kindness are unfailing towards me. I will extend mercy to those who need it in my life today, just as I have received it from You. In Jesus' name. Amen.

DAY 178

Inspiration:

"Praise the LORD. Blessed is the man who fears the LORD, who finds great delight in his commands. His children will be mighty in the land; the generation of the upright will be blessed. Wealth and riches are in his house, and his righteousness endures forever. Even in darkness light dawns for the upright, for the gracious and compassionate and righteous man. Good will come to him who is generous and lends freely, who conducts his affairs with justice." ~ Psalm 112:1-5, New International Version

Insight:

The beauty of enjoying the life God has given us lies in the fulfillment of the goals set before us each day. Those goals should not just be work related, but wealth related as well. I do not define wealth by financial or material assets alone. True wealth is found in having an intimate relationship with God, an interpersonal knowledge of self, an intentional focus upon family and friends we hold dear, and an unrelenting passion to use our skills, talents, gifts and abilities to accomplish all that God assigns to our stewardship.

Prayer to Ignite Action:

Father, You are the originator of all wealth, and You distribute it to whomever you wish by allowing us to experience the blessing of being in relationship with You, family and friends. You also allow us to enjoy opportunities to fulfill purpose by using the wealth of our talents and skills at home as well as in the marketplace. I appreciate the richness of my life, and I am determined to pass on the wealth I have received to the next generation. In Jesus' name. Amen.

DAY 179

Inspiration:

"So watch your step. Use your head. Make the most of every chance you get. These are desperate times! Don't live carelessly, unthinkingly. Make sure you understand what the Master wants." ~ Ephesians 5:15-17, The Message Bible

Insight:

Chapter 8 (Managing My Life's Time and Mission) of my book, A Woman's Journal for Joyful Living, includes the following excerpt:

"Believe in something big. Our life is worth a noble motive." ~Walter Anderson

Creating and utilizing a time management plan requires decision, discipline, and determination. Time management is really management of our life's mission as we utilize wisdom to manage the priorities, events and affairs in our lives. Determining to be good stewards of God's time afforded to us, empowers us with the ability to have control over what we do next. Our ability to distinguish between what is urgent and important and to remove unimportant tasks from our schedule, will cause us to be fruitful and fulfilled rather than frustrated and fatigued as we manage our life's time and mission. Pure joy will fill our hearts and flow to others when we believe in and serve a purpose that becomes, as Walter Anderson says, "a noble motive."

Prayer to Ignite Action:

Father, I am handpicked--chosen intentionally--to be a steward over that which only I can manage. I pray that You will give me specific instructions today for my life's mission. May the motives of my heart be pure so that my purpose is not thwarted by the misuse of time or the mismanagement of resources. I have learned that my purpose must be managed well and benefit other people to warrant Your provisions and blessing. Help me to be faithful in the stewardship of all that You've given me. In Jesus' name. Amen.

DAY 180

Inspiration:
"You have granted me life and favor, And Your care has preserved my spirit." ~ Job 10:12, New King James Version

Insight:
My definition of self-care is the intentional focus of the heart, mind and will to do what is necessary to care for the most valuable asset given to us by God other than His Son, Jesus Christ – OURSELVES. In order to care for others properly and to pursue the possibilities that resonate with our purpose, we must ensure that we intentionally focus ongoing effort not just on the work at hand and others, but on placing ourselves on our own "to-do" list daily without feeling guilty. If we take the time to nurture our own spirit, mind, and body, then we can better serve those who need what we have to offer.

Prayer to Ignite Action:
Dear Lord, You are the giver and sustainer of my life--an asset that is to be appreciated and valued by me and those closest to me. Help me to put myself on my own to-do list by carving out time to care for the health and growth of my spirit, intellect, physical body and social relationships. As I spend quality time tending to my own needs, I will be able to better serve other people within my sphere of influence. Thank You for reminding me to practice self-care today. In Jesus' name. Amen.

DAY 181

Inspiration:

"For God so loved the world that He gave His only begotten Son, that whoever believes in Him should not perish but have everlasting life. For God did not send His Son into the world to condemn the world, but that the world through Him might be saved." ~ John 3:16-17

"Therefore My Father loves Me, because I lay down My life that I may take it again. No one takes it from Me, but I lay it down of Myself. I have power to lay it down, and I have power to take it again. This command I have received from My Father." ~ John 10:17-18, New King James Version

Insight:

Isn't it awesome to think of how Jesus willingly laid His life down and died for you, me and the whole world before we could even make a decision to accept His gift of salvation? He completely obeyed the will of His Father and became the mediator between God and men to reconcile our relationship with our Creator through His shed blood. He who knew no sin became the Lamb to be slaughtered so that our sins were transferred to Him and nailed to the cross. Then, as the songwriter says, "Up from the grave He arose with a mighty triumph o'er His foes! He arose a victor from the dark domain and He lives forever with His saints to reign. He arose! He arose! Hallelujah, Christ arose!"

Because Jesus arose, we can rise above the challenges of life and the temptations of the enemy when we allow His resurrection power to live with and work through us. Death has no sting and the grave has no victory, for because of Jesus and our relationship with Him as "the redeemed," we shall reign with Him. Now, that's good news!

Prayer to Ignite Action:

Father, Your love for the world was clearly seen when You sent Your only begotten Son, Jesus, to earth on a mission to save the lost by dying on the cross. Jesus, I thank You for willingly laying down Your life for me.

The same power that resurrected Jesus now lives in me as a follower of Christ. I am so blessed to know that I can overcome any challenge because You live in me, and that I will reign with you eternally. In Jesus' name. Amen.

DAY 182

Inspiration:

"Therefore let us, as many as are mature, have this mind; and if in anything you think otherwise, God will reveal even this to you." ~ Philippians 3:15, New King James Version

Insight:

One of our quests in life should be not to allow negative thoughts to control us, but to allow our minds instead to be transformed by the power of God's Word as we adopt a purely positive mentality. The will to respond with wisdom, grace, integrity and a positive perspective to life rather than to react to what people or predicaments dictate to us, causes us to have a winning attitude come what may. The New King James Version of Proverbs 23:7 says, "For as a man [woman] thinks in his [her] heart, so is he [she]." Today, let's determine to think only the best about ourselves, others and opportunities that may come our way disguised as obstacles.

Prayer to Ignite Action:

Dear Lord, deciding not to allow negative thoughts to control me is one of the best choices I could ever make. Reveal to me those things that I have thought about that have not been helpful to my personal and professional growth. Today, I choose to be mature in my thinking by purposing to meditate on what is right, true and worthy of virtue regarding myself, other people and the circumstances of life. In Jesus' name. Amen.

DAY 183

Inspiration:

"Now to him who is able to do immeasurably more than all we ask or imagine, according to his power that is at work within us, to him be glory in the church and in Christ Jesus throughout all generations, for ever and ever! Amen." ~ Ephesians 3:20-21, New International Version

Insight:

We have inner ability that is waiting to be harnessed and channeled in the right direction daily, and God is able to increase our ability beyond our imagination when we allow Him to work through us to do what is pleasing to Him. The power within every person who confesses Jesus Christ as Lord unlocks the door to reveal what God is able to do to exceed expectations. This same power allows us to live intentionally to honor God with our life in ways that surpass what we could ever ask or think.

What have you thought about and asked God for lately? No matter what we dare to dream or how grandiose the goals to achieve it may be, God is able to top even that. So go ahead...dream big and do what is necessary to live your dream. When your motive pleases God, He will perform even greater works than you thought were possible.

Prayer to Ignite Action:

Father, You are a great and awesome God. There is no way that I can describe the enormity of Your power, nor can I fathom how Your power works through men and women to accomplish Your purposes. I pray that I would receive a glimpse of what You desire to bring to pass in my life. I ask for purity of heart, keenness of mind, and sharpness of skill to appropriate Your power in ways that are in alignment with Your plans that are larger and greater than anything I could possibly imagine. I yield my will and ways to You so that I can be a vessel through which Your power, presence and purpose will flow. In Jesus' name. Amen.

DAY 184

Inspiration:

"The law of the LORD [is] perfect, converting the soul; The testimony of the LORD [is] sure, making wise the simple; The statutes of the LORD [are] right, rejoicing the heart; The commandment of the LORD [is] pure, enlightening the eyes; The fear of the LORD is clean, enduring forever; The judgments of the LORD [are] true [and] righteous altogether. More to be desired [are they] than gold, Yea, than much fine gold; Sweeter also than honey and the honeycomb. Moreover by them Your servant is warned, [And] in keeping them [there is] great reward." ~ Psalm 19:7-11, New King James Version

Insight:

The Bible provides the spiritual, emotional and mental respite we need to be refreshed, revived, renewed and recharged so that we may possess the life that we were predestined by our Creator to experience unashamedly and unapologetically. The vicissitudes of life can catapult us into a mode of reinventing ourselves and redesigning our lives as God's Word helps us to see that we are victors rather than victims. What a wonderful reminder to awaken the power, potential and possibilities that await within us!

Prayer to Ignite Action:

Heavenly Father, I love Your Word. In it, I find the path to solace, security, stability and success. I desire to develop an even greater love for practicing the biblical principles I've read in my life. Thank You for instructing, correcting and encouraging me as I meditate on Your precepts, for then I learn more about who You are, who I am, and how I am to live. In Jesus' name. Amen.

DAY 185

Inspiration:

"You will keep in perfect peace all who trust in you, all whose thoughts are fixed on you!" ~ Isaiah 26:3, New Living Translation

"We are destroying speculations and every lofty thing raised up against the knowledge of God, and we are taking every thought captive to the obedience of Christ." ~ 2 Corinthians 10:5, New American Standard Bible

Insight:

The power of thinking positively may not change other people or our circumstances immediately, but it will inevitably alter our perspective of ourselves, others, and our surroundings for the better. It is amazing how much we can change inwardly and therefore, change the quality of life we live outwardly when we dwell on thoughts of peace, prosperity, purpose, and productivity.

Today, make a commitment to reject negative thinking patterns, and focus instead on the positive promises of God. When negative thoughts come, stop them in their tracks and take them captive according to 2 Corinthians 10:5.

Prayer to Ignite Action:

God, You have promised to keep me in perfect peace as long as my thoughts are fixed on You. Today, I commit to You every thought that will take up time and space in my mind. Out with the old and in with the new as I reject the negative and replace them with positive thoughts. I ask for the wisdom and strength to immediately dismiss wrong speculations, perceptions and opinions so that the correct mentality will prevail from this moment forward. In Jesus' name. Amen.

DAY 186

Inspiration:

"And those who know Your name will put their trust in You, For You, O LORD, have not forsaken those who seek You." ~ Psalm 9:10, New American Standard Bible

"Let me hear Your lovingkindness in the morning; For I trust in You; Teach me the way in which I should walk; For to You I lift up my soul." ~ Psalm 143:8, New American Standard Bible

Insight:

It is incredible to know that we have the power to imagine our life as we would like it to be, as well as ourselves according to what we choose to see. The way we view ourselves has a direct impact not only upon our conduct and conversation, but also on the way we interact with other people and vice versa. Our perception becomes our personal reality, so it is important to renew our minds according to what God's Word says as we trust in Him.

It is so easy to become agitated when things (or people for that matter) do not turn out the way we had hoped or expected. Instead, we must acknowledge that God has a better way for us to conduct ourselves, and a plan that is tailor-made for each of us, even when we don't quite know or understand it. Trusting in Him allows us to see from a better perspective than our own.

Prayer to Ignite Action:

Oh, my God, in You I place my trust. Teach me how to view myself and others from the perspective of Your Word as I strive to know and do what is right. Although I often miss the mark, Your ways are perfect. I am challenged, today, to rely upon You more as You show me a better way to love, live, and serve. In Jesus' name. Amen.

DAY 187

Inspiration:
"And we know that all things work together for good to them that love God, to them who are the called according to [his] purpose." ~ Romans 8:28, King James Version

"I pray that God, the source of hope, will fill you completely with joy and peace because you trust in him. Then you will overflow with confident hope through the power of the Holy Spirit." ~ Romans 15:13, New Living Translation

Insight:
Today, do not to be overwhelmed by difficult times, but know that everything that happens can be used for our good when we love God and realize that we are called according to His purpose. With this knowledge, we can endure any challenge and hold onto our inner peace and joy, regardless of circumstances. After all, happiness is dependent upon external surroundings and/or people. When those conditions change, happiness may disappear as a result. Peace and joy, on the other hand, cannot be obtained from outside influences or situations which may fluctuate. God is the Source of true peace and joy, and when He lives within us, we have unlimited access to all the peace and joy we need daily.

Prayer to Ignite Action:
Father, I believe that You are using everything in my life to work together for my good, even those things that I don't understand. Fill me now with peace and joy overflowing from the Holy Spirit that dwells in me. No matter what happens around me, my confidence is in the One who lives within me--the source of unlimited peace and joy. In Jesus' name. Amen.

DAY 188

Inspiration:

"Oh yes, you shaped me first inside, then out; you formed me in my mother's womb. I thank you, High God--you're breathtaking! Body and soul, I am marvelously made! I worship in adoration--what a creation! You know me inside and out, you know every bone in my body; You know exactly how I was made, bit by bit, how I was sculpted from nothing into something. Like an open book, you watched me grow from conception to birth; all the stages of my life were spread out before you, The days of my life all prepared before I'd even lived one day. Your thoughts--how rare, how beautiful! God, I'll never comprehend them! I couldn't begin to count them--any more than I could count the sand of the sea. Oh, let me rise in the morning and live always with you!" ~ Psalm 139:13-18, The Message Bible

Insight:

When we really think about it, our lives are immeasurably blessed beyond compare and filled with God's gracious love, peace, and joy if we will only choose to let go of the things and relationships that prevent us from focusing on the beauty in and around us. Psalm 139:13-18 paints a portrait of how wonderfully, fearfully and marvelously created we really are, so doesn't it stand to reason that we should live a life that also exemplifies those qualities? We can purposefully pursue and intentionally ensure an exquisite life beginning with the thoughts that we consistently entertain on a daily basis.

Prayer to Ignite Action:

God, You shaped me before placing me in my mother's womb. You knew everything about who I would be and wrote all the activities of my days in Your book. My spirit, mind, and body were created as a result of Your intricate handiwork. I praise You for loving, creating, watching over, and providing for me all the days of my life. I am so blessed to know that I was on Your mind before time began, and that Your plans for my present and future are secure. In Jesus' name. Amen.

DAY 189

Inspiration:
"But now, O Jacob, listen to the LORD who created you. O Israel, the one who formed you says, 'Do not be afraid, for I have ransomed you. I have called you by name; you are mine. When you go through deep waters, I will be with you. When you go through rivers of difficulty, you will not drown. When you walk through the fire of oppression, you will not be burned up; the flames will not consume you.'" ~ Isaiah 43:1-2, New Living Translation

Insight:
Problems can arise during the day which can jolt our memory of previous challenges that occurred, with the sound byte and video feed of who or what caused it and why, what was said and when, where it took place and how it all played out.

Rather than rehearsing the problems or problematic people who challenge us, let's dwell on the opportunities that present themselves as a result of the stirring of creativity within that never would have happened had it not been for problems that inevitably came our way. I've learned that sometimes we have to tell our problems, "Thank you" and concentrate on the promises of God who is our Problem Solver.

Prayer to Ignite Action:
Lord, You are always with me. Even when hardships seem to appear like rivers, I shall not be overwhelmed by them. Your presence calms my soul and Your Word brings comfort to me, regardless of the trials that come and go. Because I am Yours, I have access to wisdom that provides a solution for every difficult situation. You preserve my life, even in the midst of problems as I keep my mind focused on Your promises. God, You are my shelter in the time of storm. In Jesus' name. Amen.

DAY 190

Inspiration:

"So we built the wall, and the entire wall was joined together up to half its [height], for the people had a mind to work." ~ Nehemiah 4:6, New King James Version

"They were trying to intimidate us, imagining that they could discourage us and stop the work. So I continued the work with even greater determination." ~ Nehemiah 6:9, New Living Translation

Insight:

It takes spiritual strength, mental tenacity, physical stamina and a determined will to accomplish anything worthy of the effort and energy required to produce desired results. Nehemiah realized this, and with God's help, determination, and a strong work ethic, he rallied the Israelites to rebuild the walls of Jerusalem despite the critics and cynics who tried their best to stop their work. Nehemiah teaches us this lesson: determination dismisses distractions and detractors just as positive thoughts and affirmations alleviate wrong attitudes and attract allies to help bring the vision to fruition.

Prayer to Ignite Action:

Father, I am grateful for the value of determination and a strong work ethic. I pray that these traits infused by Your strength will cause me to stay focused on that which is most important for me to accomplish. Help me not to be distracted or deterred from what You've appointed me to do, especially when others try to sabotage me by their criticism. As I think and speak positively while following Your guidance, I believe that allies will be attracted to me for the mutual benefit and fulfillment of our God-given purpose. In Jesus' name. Amen.

DAY 191

Inspiration:

"Exercise foresight and be on the watch to look [after one another], to see that no one falls back from and fails to secure God's grace (His unmerited favor and spiritual blessing), in order that no root of resentment (rancor, bitterness, or hatred) shoots forth and causes trouble and bitter torment, and the many become contaminated and defiled by it." ~ Hebrews 12:15, Amplified Bible

Insight:

Refusing to deal with and release bitterness can become hazardous to your mental, emotional and physical health and affect those closest to you. Today, I challenge you to forgive those who have trespassed against you and to focus on purely positive thoughts that will counteract the negative influences and resistance that may have confronted you. By doing so, you can expect the truth of God's Word to help heal the wounds that caused bitterness to fester. You can meet the challenges of life head on by thinking the best and releasing the rest in your life.

Prayer to Ignite Action:

Heavenly Father, please forgive me if I have allowed bitterness in any form to fester in me, just as I choose to forgive my debtors. I release into Your care the root that may have caused bitterness to grow as a weed in my life that others, too, may have been affected by. I desire to be free from all encumbrances that would hinder forward progress for myself and those whom I consider to be my closest family, friends, and associates. I accept healing and wholeness that comes from knowing and applying biblical principles in my life. In Jesus' name. Amen.

DAY 192

Inspiration:

"Then Jesus said, 'Father, forgive them for they do not know what they do.' And they divided His garments and cast lots." ~ Luke 23:34, New King James Version

Insight:

I quoted a profound statement by Hugh Prather in Chapter 4 of my book, A Woman's Journal for Joyful Living. This particular chapter emphasizes the necessity of loving and forgiving others and ourselves as necessary. Hugh says, "There are only three things you need to let go of: judging, controlling, and being right. Release these three and you will have the whole mind and twinkly heart of a child."

Harboring unforgiveness and refusing to love fully prevents us from experiencing and enjoying the richness of life and the blessing of relationships. Realizing that we cannot and do not have the power to control the decisions and actions of others and releasing them from having control over us, frees us to live abundantly and to love extravagantly. Choosing to adopt the attitude that Jesus had when He hung on Calvary's cross will keep our hearts right before God and allow us to be healed, healthy and whole.

Prayer to Ignite Action:

Dear God, I have done nothing to deserve Your grace and mercy in my life, but I appreciate the fact that You grant both to me miraculously in spite of myself. I pray for Your help in forgiving others just as freely and quickly as Jesus forgave His accusers. I know that I am forgiven in direct proportion to my forgiveness of those who have hurt or disappointed me in some way. As I let go of the temptation to judge, control or be right, I receive healing and redemption in my heart. In Jesus' name. Amen.

DAY 194

Inspiration:
"And since we have the same spirit of faith, according to what is written, 'I believed and therefore I spoke,' we also believe and therefore speak."
~ 2 Corinthians 4:13, New King James Version

Insight:
The Clark Sisters recorded a gospel song with the following lyrics: "I'm looking for a miracle. I expect the impossible. I feel the intangible. I see the invisible." These words paint a portrait of fearless faith that breaks through boundaries and launches itself past limitations. While these lyrics may ignite and inspire us to reach for our dreams, it is quite another thing to put forth the effort necessary to fulfill them. The miracle we may be looking for is found when we can decide to become a miracle by focusing our energy toward realizing our dreams with every available opportunity afforded to us. Nothing and no one can stop a determined, destiny-driven man or woman who is full of faith that is evident in words spoken and works wrought. With that winning combination, miracles will become tangible and visible.

Prayer to Ignite Action:
Dear Lord, faith is what moves You to make the impossible possible, the intangible tangible, and the invisible visible. As I seek to walk by faith today, I will think about what can be, speak it into existence, and diligently partner with You God to bring it to pass. Doubt will not infiltrate my mind, heart or mouth because I am filled with faith and driven by destiny. May what I believe, say and do ignite faith in others today. In Jesus' name. Amen.

DAY 195

Inspiration:

"Jesus went on to make these comments: If you're honest in small things, you'll be honest in big things." ~ Luke 16:10, The Message Bible

Insight:

It is imperative that we become faithful stewards of every resource that is placed in our care. We all have been blessed with responsibilities in life to manage as we so choose. That choice must be intentionally driven by our core values, as well as by what we deem as most urgent and important for us to accomplish on a daily basis. The people and things in which we invest such as family, employment, church involvement, civic responsibilities and other individual areas of interest, represent our core values, and what we value is demonstrated by how faithfully we manage the responsibilities we've been given. When we are good stewards of what we have, we can be trusted with more.

Prayer to Ignite Action:

Father, I appreciate the responsibilities that I now have, and I thank You for what has been entrusted to me. My desire is to be a good manager of everything--from the smallest to the greatest of responsibilities and resources. Help me to be a faithful steward of my relationships as well with the knowledge that people are always more important than programs and possessions. In Jesus' name. Amen.

DAY 195

Inspiration:

"Jesus went on to make these comments: If you're honest in small things, you'll be honest in big things." ~ Luke 16:10, The Message Bible

Insight:

It is imperative that we become faithful stewards of every resource that is placed in our care. We all have been blessed with responsibilities in life to manage as we so choose. That choice must be intentionally driven by our core values, as well as by what we deem as most urgent and important for us to accomplish on a daily basis. The people and things in which we invest such as family, employment, church involvement, civic responsibilities and other individual areas of interest, represent our core values, and what we value is demonstrated by how faithfully we manage the responsibilities we've been given. When we are good steward of what we have, we can be trusted with more.

Prayer to Ignite Action:

Father, I appreciate the responsibilities that I now have, and I thank You for what has been entrusted to me. My desire is to be a good manager of everything--from the smallest to the greatest of responsibilities and resources. Help me to be a faithful steward of my relationships as well with the knowledge that people are always more important than programs and possessions. In Jesus' name. Amen.

DAY 196

Inspiration:

"Also to You, O Lord, [belongs] mercy; For You render to each one according to his work."

Insight:

There is a four-letter word that is obscene to some and obsessive to others. However, this word is the catalyst for producing results...and it's called WORK! It takes work to move our dreams and visions from the mental state of expectation to the physical state of manifestation. The process in between requires a plan with specific goals, timelines and benefits along the way, with built-in flexibility that allows God to augment the plan along the way with His creativity and ingenuity and our participation. WORK produces wonderful results when it is fueled by faith in what God is able to accomplish in and through us to create a legacy that will outlast us.

Prayer to Ignite Action:

Dear Lord, thank You for blessing me with the ability to work, and empowering me to work diligently and joyfully. I pray for consistency in doing what is necessary to follow through with each assigned task until my work is completed with excellence shown along the way. May my efforts be faithful as the fruit of my labor produces results that glorify You while blessing others, thereby allowing me to be fulfilled. In Jesus' name. Amen.

DAY 197

Inspiration:

"No discipline seems pleasant at the time, but painful. Later on, however, it produces a harvest of righteousness and peace for those who have been trained by it." ~ Hebrews 12:11, New International Version

Insight:

I've heard it said that "nothing beats a failure but a try." It's easy to give up, and even easier, to do nothing at all. It takes determination, discipline and dedication, however, to put forth hearty effort to realize a dream, vision and/or goal and to execute that effort each day with a spirit of excellence. There will be people who disagree, misunderstand and perhaps even a few who will be intentional distractions, but that should not thwart the purpose and passion that drives us to release the greatness that God has instilled in us for the benefit of His kingdom and the purpose of blessing those who are a part of our sphere of influence. Effort is the key to designing our dreams, prioritizing our plans and transforming expectations into what others think is impossible.

Prayer to Ignite Action:

Lord God, I willingly submit to the instruction and correction of Your Word which provides me with the wisdom I need to live well. Thank You for giving me the wherewithal to exercise discipline in my own life and to apply it when needed in my relationships, at work and in extracurricular activities. Allow my determination, discipline and dedication to bring my dreams to pass, and to set necessary boundaries and structure in my life for the sake of my and others' growth and development. In Jesus' name. Amen.

DAY 198

Inspiration:

"He has made everything beautiful in its time. He has also set eternity in the hearts of men; yet they cannot fathom what God has done from beginning to end. I know that there is nothing better for men than to be happy and do good while they live. That everyone may eat and drink, and find satisfaction in all his toil--this is the gift of God." ~ Ecclesiastes 3:11-13, New International Version

Insight:

Dr. Rita Twiggs stated the following: "Success woke me up, motivation made me breakfast, destiny gave me my agenda, and the Lord gave me His blessings!" What a powerful statement to acknowledge that the driving force behind everything we do is God who works in and through us to accomplish His purpose and our expectations. Our motive and mission must agree with His agenda for our day and destiny. Life is worth living when we function with a purpose-filled reason in mind, and operate in God's divine season and time.

Prayer to Ignite Action:

Father, my prayer today is that my motive and mission will agree with the agenda and destiny You have in store for me. Let me operate in Your divine timing and season for my life with a singular focus on my distinct purpose which You know from beginning to end. You have blessed me abundantly, and I take pleasure in the gift of life and sense of purpose You've given me. In Jesus' name. Amen.

DAY 199

Inspiration:

"And don't forget to do good and to share with those in need. These are the sacrifices that please God." ~ Hebrews 13:16, New Living Translation

Insight:

Whenever there is a need of any kind, it serves as a reminder that there is a vacuum waiting to be filled. When we focus on the need in our own lives, we are deterred from pursuing the possibilities that exist to find and fill a need that others may have. Placing our trust explicitly in God as our Provider and striving to serve Him, opens a doorway into our lives for Him to fill the vacuum of our need. We should not worry or become anxious when we have a personal need. Employing what brings us joy allows us to live a life of purpose, on purpose, that pleases God and blesses other people. God will supply what is lacking when we continue to focus on what truly matters.

Prayer to Ignite Action:

Heavenly Father, Your word compels us to help those who are in need by practicing hospitality and giving of our resources as necessary. I pray for discernment today so that I can identify people who are in need and help to fill those needs by offering whatever I have as I am led by You. Let the love of God be seen in me as I spread it abroad today. In Jesus' name. Amen.

DAY 200

Inspiration:

"A man's gift makes room for him, And brings him before great men."
~ Proverbs 18:16, New King James Version

Insight:

There is a difference between an occupation and a vocation. An occupation is the employment that provides the financial means to meet the obligations of one's household and creditors, and therefore, becomes the means to an end of satisfying debt and hopefully, securing a future with benefits that include retirement investments as well as health, dental and life insurance options. A vocation, however, is not just a means to an end on earth, but it has far greater implications with the end of one's eternal destiny in mind.

A vocation is a calling that has been predestined by God to align with one's potential, passion and purpose. Ideally, one's occupation and vocation should intersect so that what one loves to do becomes his or her magnificent obsession in that it is no longer viewed as employment, but rather, as meaningful life's work that adds value to oneself and others. When this becomes the impetus and motivation for waking up each morning, the assertion can be made that this is what one can do for the rest of his or her life, whether compensated for it or not. One can say, "This is the life for me, and I would live it for free." As one's gifts continue to make room for him or her, God will also provide an overflow of blessings to include people, resources, finances and favor to supply every need and heart's desire in agreement with His Word and will.

Prayer to Ignite Action:

God, You are the giver of every good and perfect gift. I praise You for equipping me with gifts and abilities I need to serve a greater purpose to fulfill destiny. When I use the talents I have, You open doors of opportunity and favor for me so that my gifts will have a greater impact in the future. Thank You not only for more opportunities, but for bringing more people and resources into my life today and in time to come. In Jesus' name. Amen.

DAY 201

Inspiration:
"Ah Lord GOD! behold, thou hast made the heaven and the earth by thy great power and stretched out arm, [and] there is nothing too hard for thee." ~ Jeremiah 32:17, King James Version

"But Jesus beheld [them], and said unto them, With men this is impossible; but with God all things are possible." ~ Matthew 19:26, King James Version

Insight:
All things are possible to those who believe, just as all things are impossible to those whose belief system produces only what has been accepted as their personal truth. In order to get different results, we must think, and therefore act, differently. Our thoughts can become a barrier to keep us from attaining, or a bridge to connect us to achieving what is possible if we only believe. There is nothing too difficult for God, and since He lives within us, there is nothing too difficult for us to accomplish if we will consistently think, speak and act in a manner that will produce the results we desire and deserve.

Prayer to Ignite Action:
Lord God, You created the vast expanse of space and time--the world that we can see and the universe that exists beyond our galaxy. You have proven by Your infinite wisdom and unsurpassed power that nothing is too difficult for You. I praise You because of who You are and am awed by all You have done and will do to express love and care for all of creation. I pray that Your wisdom and power will emanate from me to do what others thought was impossible. I believe that I can do anything that You lead me to do because You are with me. In Jesus' name. Amen.

DAY 202

Inspiration:

"But also for this very reason, giving all diligence, add to your faith virtue, to virtue knowledge, to knowledge self-control, to self-control perseverance, to perseverance godliness, to godliness brotherly kindness, and to brotherly kindness love." ~ 2 Peter 1:5-7, New King James Version

Insight:

Happiness is dependent upon external circumstances or people which may change at a moment's notice beyond our control. Joy, however, comes as a result of an inner resource that feeds our mind and spirit regardless of what and who surrounds us. God desires to be our Source and resource from whom all joy, wisdom, strength, grace, favor, and creativity flow. When we allow Him to fill the recesses of our soul with His Spirit, we then have Him to depend on and to trust for present and future prevision and provision. Knowing that God is in control of all that concerns us, and that He has given us the power and ability to control ourselves with His help, frees us from the need to control anything and anyone outside of our assigned area of influence. Now that is enough to keep us joyful!

Prayer to Ignite Action:

Heavenly Father, You have given me the ability and grace to control my thoughts, feelings as well as my choice of words and actions. I do not have, however, the ability or grace to change what is beyond my control. Today, I am reminded to be grateful for self-control and to exercise it as needed while releasing what I do not have the responsibility to control to You. As I accept the influence that I have by diligently practicing self-control along with virtue, knowledge, perseverance, godliness, kindness and love, my life will be richer and the world will become better. In Jesus' name. Amen.

DAY 203

Inspiration:
"But remember the LORD your God, for it is he who gives you the ability to produce wealth, and so confirms his covenant, which he swore to your forefathers, as it is today." ~ Deuteronomy 8:18, New International Version

Insight:
It has been said that we may not know what the future holds, but we know who holds the future. God who designed our future, is also concerned about our present. He will also use our past to shape and mold us into who He desires for us to be so that we are equipped and empowered to function with excellence in our endeavors today, which will in turn impact our future. No matter what happened in our past, the time we have right now is most important. How we utilize our creative abilities, natural gifts and honed skills today will determine our level of productivity personally, professionally, socially and even emotionally. If we really desire to reach our long-term goals in the next one, three and five years and beyond, we must be intentional about setting and accomplishing our daily, weekly and monthly short-term goals. Doing so will not only increase our sense of self-worth and level of productivity, but it will add great value to the world in which we live.

Prayer to Ignite Action:
Father, You blessed us from the beginning with the ability to be fruitful and productive by using what we were given and multiplying it to increase the value of ourselves, others and earth. The original command you gave to Adam and Eve applies to us today. I take that responsibility seriously, and agree with Your decree that I am blessed to be fruitful and productive so that I can experience health and wealth in every area of my life both now and in the future. In Jesus' name. Amen.

DAY 204

Inspiration:

"But the seed on good soil stands for those with a noble and good heart, who hear the word, retain it, and by persevering produce a crop." ~ Luke 8:15, New International Version

Insight:

Once a seed of any kind has been planted, it takes a little while before the evidence of the labor of tilling, cultivating, fertilizing and watering begins to show. In the meantime, there is a root system underneath the surface of the ground that allows the seedling to grow and produce what was originally intended with steady, proper care.

So it is with the labor of our efforts toward any endeavor. We cannot see the fruit right away, and sometimes we may wonder if it will ever appear. However, we must remain consistent and persistent in our efforts, knowing that although nothing may be seen with the naked eye right away, there is a root system that is being established to undergird and support the fruit that will eventually appear and remain as we continue to work our plans with God's leading. "Faith without works is dead" as James chapter 2 verses 20 and 26 declare. Let's allow the dynamic duo of our faith and work and produce the hidden treasures that are just beneath the surface waiting to burst forth according to the divine time and season that God has ordained.

Prayer to Ignite Action:

Father, I realize that all of my labor is as a seed that is planted in the ground or the water that nurtures seeds planted by other people. Having faith pleases you, but adding deeds to our faith produces a harvest of blessings. By Your grace, I will persevere to produce good results with the seeds I plant and water so that I may prosper spiritually, intellectually, emotionally, physically, socially and financially today and beyond. In Jesus' name. Amen.

DAY 205

Inspiration:

"In the crowd that day there was a woman who for twelve years had been afflicted with hemorrhages. She had spent every penny she had on doctors but not one had been able to help her. She slipped in from behind and touched the edge of Jesus' robe. At that very moment her hemorrhaging stopped...Jesus insisted, 'Someone touched me. I felt power discharging from me.' When the woman realized that she couldn't remain hidden, she knelt trembling before him. In front of all the people, she blurted out her story--why she touched him and how at that same moment she was healed. Jesus said, 'Daughter, you took a risk trusting me, and now you're healed and whole. Live well, live blessed!'" ~ Luke 8:43-44, 46-48, The Message Bible

Insight:

This woman who remains nameless in the Bible had an issue of blood which caused her to be in a weak, bent over position of pain because of the unending hemorrhaging she experienced--until she met Jesus and touched the hem of His garment. Her change in focus caused a change in her position. No longer was she hemorrhaging endlessly; she was now healed and whole which she declared emphatically!

Our present issue or condition does not equate to our future position. There are many possibilities that can be pushed out of pain or problems if we but change our perspective and allow them to propel us closer to Jesus and further toward the fulfillment of our purpose. Creativity is sometimes birthed from crisis just as "necessity is the mother of invention."

Don't become isolated because of your issue or boxed in by your problem. Instead, think outside of the box and explore the unique opportunities that will arise when your focus is changed and redirected.

Prayer to Ignite Action:

Dear Lord, I bring the issues and problems that I have and those that I'm aware of as I intercede for others to You today. I have the faith to believe that You can provide hope, help, healing and wholeness in any situation that desperately needs Your intervention. I now know that a change in focus will produce a change in condition and position. My trust is in You and my eyes are upon You, O Lord, for You are my Strength and my Redeemer. In Jesus' name. Amen.

DAY 206

Inspiration:

"And be not conformed to this world: but be ye transformed by the renewing of your mind, that ye may prove what [is] that good, and acceptable, and perfect, will of God." ~ Romans 12:2, King James Version

Insight:

What we perceive is what we believe, and what we believe is what we will eventually receive. The mind is a powerful tool that can work for or against us in the formulation and determination of what will become our own reality. Although God has a good, and acceptable, and perfect will for our lives according to Romans 12:2, we are the ones who have the responsibility of choosing what path to follow and who we will allow to either help or hinder us along the way. Let us be good stewards of our thoughts, friendships, words and actions today so that what we perceive, believe and receive will produce the perfect will of God rather than our own.

Prayer to Ignite Action:

Father, I delight in Your Word and desire to be found in Your perfect will. Let me not become so influenced by the world that I adjust my beliefs and actions to fit in with society's status quo. Transform my thoughts so that I can think with clarity and act with conviction as I meditate upon Your principles and precepts. In You, my mind and spirit are renewed each day, and for this, I give You praise. In Jesus' name. Amen.

DAY 207

Inspiration:
"I must work the works of Him who sent Me while it is day; [the] night is coming when no one can work." ~ John 9:4, New King James Version

Insight:
I really don't believe in making wishes and expecting them to randomly come true. I do, however, believe in having a strong desire to achieve something for a purpose greater than oneself to influence and impact others for good. Desire alone is not enough. A work ethic is needed to implement a strategic plan in order to manifest the reality of what is desired. To dream is better than wishing, and being determined to consistently accomplish the work that is necessary in order to achieve what is desired will produce results.

Prayer to Ignite Action:
Heavenly Father, Your Son Jesus served as the Perfect example of what it means to have a work ethic. He worked diligently during the day to fulfill Your will, realizing that His time was valuable and precious, and would be cut short when the night season in His life arrived. Thank you for giving me discernment to know what to do and when as I work with fervor "while it is day." Help me to manage my time and resources well, and to put forth my best efforts in every endeavor assigned to my stewardship. In Jesus' name. Amen.

DAY 208

Inspiration:

"Be assured that from the first day we heard of you, we haven't stopped praying for you, asking God to give you wise minds and spirits attuned to his will, and so acquire a thorough understanding of the ways in which God works. We pray that you'll live well for the Master, making him proud of you as you work hard in his orchard. As you learn more and more how God works, you will learn how to do your work." ~ Colossians 1:9-10, The Message Bible

Insight:

We all should dare to dream and desire to set goals to make our dreams a reality. Dreaming is one thing, and talking about what we will do one day is another, but doing the work to develop a strategy that is in concert with God's plans for our lives is much more difficult. Anything worth having is worth working for, which lets us know to expect resistance and uneasiness along the way. If we can expect that our life will not always be one of comfort and ease, then we will not be surprised by challenges when they arise. In fact, the challenges will not be seen as obstacles or impossibilities, but as opportunities and possibilities waiting for us to tackle them head on with courage, confidence and the strength that comes from the ability that God supplies as we yield our dreams and goals to Him in exchange for His will.

Prayer to Ignite Action:

Heavenly Father, some may consider work to be old-fashioned and outdated, but I know that You see it as the pathway to progress. Those who work with intentionality do not just dream at night, but their vision causes them to dream and to do the necessary work by day to fulfill destiny even in the midst of difficulty. When my motive is to know and follow Your perfect will, then my works will be blessed beyond measure. Undergird me with the resolve to be found in Your will as I seek to be faithful in the work I'm called to do. In Jesus' name. Amen.

DAY 209

Inspiration:

"You are of God, little children, and have overcome them, because He who is in you is greater than he who is in the world." ~ 1 John 4:4, New King James Version

Insight:

We are God's handiwork, intricately woven to represent the best of who He is to the world each day. To possess such an attitude of confidence is to recognize that greatness has been invested in us so that it can be shared with those assigned to us and vice versa. There is no value in rehearsing what we could, would or should have done or who we might have been if only things were different in our past. All that matters is the character, integrity, responsibility and accountability with which we choose to govern our lives today, and the anticipation of making a difference as we determine to settle for nothing less than being our best. And we can do anything because of the Greater One who lives in us.

Prayer to Ignite Action:

Heavenly Father, it is a privilege to know that You are my God. Because You created me and live in me, there is greatness within waiting to be released. My past does not control my present or future, because I have overcome it by Your grace. I pray that the greatness You placed in me will be represented by my character, conversation, conduct, compassion for people and contribution to the world. In Jesus' name. Amen.

DAY 210

Inspiration:

"Behold, I intend to build a house for the name of the LORD my God, as the LORD spoke to David my father, saying, 'Your son, whom I will set on your throne in your place, he will build the house for My name.'" ~ 1 Kings 5:5, New American Standard Bible

Insight:

King Solomon's desire to build a temple was not just a pipe dream handed down from his father David who was the King of Israel who preceded him. His intent was inspired by God Himself within his and his father's hearts because it agreed with what Solomon was predestined to do. His intentionality drove him to make the building of God's temple a reality.

Someone once asked me to describe my life and what I do in one word as I was introducing myself to a group of professional colleagues. I chose to use the word intentional because it denotes the expressed emphasis of thinking, acting and living with and for a specific purpose. Being intentional about our decisions and how we carry them out eliminates distractions that could sidetrack us and cause us to stray from the path that has been set before us to reach our destiny. Focusing on who God originally intended for us to be and all that He has equipped and empowered us to do, serves as the fuel to ignite our engine of expectation as we eagerly pursue our dreams with the best of effort each day.

Prayer to Ignite Action:

Dear God, more than anything I desire to be intentional about my love for You and sharing my faith with those who need You. I also want to intentionally serve the purpose for which I exist on earth as I maximize the life I've been given. Ignite me to execute the dreams inspired by You so that my destiny becomes reality. In Jesus' name. Amen.

DAY 211

Inspiration:

"As for these four children, God gave them knowledge and skill in all learning and wisdom: and Daniel had understanding in all visions and dreams." ~ Daniel 1:17, King James Version

Insight:

Daniel, Hananiah, Mishael and Azariah were young adolescents from Judah who were being held captive in Babylon. Although they were in a less than ideal situation, their determination to represent God by not compromising their faith or defiling their bodies caused them to have favor with the King of kings as well as Nebuchadnezzar the king of Babylon.

We also have the ability and opportunity each day to determine what we will give to and receive out of life without compromising our values. Seeking to understand rather than to be understood, to listen in order to learn, to speak in order to share solutions, and to act in ways that will affect people and effect our surroundings for God and for the common good, are decisions that will determine the quality of our living and the value of our giving.

Some people allow life to pass them by as they wait for perfect conditions to appear. Instead of waiting, let's start creating opportunities by ensuring that we are wise, knowledgeable and skillful in our respective areas of expertise. *Carpe diem* (seize the day)!

Prayer to Ignite Action:

Father, all wisdom, knowledge, understanding and skill ultimately comes from You--the God of all creation. May these virtues be deepened and sharpened in me as I seize each moment to serve and to ensure a better quality of life for this and the next generation without compromising who I am or what I believe. In Jesus' name. Amen.

DAY 212

Inspiration:

"The God who made the world and everything in it, this Master of sky and land, doesn't live in custom-made shrines or need the human race to run errands for him, as if he couldn't take care of himself. He makes the creatures; the creatures don't make him. Starting from scratch, he made the entire human race and made the earth hospitable, with plenty of time and space for living so we could seek after God, and not just grope around in the dark but actually find him. He doesn't play hide-and-seek with us. He's not remote; he's near. We live and move in him, can't get away from him! One of your poets said it well: 'We're the God-created.'" ~ Acts 17:24-28, The Message Bible

Insight:

We live, move and have our being only because of God's grace, mercy and gift of life. We are present in this moment as a result of His presence and purpose that pushes us to live, love, laugh and learn each day. It is not what we own, who we know, when we were born, or where we live that matters the most. The most important factors to consider are: why are we living, and what will we do with the knowledge, natural talents and acquired skills we possess to add value to the world. Our influence in the world begins at home and extends to our community, nation and world.

Acts 1:8 says, "But you shall receive power when the Holy Spirit has come upon you; and you shall be witnesses to Me in Jerusalem, and in all Judea and Samaria, and to the end of the earth." The breath and power of God within us was given to represent who God is to those within our sphere of influence in a way that is as distinct as our personalities and gifts. Let's take God's presence--a present to us--and share it today and always.

Prayer to Ignite Action:

Dear Lord, in You I live, move and breathe. Without You I can do nothing, but with Your presence and by Your power, I can share my faith at home, at work, in my community and wherever else You lead me. I am grateful for opportunities that You will provide today for me to love, listen, learn and laugh as I live for You. In Jesus' name. Amen.

DAY 213

Inspiration:

"Do you not know that those who run in a race all run, but one receives the prize? Run in such a way that you may obtain [it]." ~ 1 Corinthians 9:24, New King James Version

"Therefore we also, since we are surrounded by so great a cloud of witnesses, let us lay aside every weight, and the sin which so easily ensnares [us], and let us run with endurance the race that is set before us, looking unto Jesus, the author and finisher of [our] faith, who for the joy that was set before Him endured the cross, despising the shame, and has sat down at the right hand of the throne of God." ~ Hebrews 12:1-2, New King James Version

Insight:

Stamina, endurance, persistence and consistency are qualities that we need to embrace as we run the race of life set before us. It is not how fast we run, but how well we run and the attitude we have along the way that makes all the difference. No matter how difficult the race becomes, we must not allow ourselves to become distracted, deterred, distressed or derailed to the point of giving up. Maintaining our momentum and fine tuning our focus keeps our eyes on the prize as our purpose draws nearer and our passion becomes dearer.

Prayer to Ignite Action:

Father, thank You for the race You've set before me--a race that is specifically designed for me to run. I pray that You would grant me the stamina, endurance, persistence and consistency needed to stay the course while remaining focused on the prize of reaching my destiny. Help me to recognize distractions and deterrents along the way so that I do not succumb to them, but rather, overcome them. I follow the example of Jesus--the author and finisher of our faith--who ran the race set before Him because of the joy ahead that guided Him. In Jesus' name. Amen.

DAY 214

Inspiration:

"I call heaven and earth as witnesses today against you, [that] I have set before you life and death, blessing and cursing; therefore choose life, that both you and your descendants may live; that you may love the LORD your God, that you may obey His voice, and that you may cling to Him, for He [is] your life and the length of your days; and that you may dwell in the land which the LORD swore to your fathers, to Abraham, Isaac, and Jacob, to give them." ~ Deuteronomy 30:19-20, New King James Version

Insight:

The power of choice is a phenomenal gift from God to mankind. No other creation has the ability to think logically and rationally, and then to make a decision based on the processing center of the mind. This gift can be used for good to elevate our standard of living as well as our approach to life. We cannot make decisions for others, but we most certainly have the responsibility to choose for ourselves. That is the opportunity given to us by our Creator as stated in Deuteronomy 30:19 which determines the course of our day and destiny.

Prayer to Ignite Action:

Dear God, the ability to choose life and blessings is a gift given by You but accepted and acted on only by us when we follow through with our own decision. Today, I firmly decide to choose a blessed life that is to be lived not for my sake alone, but for the sake of generations following me as I leave the blessing of a godly legacy. I receive every good and perfect gift from You, and vow to become a blessing to others with what I have received spiritually and naturally. In Jesus' name. Amen.

DAY 215

Inspiration:

"Dear friends, don't be surprised at the fiery trials you are going through, as if something strange were happening to you. Instead, be very glad--for these trials make you partners with Christ in his suffering, so that you will have the wonderful joy of seeing his glory when it is revealed to all the world." ~ 1 Peter 4:12-13, New Living Translation

Insight:

Life presents with it both joy and sorrow, opportunities and obstacles, and often times crisis that forces things in and around us to change. Fighting against the current of life's challenges can cause frustration and fatigue to overwhelm us. However, when we choose to flow with God's plan and the path that He predestined rather than our own or what others may have chosen for us, then we find unparalleled freedom and joy by using our energy and talents in the best possible way to honor God and add value to the world. In this way, even our trials can be used to remind us that we can be thankful and joyful in the midst of trying times as God reveals His glory.

Prayer to Ignite Action:

Father, I do not always understand why difficulties arise in my life, but I know that You will never forsake me. Help me to remain thankful by remembering how You brought me through before as I focus on triumphing over trials now and in the future. I will not be discouraged by what I see, hear or feel. Instead, I am encouraged by what I believe by faith in expectation of what You will do to show your glory through my life's story. In Jesus' name. Amen.

Day 216

Inspiration:

"This [is] the day the LORD has made; We will rejoice and be glad in it."
~ Psalm 118:24, New King James Version

Insight:

This is a day of profound possibilities with limitless opportunities to learn, laugh and show love with our conversation and conduct to those closest to us. Whatever was left undone yesterday is not as important as what we determine to do with the time allotted to us today. Let's seize each moment with eager expectation, knowing that the decisions we make and the actions we execute will determine our quality of life and leave a legacy for others to emulate.

Prayer to Ignite Action:

Dear God, I acknowledge that You are the maker and giver of this day, and I am determined to enjoy every minute of it! Let my eyes, ears and heart be open to behold, hear and feel the joy of living in the moment. I will make an extra effort to embrace the beauty that is encapsulated in this day with a positive mindset and a heart full of thanksgiving. In Jesus' name. Amen.

DAY 217

Inspiration:

"[He is] the Rock, His work [is] perfect; For all His ways [are] justice, A God of truth and without injustice; Righteous and upright [is] He." ~ Deuteronomy 32:4, New King James Version

"The LORD will perfect [that which] concerns me; Your mercy, O LORD, [endures] forever; Do not forsake the works of Your hands." ~ Psalm 138:8, New King James Version

Insight:

I have learned that perfection is impossible to achieve in this life, but excellence is certainly within our grasp. To strive for excellence rather than perfection frees us from unrealistic goal-setting for ourselves as well as unfair expectations that we may have of others. Our preoccupation should not be with perfection, but rather, with pursuing and receiving the peace that comes from knowing that we are doing the best that we possibly can with the knowledge, skills and resources that are at our disposal. Embracing the reality of that as our truth, will add to our inner self-worth and create value for those closest to us. A quote from Anna Quindlen that emphasizes the lesson I've learned: "The thing that is really hard, and really amazing, is giving up on being perfect and beginning the work of becoming yourself."

Prayer to Ignite Action:

God, You are my Rock and my Fortress. As imperfect as I am, I still trust in You whose ways are perfect. I am awed by the fact that You love, provide for and use me regardless of my frailties and failures. Your mercy towards me is shown each time I am forgiven and my sins are forgotten. Thank you for perfecting and maturing me so that You can complete what You started in me. How I love You, Lord, and I am so honored to serve You. In Jesus' name. Amen.

DAY 218

Inspiration:

"Happy [is] the man [who] finds wisdom, And the man [who] gains understanding; For her proceeds [are] better than the profits of silver, And her gain than fine gold. She [is] more precious than rubies, And all the things you may desire cannot compare with her. Length of days [is] in her right hand, In her left hand riches and honor. Her ways [are] ways of pleasantness, And all her paths [are] peace." ~ Proverbs 3:13-17, New King James Version

Insight:

Many people seek to be happy based on their personal and professional relationships as well as their possessions. However, true happiness cannot be attained from external means or measures alone. Basing one's happiness on the status of people, circumstances and material things which can and do change, is an unstable and unsure foundation. Pursuing joy and peace from an inner wellspring and resource that is greater than oneself is the key to a fulfilling and blessed life. "Greater is He that is within...[God who is our Ultimate Source and Resource] than he that is in the world [external means and measures]."

Prayer to Ignite Action:

Heavenly Father, I magnify Your name and Your Word in my life so that what is contrary to Your will decreases as wisdom and discernment to do what is right increases. Wisdom brings with it the companions of understanding, joy, peace and a long life that is rich and rewarding. Teach me the ways of wisdom today. I commit myself to learn and follow Your instructions, and to receive the benefits of my obedience. In Jesus' name. Amen.

DAY 219

Inspiration:

"In view of all this, make every effort to respond to God's promises. Supplement your faith with a generous provision of moral excellence, and moral excellence with knowledge, and knowledge with self-control, and self-control with patient endurance, and patient endurance with godliness, and godliness with brotherly affection, and brotherly affection with love for everyone. The more you grow like this, the more productive and useful you will be in your knowledge of our Lord Jesus Christ." ~ 2 Peter 1:5-8, New Living Translation

Insight:

We should make every effort to seek to be empowered so that we may empower others in return. A work ethic guided by morality and integrity and ignited by God's purpose for our lives, speaks volumes to those who are always watching and listening. The more effort we exert, the more impact we'll have to influence our corner of the world for God and for good.

Prayer to Ignite Action:

Father, You created us to work so that we can lead a rich and rewarding life. Thank you for empowering me to do what I love so that I can empower others to do the same. In Jesus' name. Amen.

DAY 220

Inspiration:

"Turn away from evil and do good. Search for peace, and work to maintain it." ~ Psalm 34:14, New Living Translation

"I listen carefully to what God the LORD is saying, for he speaks peace to his faithful people. But let them not return to their foolish ways." ~ Psalm 85:8, New Living Translation

Insight:

The peace of God is available and attainable for us to possess when we position ourselves to receive it by releasing all worry, anxiety and stress. The way to let go of these useless feelings and thoughts is to pray to God with honest, sincere communication, letting Him know how we feel and giving to Him all that concerns us. As we trust God to take what we offer to Him in prayer without taking it back from Him, in exchange we will receive peace that calms our minds and guards our spirits, and an assurance that God's will shall be done. Perfect peace becomes our possession when our minds are focused on God's promises rather than our problems.

Prayer to Ignite Action:

Lord God, You are my burden bearer so that I no longer need to carry what caused me to worry. I release into Your hands all my anxiety and stress in exchange for perfect peace. I thank You for the sense of relief I have from knowing that You are in control and can handle what I cannot. I will not take back what I have given to You. I have peace of mind because I trust You. In Jesus' name. Amen.

DAY 221

Inspiration:

"No temptation has overtaken you except such as is common to man; but God [is] faithful, who will not allow you to be tempted beyond what you are able, but with the temptation will also make the way of escape, that you may be able to bear [it]." ~ 1 Corinthians 10:13, New King James Version

Insight:

Life presents itself in the form of circumstantial ups and downs, triumphs and tragedies, that can, if we allow it to be so, throw us into a tailspin or cause us to move forward with the knowledge that with God, we already win! That is not to say that we are impervious to pain and immune to problems. The fact of the matter is that our Creator knows what we can and cannot handle, and He has equipped us with the inner witness of the Holy Spirit and the inspiration of His Holy Word to endure every trial while still choosing to enjoy life.

There is no temptation or tribulation that we cannot bear with God working faithfully in, through and around us. We do not have to succumb to or bow beneath the pressure of circumstances because God has made a way for us to ascend above them daily in our thoughts, words and deeds.

Prayer to Ignite Action:

Father, I know that I am not alone in the things that I experience. Life happens to us all, but You are faithful to provide a way of escape so that we do not have to be overtaken by any temptation. Thank You for giving me the power to resist temptations that come as I continue to rely on You. In Jesus' name. Amen.

DAY 222

Inspiration:

"'I tell you the truth, Jesus answered, 'this very night, before the rooster crows, you will disown me three times.' But declared, 'Even if I have to die with you, I will never disown you.' And all the disciples said the same...Then Peter remembered the word Jesus had spoken: 'Before the rooster crows, you will disown me three times.' And he went outside and wept bitterly." ~ Matthew 26:34-35, 75, New International Version

Insight:

Agonizing over past failures of ourselves or others, disheartening disappointments, as well as meandering through the maze of mistakes and misunderstandings repetitively in our minds, will not add any virtue to our present circumstance, nor will we gain any added value whatsoever from doing so in our future. The best choice we can make is to learn from our past so as not to repeat the same mistakes and to move on by sharing lessons learned with others as we focus upon what lies ahead with a positive perspective and principle-driven behavior. Now that's what enhances our quality of life.

Prayer to Ignite Action:

Heavenly Father, I have made many mistakes and have agonized over them, but I rejoice in the fact that I do not have to be weighed down by guilt, shame or sorrow when I ask for and receive Your forgiveness. Because of Your mercy and grace, I can release my past and begin again with this new day. In Jesus' name. Amen.

DAY 223

Inspiration:

"You know me inside and out, you know every bone in my body; You know exactly how I was made, bit by bit, how I was sculpted from nothing into something. Like an open book, you watched me grow from conception to birth; all the stages of my life were spread out before you, The days of my life all prepared before I'd even lived one day. Your thoughts--how rare, how beautiful! God, I'll never comprehend them! I couldn't even begin to count them--any more than I could count the sand of the sea. Oh, let me rise in the morning and live always with you!" ~ Psalm 139:15-18, New International Version

Insight:

God loves us so much that His thoughts toward us are innumerable and His love toward us is limitless. He took the time to fashion every detail and day of our lives, and to record them all in His book. It is mind-boggling to think that we are always on the mind and heart of God, and that His masterful handiwork (including you and me) is marvelous in His eyes. We were marvelous (incredible, extraordinary, astonishing, surprising, superb and excellent) to God before we were placed in the wombs of our mothers. We should remind ourselves to value what God values and to love what God loves as a cherished treasure--and that begins with valuing and loving ourselves here and now so that we may also value and love others.

Prayer to Ignite Action:

Loving Father, Your thoughts about me and your plans for me are constantly on display every time I awaken to receive Your provisions--life, health, strength, joy, peace, protection, valued relationships, finances, favor--that are always on time and without fail. You know all about me, and love me enough to gently push me so that I am propelled into my future without being held captive by my past. Thank You for knowing what I am capable of to fulfill each day's destiny as recorded in the annals of heaven. In Jesus' name. Amen.

DAY 224

Inspiration:

"But as for you, you meant evil against me; [but] God meant it for good, in order to bring it about as [it is] this day, to save many people alive." ~ Genesis 50:20, New King James Version

Insight:

In the book of Genesis, Joseph had endured very harsh treatment from his brothers who sold him into slavery. Although Joseph experienced hardship in the bottom of a pit, in Potipher's house as he was wrongfully accused by his master's wife of trying to rape her, and in the cold dungeon of a prison, the favor of God was with him in each place, which eventually led him to the palace as second in command to Pharoah, king of Egypt. Did you notice that all of the places where Joseph found himself in pain begin with the letter "p'?" It's important to note that Joseph's potential could not be fully released unless he pursued this particular path in order to propel him into his predestined purpose! The same holds true for us oftentimes. Purpose may be birthed through the pain of disappointment. The sooner we realize that everything and everyone we encounter can be used by God to work together for our good (Romans 8:28), then we can, like Joseph, rest assured that what God allows to happen will be used to shape us for the season in our lives that is to come--a season when we are able to be a blessing to many because of the lessons we've learned.

Prayer to Ignite Action:

Father, You are the One who knows the path I must take as well as the potholes and pitfalls along the way. Lead me so that I will stay on the road that is meant for me, and help me to endure the rocks that may be thrown without stumbling over them. I need Your strength so that I remain focused and faithful, remembering that You will take what was meant for evil and use it for a purpose that is good for me and those that I will be a blessing to because I persevered. In Jesus' name. Amen.

DAY 225

Inspiration:
"But make sure that you don't get so absorbed and exhausted in taking care of all your day-by-day obligations that you lose track of the time and doze off, oblivious to God. The night is about over, dawn is about to break. Be up and awake to what God is doing! God is putting the finishing touches on the salvation work he began when we first believed." ~ Romans 13:11-12, The Message Bible

Insight:
The most important moment in time is not already past, but it is right now. Now is the opportunity to think, speak, act and feel in such a way that times before pale in comparison to the possibilities that this present moment in time brings. This is a day we've never seen before, with brand new mercy extended to us to finish what we started, and to begin afresh and anew with innovative goals and strategies that will provide solutions and garner success, not just for ourselves, but for those who willingly step into our sphere of influence. Now is the time to share our faith by the way we live and the service we give. Let's make our NOW moment, a WOW moment!

Prayer to Ignite Action:
Father, thank You for giving me another chance to make good use of time by valuing this day and refusing to waste one minute of it. Help me to be awake and alert to what You are doing and how I can fit into Your work of salvation. Use my voice, hands, gifts and resources as only You can today. In Jesus' name. Amen.

DAY 226

Inspiration:

"Teach me, O Lord, the way of Your statues, and I will keep it to the end [steadfastly]. Give me understanding, that I may keep your law; yes, I will observe it with my whole heart. Make me go in the path of Your commandments, for in them do I delight." ~ Psalm 119:33-35, Amplified Bible

Insight:

Our destination (where we end up in our future) is determined by our decisions (where we choose to place our focus). Whatever we constantly think about is what we will allow to manifest in and around us. Therefore, it is imperative that we focus on God's best for our lives so that we will not settle for anything less. Our thoughts, words and actions should be centered on biblically sound principles and positive affirmations that are in agreement with God's purpose and intent for us. As we continue to pursue God's presence through a relationship of prayerful communication to seek and search for Him with our whole heart, He will in return reveal His plans for our future and a hope that extends beyond our present into eternity. Listening to God's Word and following His will increases our faith and sharpens our focus.

Prayer to Ignite Action:

Dear Lord, Your Word is life to me. I love Your precepts and desire to live by godly principles. Hearing and obeying Your Word reveals more of You, increases my faith, renews my spirit, and leads me toward my destiny. Thank You for teaching me how to walk in Your ways as I meditate on Your Holy Word. In Jesus' name. Amen.

DAY 227

Inspiration:

"Your words all add up to the sum total: Truth. Your righteous decisions are eternal...I'm ecstatic over what you say, like one who strikes it rich. I hate lies-can't stand them!-but I love what you have revealed." ~ Psalm 119:160, 162-163, The Message Bible

Insight:

My daughter Lesley stated in a sermon once, "What may be perceived as true is not necessarily THE TRUTH." What a powerful statement! Often times, we perceive perhaps what we've heard or have told ourselves repeatedly based on our upbringing or surroundings as true without questioning it or examining it from different perspectives. It is important to compare what we see, hear and feel to the truth of God's Word which is a solid and reliable foundation. God's Word will never lead us astray when we use it as the compass by which our lives are guided each day.

Prayer to Ignite Action:

Father, there are many forces of influence around me such as the media, music, positive peers, and critical cynics. The most precious influence to me is Your Holy Word, for from ages past to the present and into the future, it has been and will be tested, tried and found to be the truth. Please grant me discernment so that I will not mistake or confuse what may appear to be true with the truth of Your Word for my life. In Jesus' name. Amen.

DAY 228

Inspiration:

"Your beginnings will seem humble, so prosperous will your future be."
~ Job 8:7, New International Version

"Know also that wisdom is sweet to your soul; if you find it, there is a future hope for you, and your hope will not be cut off." ~ Proverbs 24:14, New International Version

Insight:

"Que sera', sera'; whatever will be, will be. The future's not ours to see. Que sera', sera'." These are the lyrics of a song that actress Doris Day sang. Whereas some may think that adopting this attitude is best, the truth is that we have a hand in the future that God has predestined for us to enjoy. Whatever will be is really up to you and me when we seek God's will and "get in where we fit in." We can and will see our future, and it will be so bright that we'll want to wear shades to enjoy the Son!

Prayer to Ignite Action:

Heavenly Father, I praise You whose wisdom existed before time began. You hold the future in the palm of Your hands, and are aware of the way in which I should walk because it was planned with me in mind. Thank You for allowing me to participate in my own future here on earth and in eternity as a result of having a relationship with You. In Jesus' name. Amen.

DAY 229

Inspiration:

"But no weapon that is formed against you shall prosper, and every tongue that shall rise against you in judgment you shall show to be in the wrong. This [peace, righteousness, security, triumph over opposition] is the heritage of the servants of the Lord [those in whom the ideal Servant of the Lord is reproduced]; this is the righteousness or the vindication which they obtain from Me [this is that which I impart to them as their justification], says the Lord." ~ Isaiah 54:17, Amplified Bible

Insight:

When you know who you are according to God's Word and confidently walk in that knowledge, there is nothing that you cannot accomplish. You can go anywhere and do anything, and attract the kind of people and relationships in your life that are in alignment with your conscious thoughts, conversation, conduct and character--all of which will work synergistically to keep you on the pathway of purpose. God working in and through us, will see to it that we supersede all odds, obstacles and opposition that could ever come against us.

Prayer to Ignite Action:

Omnipotent God, I worship You, my Creator and Sustainer. I shall not fear, for Your hand protects and provides for me. I have peace because You are aware of those who are for and against me, and You will keep me safe in Your hallowed hand. Hurt, harm and danger may try to come near me and those closest to me today, but no weapon that is formed will prosper against those who serve You. In Jesus' name. Amen.

DAY 230

Inspiration:

"I have shown you in every way, by laboring like this, that you must support the weak. And remember the words of the Lord Jesus, that He said, 'It is more blessed to give than to receive.'" ~ Acts 20:35, New King James Version

Insight:

More effort should be spent in giving rather than receiving--giving of our time, talents and treasures as an investment that will yield both temporal and eternal dividends. We should do our best to live a quality of life that would make God smile and attract others to Him. We have more to give than we think, and in order to release what is valuable to us and others, we must make an assessment of what we have to offer and be intentional about giving it away. Generous love and great joy are gained as a result of our giving. Ready...set...GIVE!

Prayer to Ignite Action:

Oh Lord, You have shown us the way in which we should live by Your own example. Jesus said, "It is more blessed to give than to receive," and demonstrated it so that we could do the same as disciples. Today, I pray for a head, heart and hands of compassion to identify and empathize with the needs of the weak, and to give what I can to meet them where they are. I am determined to reflect Your love and light in the world. In Jesus' name. Amen.

DAY 231

Inspiration:
"That precious memory triggers another: your honest faith--and what a rich faith it is, handed down from your grandmother Lois to your mother Eunice, and now to you! And the special gift of ministry you received when I laid hands on you and prayed--keep that ablaze! God doesn't want us to be shy with his gifts, but bold and loving and sensible." ~ 2 Timothy 1:5-7, The Message Bible

Insight:
Pursuing what gives our life meaning and value while staying true to what stirs our gifts and feeds our soul, will lead us to the path of purpose that God has predestined for us. Timothy learned this from his grandmother and mother, as well as from the apostle Paul who served as his spiritual mentor. Following that path brought Timothy joy and fulfillment, even though there were difficulties along the way. When we stir up our gifts by acknowledging and using them for a cause greater than ourselves, then we will also experience joy and fulfillment that will overflow into the lives of others.

Prayer to Ignite Action:
Dear God, today I pray for the boldness, love and sensibilities to serve You fully with the gifts and abilities I have. Thank You for the indelible mark made by others You've placed in my life to help me recognize my natural talents and sharpen my skills so that I can be effective in using what I've been given to represent You and reach those in my sphere of influence. In Jesus' name. Amen.

DAY 232

Inspiration:

"As for you, you meant evil against me, but God meant it for good in order to bring about this present result, to preserve many people alive."
~ Genesis 50:20, New American Standard Bible

Insight:

Have you ever heard the expression, "The world is going to hell in a hand basket?" While it seems that depravity is on the rise as a result of sin's devastating imprint, God's grace is still able to abound and turn a negative situation around. Even in the most dire of circumstances, deliverance is available when we follow God's directive and maintain a positive perspective. Joseph shows us this life-giving principle in Genesis 50:20. He had every right to be upset about the way his brothers mistreated him, but he took the high road because God had a greater purpose. We can do the same when we understand that purpose can still be revealed and that we can be healed in the aftermath of pain and difficulty.

Prayer to Ignite Action:

Heavenly Father, I believe that You are in control of every situation and circumstance that I will face today. Fill me with the ability to strengthen others with the lessons I've learned as I take the high road by thinking, speaking and acting in ways that represent Your character and nature. Today, I choose to be filled with Your Spirit, healed by Your power, and sealed by the promises of Your Word. In Jesus' name. Amen.

DAY 233

Inspiration:

"God's gifts and God's call are under full warranty--never canceled, never rescinded." ~ Romans 11:29, The Message Bible

"Every good gift and every perfect gift is from above, and cometh down from the Father of lights, with whom is no variableness, neither shadow of turning." ~ James 1:17, King James Version

Insight:

When I was a little girl, I used to draw quite frequently, and I seemed to be very good at it. I remember drawing my father as he sat in his recliner fast asleep, as well as a myriad of animal and human caricatures for my mother's third grade classroom bulletin boards for many years. My mother was so wonderful in allowing me to unleash hidden gifts that would have remained dormant had she not made a demand on my potential. I didn't know at the time that she was preparing me to release creative gifts not only in music and arts, but also in teaching and writing that would manifest years later.

You also have creative possibilities that are waiting to be discovered and shared with the world around you. Unleashing the creativity in you will also allow seeds to be planted in others that may blossom later. Take the time to evaluate your gifts and to also help to nurture the gifts in those around you.

Prayer to Ignite Action:

Dear Lord, You have given every man, woman, boy and girl talents and abilities that are as unique as each personality and fingerprint. The origin of every gift is perfect, for it came from You and will never be taken away. Help me and others today to perfect the gifts we have by using them with regularity and skill. The original intent of every talent was given so that we may honor You and be a blessing to others with it. Thank You for the perfecting process that is needed so that I can continue to grow and develop into full maturity as a follower of Christ. In Jesus' name. Amen.

DAY 234

Inspiration:

"Now that I've put you there on a hilltop, on a light stand--shine! Keep open house; be generous with your lives. By opening up to others, you'll prompt people to open up with God, this generous Father in heaven." ~ Matthew 5:16, The Message Bible

Insight:

The past has passed and the future is beyond us. What we have for certain is today, this moment, right now. There are plenty of opportunities to take in the beauty, brightness and brilliance of what is in front of us if we give proper priority and perspective to the people, places and things that enrich our lives as well as the ways in which we can enrich the lives of others. What matters most is how well we use the resources within and around us to increase God's kingdom here on earth which will in return yield eternal dividends. True splendor lies in what we do for God, for only what we do for Him will last.

Prayer to Ignite Action:

Father God, You have given me another day, and with it another opportunity to shine brightly for You. Allow me to be transparent enough for people to see that You live in me and will come to dwell in all who denounce sin and declare faith in Jesus Christ. May I be reminded that only what I do for You today will speak in eternity. In Jesus' name. Amen.

DAY 235

Inspiration:
"Then Saul said to Samuel, 'I have sinned, for I have transgressed the commandment of the LORD and your words, because I feared the people and obeyed their voice.'" ~ 1 Samuel 15:24, New King James Version

Insight:
It is apparent that Saul feared the people in his kingdom. He was controlled by their whims and wishes, and therefore, he had abdicated his throne without even knowing it. Instead of leading the nation of Israel, he assumed the position of following them. Good leadership requires wisdom, knowledge, understanding and counsel from a source higher and greater than oneself. Having mentors and aspiring to learn from exceptional leaders is commendable, but the greatest Leader of all time is God who knows our calling, character and capabilities and can lead us in the right direction when we allow Him to do so.

Prayer to Ignite Action:
Oh Lord, You are full of wisdom, knowledge, understanding, counsel and might. Everything that is needed and desired is found in You--the God who created and approved of us before anyone ever expressed criticism or disapproval against us. I am so grateful that You approve of me, and that Your Word gives clear instructions for me to follow. Lead me in the path of righteousness today so that Your voice supersedes the voices of others. You are the audience of One that I desire to please. In Jesus' name. Amen.

DAY 236

Inspiration:

"You open Your hand and satisfy the desire of every living thing...He will fulfill the desire of those who fear Him; He also will hear their cry and save them." ~ Psalm 145:16 & 19, New King James Version

Insight:

Anything worth having is worth working for, which requires extra effort, due diligence and commitment that is crucial to significant success. Doing our part to create the life we desire cannot be delegated to anyone else. We have the power to choose and then to act upon the decisions we make that are in agreement with the vision that we see and seek. We must ensure that our vision is God-inspired so that when disappointments come, we can press on while keeping our eyes on the prize that requires our full participation.

Prayer to Ignite Action:

Father, You are concerned about and desire to fulfill the desire of every living thing. You've promised to fulfill the desire of all who reverence You. Today, I pray that the cry of those who need salvation and a sense of purposeful living will be heard and answered. I avail myself to be used today to fulfill Your plan and to meet a need in the life of someone else. In Jesus' name. Amen.

DAY 237

Inspiration:
"A fool vents all his feelings, But a wise [man] holds them back." ~ Proverbs 29:11, New King James Version

Insight:
Relying on our feelings to dictate our actions is the same as trying to walk a tight rope, knowing that we can fall or fail at any second. Although God wired us, especially as women, to experience emotion intensely, we are not to base our decisions and actions on feelings that can change directions like the wind. Emotions are intricately interwoven into the fabric of our soul, but we must also realize that our soul consists of other components such as our mind, will, intellect and imagination which are equally important and beneficial as we cultivate each component with intention and precision. Maintaining balance is the key to living a life of joy that overflows onto our path of purpose and into the people who happen to cross our pathway each day.

Prayer to Ignite Action:
Father, it is so difficult to maintain balance in life with the relationships and responsibilities that I have. Yet, I find wisdom and strength in You to manage not only my relationships and responsibilities, but also myself. Let me not be driven by my emotions in decisions made and actions taken today. Instead, allow me to recognize the source and reason behind feelings that may arise, and to respond in the appropriate manner at the right time. In Jesus' name. Amen.

DAY 238

Inspiration:
"For His anger is but for a moment, but His favor is for a lifetime or in His favor is life. Weeping may endure for a night, but joy comes in the morning." ~ Psalm 30:5, Amplified Bible

Insight:
Life is given to us so that it can be enjoyed immensely. People, conditions and circumstances encountered will not be perfect, but they can become possibilities once presented to us when we choose to make the best out of what could be considered a less than desirable situation. Sometimes the most valuable lessons can be learned from the most challenging situations, and the most creative innovations and strategies are often birthed because of an old adage that says, "Necessity is the mother of invention." Joy is the aftermath of all the lessons, innovations and strategies we implement to increase productivity and our own maturity. Take time today to enjoy the fruit of your labor and to appreciate the richness of life and all of its lessons. And as Maya Angelou would say, "Once you learn, teach!"

Prayer to Ignite Action:
Father God, Your favor even during the most trying times of my life keep me focused on what You are able to do because of the track record of Your faithfulness. Today, I am determined to learn valuable lessons from the people and predicaments that surround me so that I can sharpen myself and teach them to those around me. In Jesus' name. Amen.

Inspiration:

"You yourselves are all the endorsement we need. Your very lives are a letter that anyone can read by just looking at you. Christ himself wrote it--not with ink, but with God's living Spirit; not chiseled into stone, but carved into human lives--and we publish it. We couldn't be more sure of ourselves in this--that you, written by Christ himself for God, are our letter of recommendation." ~ 2 Corinthians 3:2-4, The Message Bible

Insight:

Birthdays are a blessed occasions, for they often provide opportunities for us to experience love expressed by those whose lives have been touched in some way by ours. It is wonderful to know that our life can impact others. We can choose to influence and mentor as many people as we can by our words, works, mentoring, faith and friendship, God desires to use our lives as an open book for others to read and relate to as we point the way to Christ and the abundant life that is available in Him. After all, His gift to us was life, and the least that we can do in return is to offer it to God afresh to be shaped and molded continuously into what He predestined for it to be.

Prayer to Ignite Action:

Heavenly Father, I do not take any day for granted, for everyday that I awaken to breathe is a blessing that comes from You. Thank You for this day and for days past when my life has touched someone else's and made a difference. Today, I will seize every available moment to live in such a way that my life becomes an open book for others to read and learn from as I point them to You. In Jesus' name. Amen.

DAY 240

Inspiration:

"And God heard the voice of the lad. Then the angel of God called to Hagar out of heaven, and said to her, 'What ails you, Hagar? Fear not, for God has heard the voice of the lad where he [is]. Arise, lift up the lad and hold him with your hand, for I will make him a great nation." ~ Genesis 21:17-18, New King James Version

Insight:

How are you allowing your voice to be heard? We have a responsibility to teach others what we have learned ourselves. We do not exist merely to live, but to value our life's lessons as our legacy to give. Our voice can be shared by what we speak and do, and most importantly, by how we live each day. What are we doing to pass on a legacy of hope to others? Is our voice being shared or silenced? Let's make every effort to speak clearly with purpose and intentionality not just verbally, but with nonverbal language as well that communicates the character and nature of our Creator.

Prayer to Ignite Action:

Father, I lift my voice to You in this prayer of thanksgiving. You have given me a voice to use for righteousness and courage enough to express what needs to be addressed in the right setting and season. Thank You for listening when I call on You, and for knowing not just what I need, but for hearing the requests made on behalf of others with even greater needs and providing for all of us so faithfully. Let my voice be a resounding trumpet for justice and mercy wherever I go today. In Jesus' name. Amen.

DAY 241

Inspiration:

"He trained us first, passed us like silver through refining fires, Brought us into hardscrabble country, pushed us to our very limit, Road-tested us inside and out, took us to hell and back; Finally he brought us to this well-watered place." ~ Psalm 66:10-12, The Message Bible

Insight:

Life has winding roads and turns that we could have never predicted, yet when we embrace them with our heart and soul, we will find that they will lead to acquiring a better understanding of who we are and all the opportunities that are made available to us in the most unexpected ways. There is something to be said for having knowledge and experience, but we must also possess a passionate heart that will lead us to the path God has ordained for us. "Trusting God when we can't trace Him" is difficult, but the rewards will be well worth the exercising of our faith and efforts.

Prayer to Ignite Action:

Father, nothing that has occurred in my life has been without Your infinite knowledge and permission. I am thankful that You have been, are, and will be with me through my triumphs and tragedies. You've been my shelter and strength through times of testing that were turned into opportunities of blessing. You have cultivated in me a heart of passion for life and compassion for people in this well-watered place, and for that I am extremely grateful. In Jesus' name. Amen

DAY 242

Inspiration:
"And though you started with little, you will end with much." ~ Job 8:7, New Living Translation

Insight:
Success does not happen by chance. It occurs as a result of a series of small goals accomplished one step at a time. Never despise small beginnings, for those who start small and remain consistent in their efforts without being swayed will achieve greatness that others only dream about. More important, those who start small and finish strong by following God's plan for their lives will hear Him say, "Well done, good and faithful servant." And that is the ultimate joy and definition of success.

Prayer to Ignite Action:
Father, every moment of time is given by You for creation to use to fulfill purpose. No one and nothing is too small or insignificant, for every detail of our lives is important to You. Just as Your watchful gaze is upon all You've created, so I desire to focus on the details of what You've placed within my hands. Help me to be faithful with what You've given me-- whether it be little or much--and to manage it all well. In Jesus' name. Amen.

DAY 243

Inspiration:

"So think clearly and exercise self-control. Look forward to the gracious salvation that will come to you when Jesus Christ is revealed." ~ 1 Peter 1:13, New Living Translation

Insight:

I must confess that I can be strong-willed at times. Once my mind is set on something, be it a goal, vision, project or purpose, nothing can stop me unless God Himself intervenes. Perhaps you are the same way, or know someone who is. (Ironically, my husband and I are alike in this area.)

Refusing to be swayed in our opinions, focus and destiny is a good thing only when we are influenced and guided by the wisdom and inspiration of God. It takes that kind of an attitude to remain a Christian in the midst of a society and world that downplays the tenets of Christianity and even more so, the Person of Jesus Christ. It takes a strong will to resist temptations and to withstand and pass the tests that come our way--tests that will strengthen and equip us so that we may reach a greater level of maturity. We must be totally convinced of who we are (not apart from God, but because of God), what we are called to do and who we are called to reach. Once we have this confidence, we become a force to be reckoned with as we focus on fulfilling the will of God and not just our own.

Prayer to Ignite Action:

Dear Lord, I realize that my life has the power to impact my present and future. Please help me to steady my will so that I can resist temptation and pass the tests of life that come to develop maturity in me. I will exercise self-control in the arena of my thoughts as well as in my actions to fulfill Your will today. In Jesus' name. Amen.

DAY 244

Inspiration:

"Who gives intuition to the heart and instinct to the mind?" ~ Job 38:36, New Living Translation

Insight:

Ah, the beauty of a creative mind! Isn't it wonderful to know that we have the power to imagine life, not as it is, but as we desire for it to be and then live it accordingly? No other creature possesses the intuitive and imaginative prowess of the human brain with reasoning ability that can actually alter reality. Today, let's determine to imagine our life with precision down to the smallest detail, and make sure that we are mission-minded and purpose-driven. When we commit to following through with what it takes to achieve what we have imagined and give of ourselves to make the world a better place, then we will be abundantly blessed in return.

Prayer to Ignite Action:

Father, the capabilities of the human mind to imagine and the capacity of the human heart to love are evidence of Your sovereignty and creativity. I never want to take the functionality of my mind and heart for granted, for they operate at Your pleasure. Influence my imagination with Your inspiration to live as You originally designed on purpose, for a purpose. In Jesus' name. Amen.

DAY 245

Inspiration:
"I was cast upon You from my very birth; from my mother's womb You have been my God." ~ Psalm 22:10, Amplified Bible

Insight:
What separates us from every other individual on earth? We can certainly surmise that our DNA, fingerprints and teeth are used to identify us and to distinguish us from any other person. Likewise, we were created with unique personalities, talents, gifts and abilities--some innate and others that are to be developed and honed--to reiterate our individuality while we are dependent upon God for wisdom and direction and interdependently connected to others for partnership and relationship. Being in relationship with God and others while knowing ourselves, requires honesty, integrity, transparency and authenticity--qualities that will thrust us into our divine destiny.

Prayer to Ignite Action:
Dear God, You have known me from my inception to my conception, and are aware of my individuality and every idiosyncrasy. Thank You for loving me unconditionally and for granting me the ability to be authentic and genuine as I depend on You and connect with others who are integral in my life. I honor You for allowing me to embrace this day fully with every breath and step taken. In Jesus' name. Amen.

DAY 246

Inspiration:

"Words satisfy the mind as much as fruit does the stomach; good talk is as gratifying as a good harvest. Words kill, words give life; they're either poison or fruit--you choose." ~ Proverbs 18:20-21, The Message Bible

Insight:

Proverbs 18:20-21 tells us in essence to expect to attract into our lives that which we love the most. The power of positivity or negativity, blessing or cursing, life or death, is in our mouths. However, before the words roll off our tongue, the decision is first made within our minds as to what kind of words we will choose. We will produce positive results when our words which are directly linked to our thoughts, are positive. Such a perspective not only transforms us, but it also transforms the world around us.

Prayer to Ignite Action:

Lord God, You have given us the power to choose as a gift to use with wisdom and discretion. Today, I choose to speak and embrace life and to acknowledge the blessings all around me with appreciation. Since the choices I will make today have the power to affect the atmosphere, please help me to make choices that will produce positive results in the stewardship of my relationships and responsibilities. In Jesus' name. Amen.

DAY 247

Inspiration:

"You will still be eating last year's harvest when you will have to move it out to make room for the new." ~ Leviticus 26:10, New International Version

"See, the former things have taken place, and new things I declare; before they spring into being I announce them to you." ~ Isaiah 42:9, New International Version

"See, I am doing a new thing! Now it springs up; do you not perceive it? I am making a way in the desert and streams in the wasteland." ~ Isaiah 43:19, New International Version

Insight:

When we cross the threshold of a brand new day, we leave yesterday behind in our rearview mirror. Now we have fresh opportunities awaiting on the horizon to challenge, strengthen, sharpen and motivate us to live our best lives and to become our best selves. This is the day to begin again and to put an end to the things, relationships and circumstances that engendered frustration rather than fruitfulness and perplexity rather than peace. Today is the catalyst that will catapult us into greater purpose-driven possibilities than ever before when we imagine what we can do and follow through by replacing fear with faith, fervor and the freedom to be who God originally intended us to be.

Prayer to Ignite Action:

Father, Your Word says, "Jesus is the same yesterday, today and forever." You have been and will be with me always. Teach me not dwell on the old that should be forgotten and to embrace the new that You have promised to reveal to me. I will not be hindered by my past, for I cannot change it. Thank You for the grace to accept what has been while I anticipate the fresh opportunities and great things in store for me and those I meet today. In Jesus' name. Amen.

DAY 248

Inspiration:

"You have heard these things; look at them all. Will you not admit them? 'From now on I will tell you of new things, of hidden things unknown to you.'" ~ Isaiah 48:6, New International Version

Insight:

As you embark upon the dawning of this new day, remember that you have the ability to choose the life you dare to leave behind as well as the new life you are determined to live now. What aspirations do you have for today? What inspiration will you offer to others? How will you sharpen your skills and utilize your gifts more fully to impact more people for God's glory? What do you need to leave in the past, and what should you pursue to secure your desired future? All these decisions and more will determine the quality of life that awaits you and the peace that will most definitely follow when you choose wisely.

Prayer to Ignite Action:

Heavenly Father, reveal to me what has been hidden so that I will receive clarity of focus, direction, purpose and timing as I move forward and leave my past behind. I will intently listen for Your voice and intentionally watch for the ways in which You choose to speak to me today. My desire is to be used as the vessel through which Your love, kindness and generosity can flow to those who need it most. Let my life become a bridge to connect others to You. In Jesus' name. Amen.

DAY 249

Inspiration:

"Therefore you have no excuse or defense or justification, O man, whoever you are who judges and condemns another. For in posing as judge and passing sentence on another, you condemn yourself, because you who judge are habitually practicing the very same things [that you censure and denounce]." ~ Romans 2:1, Amplified Version

Insight:

It really is possible to live life on our own terms, which simply means that we choose to take control of our own decisions and actions without delegating them to others and subsequently blaming them for the outcome. After all, we are responsible for the choices we make daily and the consequences of those choices. Procrastination, lack of motivation, intimidation and stagnation are thieves that come to rob us of our time, energy, confidence and progress. They are merely excuses for not moving forward and allowing the brilliance of God's light to shine through us. When we reject and eject the excuse-laden mentality that points the finger at others for what we should take responsibility for ourselves, we'll find that excellence will make its abode with us and the results will be incredible. Now that is what it means to truly live life on our own terms!

Prayer to Ignite Action:

Loving Father, in You there is forgiveness of sins past, present and yet to be committed. I ask for You to forgive me for my judgment of others and when I should have pointed my finger toward myself. Please grant me the grace to also forgive myself, and to extend mercy to others as I see them through Your eyes. I take responsibility for my own actions alone, and will not make excuses for unacceptable behavior. May I be led by my moral conscience today as I am empowered to live righteously and to love unconditionally. In Jesus' name. Amen.

DAY 250

Inspiration:

"Don't let anyone under pressure to give in to evil say, 'God is trying to trip me up.' God is impervious to evil, and puts evil in no one's way. The temptation to give in to evil comes from us and only us. We have no one to blame but the leering, seducing flare-up of our own lust." ~ James 1:13-14, The Message Bible

Insight:

We never know how strong we really are until we are tempted and tested. God would never tempt us, for He could never be tempted with evil or use temptation as a trap to ensnare His children. However, God will utilize circumstances, people and the vicissitudes of life to test our resolve, strengthen our character, and bring out what He values most in us. Today, let's make every effort to acknowledge whether we are being tempted or tested, and then pull from the reservoir of strength within not to yield to the temptation but to pass the test with flying colors and keep moving forward with God's help.

Prayer to Ignite Action:

Heavenly Father, You are the joy and the strength of my life--my place of refuge where I find comfort and courage when I am tempted and tested. Thank You for giving me the resolve to stand by my moral convictions and to stand against what is contrary to Your Word and will in my life. Infuse me with Your power and ignite me with purpose so that I will not be thwarted by temptations. Test my heart and try my motives, for I desire to live holy as the Holy One lives in me. In Jesus' name. Amen.

DAY 251

Inspiration:

"But you who held fast to the LORD your God are alive today, every one of you." ~ Deuteronomy 4:4, New King James Version

"And these words which I command you today shall be in your heart." ~ Deuteronomy 6:6, New King James Version

Insight:

Today is special in that it has never existed before. This day is God's gift to us, and wrapped within it is 24 hours, 1,444 minutes or 86,640 seconds to be used at our discretion to fulfill God's purpose and produce peace, joy and lasting benefits for us and others to enjoy. We have the opportunity to create a legacy that will outlast us beyond this day when we value the gift of time given to us and embrace it with the life and love of all that we hold dear. This day, and each moment, is a miracle to behold and unfold when we seize it with contemplation, creativity, character and courage inspired by God.

Prayer to Ignite Action:

Dear Lord, I graciously accept today as a gift from You in which purpose is to be fulfilled--not just for my sake, but also for the sake of others I will influence. As I treasure this day and value the time that comes with it, I ask for Your assistance to guide me in the management of what matters most. Give me the inspiration to prioritize, organize and strategize today, I pray. In Jesus' name. Amen.

DAY 252

Inspiration:

"I'm off and running, and I'm not turning back. So let's keep focused on that goal, those of us who want everything God has for us. If any of you have something else in mind, God will clear your blurred vision--you'll see it yet! Now that we're on the right track, let's stay on it." ~ Philippians 3:14-16

Insight:

Israel Houghton and New Breed sing a prophetic song entitled, "Moving Forward." The song emphatically states, "I'm not going back, I'm moving ahead. I'm hear to declare to you, the past is over...You've made all things new, yes, You've made all things new and I will follow You forward!"

No matter what occurred yesterday or in yesteryear, the promise ahead is greater than the pain of our past when we choose to push on and press forward with the knowledge and assurance that God can take the old and make it brand new. As God does His part, He expects us to make progress by constantly moving toward the plan that He predestined for us. Nothing and no one else will satisfy our soul's longing to "press toward the mark for the prize of the high calling of God" for our lives. That "high calling" is not behind us but in front of us, waiting for us to pursue it.

Prayer to Ignite Action:

Father God, I make a commitment to move forward today by Your grace. My eyes are firmly fixed and focused on the goal that You have set for me--a life of abundance here on earth and life everlasting in Your presence. I will run the race that is set for me without being sidetracked by others who are following their own paths and choosing their own goals. Help me to stay in my lane so that I do not distract or deter others from following You. Let my race inspire others to run their own in pursuit of You today. In Jesus' name. Amen.

DAY 253

Inspiration:

"Have no fear of sudden disaster or of the ruin that overtakes the wicked, for the LORD will be your confidence and will keep your foot from being snared." ~ Proverbs 3:25-26, New International Version

Insight:

There will always be challenges for us to face. No matter how difficult a day may seem, we can make a conscious decision not to be overwhelmed but to overcome any challenges that exist by transforming our thoughts and adjusting our attitude. As Christians, we have the power of Christ within us and the Word of God to guide us as we forge ahead to do what needs to be done. Staying focused on our God-given purpose is what motivates us to think positively and act proactively without allowing our energy to be halted by hard times. As long as we have the right mindset, we will put in motion what is necessary to confront any challenge with confidence, knowing that "this too shall pass."

Prayer to Ignite Action:

Lord God, I will not be overwhelmed by what I see or hear, for I know that You will not allow me to be overtaken by it because my trust is in You. Your presence and power enables me to confront any challenge with confidence as I take on this day with pure gratitude and a positive attitude. I am expecting great things to happen for me and those closest to me today. In Jesus' name. Amen!

DAY 254

Inspiration:

"The LORD redeems his servants; no one will be condemned who takes refuge in him." ~ Psalm 34:22, New International Version

"Praise the LORD, O my soul, and forget not all his benefits--who forgives all your sins and heals all your diseases, who redeems your life from the pit and crowns you with love and compassion, who satisfies your desires with good things so that your youth is renewed like the eagle's." ~ Psalm 103:2-5, New International Version

Insight:

Your current situation is not your destination and your present condition is not the same as your purpose-filled position. God sent His Son Jesus to earth to redeem us--to purchase us with the blood of Christ that cleanses, purifies, heals and restores us to God's original intent--justified rather than condemned as we accept Jesus as our Lord and Savior. We are winners through Christ, and God's plan for us supersedes anything we could ever imagine for ourselves on earth and into eternity.

Prayer to Ignite Action:

Father, my soul praises You for all the many benefits You lovingly give to those whose hearts safely trust in You--benefits of forgiveness, healing, redemption, compassion, satisfaction of desires granted and renovation of mind, body and spirit. Your lovingkindness is unfathomable! I accept the benefits of Your provisions today as Your heir and a joint-heir with Jesus Christ. You are my Lord, and with my life and lifestyle I willingly worship You. In Jesus' name. Amen.

DAY 255

Inspiration:

"Seek the Kingdom of God above all else, and live righteously, and he will give you everything you need. So don't worry about tomorrow, for tomorrow will bring its own worries. Today's trouble is enough for today."
~ Matthew 6:33-34, New Living Translation

Insight:

Keeping the main thing the main thing is often thought of as a reminder to stay focused on what really matters by not majoring on what is minor, but by knowing our priorities and concentrating on that which is most important. That is really the clarion call for each person who desires to be single-minded, or rather, single-hearted so that our life's work is motivated by our greatest passion. That passion will drive all that we do full-time, for it is what captivates our mind, captures our heart and catapults us toward our destiny.

Prayer to Ignite Action:

Dear God, I give You first place in my life. My love for and relationship with You is more important to me than anything. As I seek to please You by the life I live and the service I give, I pray that You would provide for the needs of my loved ones, friends, household, church, business and activities in which I am involved. Let my purpose intersect with every area of my life to expand Your Kingdom. In Jesus' name. Amen.

DAY 256

Inspiration:

"Jesus replied, 'You must love the LORD your God with all your heart, all your soul, and all your mind." ~ Matthew 22:37, New Living Translation

"When wisdom enters your heart, And knowledge is pleasant to your soul, Discretion will preserve you; Understanding will keep you." ~ Proverbs 2:10-11, New King James Version

Insight:

it has been said that "a mind is a terrible thing to waste." That is a true statement, for we were given a brain so that we can utilize our intellect to ponder, learn from and contribute to life. However, God also equipped us with the capacity to discern with our heart which is the seat of our emotions. Everything cannot be dissected and computed logically with our minds, which is why at times, we must also consider our feelings. Now we should not make a habit of basing decisions on emotions alone, but if they are speaking loudly, we must not ignore them either. Our feelings are an important part of us, which enables us to discover and embrace life more fully. We are tripartite beings consisting of spirit, soul (mind, will, intellect, emotions and imagination) and body, and every component is vital, never to be neglected.

Prayer to Ignite Action:

Father, I know that I am not to be led by my feelings alone in the decisions I make, neither should I ignore them or take them for granted. Thank You for the emotions that I am able to feel through my senses, for You allow me to feel happiness, sadness, anger, fear and shame so that I can recognize the root cause of these emotions and manage them appropriately as I care for the wellbeing of my soul, spirit and body. Help me to respond to every person and situation that I face today by making sure that my decisions and actions follow Your Golden Rule of treating others the way I desire to be treated. In Jesus' name. Amen.

DAY 257

Inspiration:

"But you are the ones chosen by God, chosen for the high calling of priestly work, chosen to be a holy people, God's instruments to do his work and speak out for him, to tell others of the night-and-day difference he made for you--from nothing to something, from rejected to accepted."
~ 1 Peter 2:9, The Message Bible

Insight:

No one can do what you can do quite like you. The reason is because you are a designer's original, specifically created by God with intricate details of spirit, character, and a body frame that was meant to distinguish you from every other person. You are peculiar on purpose with distinct factors that separate you from the rest of humanity such as your physical appearance, personality and purpose. Be authentically you and genuine, and celebrate the reality and beauty of who you really are and all the endless possibilities of what only you can accomplish today.

Prayer to Ignite Action:

Heavenly Father, my desire is to be what You've called me to be. I say, yes, to Your way and Your plan for my life, accepting that which You have ordained for me to do for Your glory. Use my life as a beacon of light to attract those to You who are seeking love, acceptance, purpose and destiny. I pray that they, too, will agree to become who You originally called them to be--children of the Most High God. In Jesus' name. Amen.

DAY 258

Inspiration:

"GOD was wonderful to us; we are one happy people. And now, GOD, do it again--bring rains to our drought-stricken lives So those who planted their crops in despair will shout hurrahs at the harvest, So those who went off with heavy hearts will come home laughing, with armloads of blessing." ~ Psalm 126: 3-6, The Message Bible

Insight:

There are certainly times when we experience disappointment, frustration and perhaps anxiety during stressful situations. However, we have the power to turn stress into what will work best for us and those closest to us by seeing from a different perspective and creating opportunities out of what could have been perceived as obstacles. Let's take the time today to imagine an ideal life filled with love, laughter and learning, and then choose to live it unapologetically.

Prayer to Ignite Action:

Dear God, every day that I awaken to see the sun rise and the season greet me--whether it be winter, spring, summer or fall--is a blessing. Just as the earth must experience seasons and climates of change, so must Your people. Today, I am thankful for this season of my life and all that it brings. Help me to work through even the most difficult of changes without giving in to stress by maintaining a positive perspective governed by the surety of Your promises as I live by biblical principles that never change. Fill my heart with love and laughter as I learn valuable lessons in this season of my life that are meant not just for me, but to be passed on to others. In Jesus' name. Amen.

DAY 259

Inspiration:
"To the Chief Musician. A Psalm of David. The heavens declare the glory of God; And the firmament shows His handiwork. Day unto day utters speech, And night unto night reveals knowledge. [There is] no speech nor language [Where] their voice is not heard." ~ Psalm 18:1-3, New King James Version

Insight:
It takes a transformed mind to see the world as beautiful despite what we see and hear via the media. Amidst the sin of mankind, the heavens and earth still declare the glory and splendor of God when we choose to see through our spiritual eyes. Every thought we have and decision we make directly impacts how we view God, His plan for our lives, the world and the people we encounter. Today, let's see the beauty in everything and everyone by looking past the surface and being thankful for the originality of God's intent and design for ourselves and others.

Prayer to Ignite Action:
Oh Lord, I see the beauty of Your creation all around me--the work of Your hands can be seen in everything that exists. I also look in the mirror and am reminded that I am Your handiwork created to declare Your glory everywhere I go in all that I say and do. Today, I will be more mindful of the splendor of Your world, for Your wisdom, knowledge and power cannot be denied. The fact that I am living and breathing is enough of a miracle for me to marvel at and magnify You. In Jesus' name. Amen.

DAY 260

Inspiration:
"Serve the LORD with gladness; Come before His presence with singing."
~ Psalm 100:2, New King James Version

Insight:
There is no greater freedom than what we experience in God's gift of the power of choice. We have the liberty of choosing whether we will serve God (the most important choice of all), and that decision will have a profound effect upon every other choice that we make. When we wisely choose to honor God by accepting His Son Jesus Christ as Lord of our lives, then we have access to a wealth of wisdom concerning all of life as well as how we will live and learn from it.

Every day affords us opportunities to choose again for either the betterment or the detriment of ourselves and others. I once heard a wise man say that, "Life is choice-driven. The quality of our choices [or decisions] will determine the quality of our lives." ~Bishop L. W. Francisco III

Prayer to Ignite Action:
Dear God, I am so very grateful for the gift of choice that I have, and the wisdom You've given me to choose wisely. I gladly choose to serve You with my whole heart today, knowing that this is the most important and the best decision I could ever make, for it impacts my life now and eternally, as well as those who see that You are living in me. God, I thank You for the opportunity to serve You in everything I say and do, for it fills me with joy. In Jesus' name. Amen.

DAY 261

Inspiration:
"I wisdom dwell with prudence, and find out knowledge of witty inventions." ~ Proverbs 8:12, King James Version

Insight:
Because we are God's children made in His image, we have the imprint of His character and creativity when we choose to recognize and be energized by His wisdom. There are limitless possibilities for us to realize, just as there is latent potential waiting to be released. Tapping into the uniqueness of our thoughts, feelings, and gifts will unleash the desire to hone our skills and offer the best of who we are to the world. After all, God created us so that we can allow our creativity to infiltrate our circle of influence in positive and profound ways.

Prayer to Ignite Action:
Father, You are the epitome of wisdom, prudence, knowledge and understanding. Because You live in me, all that You are now dwells within me. Thank you for allowing me to tap into the vast resources that accompany wisdom and to apply it with the uniqueness of my personality and potential in ways that demonstrate divine creativity and ingenuity as I add value to the people, projects and places assigned to me today. In Jesus' name. Amen.

DAY 262

Inspiration:

"That's why we can be sure that every detail in our lives of love for God is worked into something good. God knew what he was doing from the very beginning. He decided from the outset to shape the lives of those who love him along the same lines as the life of His Son. The Son stands first in the line of humanity he restored. We see the original and intended shape of our lives there in him. After God made that decision of what his children should be like, he followed it up by calling people by name. After he called them by name, he set them on a solid basis with himself. And then, after getting them established, he stayed with them to the end, gloriously completing what he had begun. So what do you think? With God on our side like this, how can we lose? ~ Romans 8:28-31, The Message Bible

Insight:

God often uses our past experiences, whether painful or precious, for a greater purpose. Even the people in our lives whom I call character builders, are strategically placed in our presence to make us better. With this knowledge, we can be assured that we are where we are, doing what we doing, for a reason. Our lives are open letters consisting of lessons to be learned for ourselves and others. Isn't it good to know that God uses all things to work together for our good and His purpose when we love Him and walk in our calling?

Prayer to Ignite Action:

Heavenly Father, I trust You completely to take every experience in my life--whether good, bad or indifferent--and piece it together to create a miraculous masterpiece of Your power and glory working to produce what's best for me. You know the road that I must take to reach the destination You've planned for my good. My hope and expectation remain in You, for I know with confidence that You will complete the work that has begun in me. In Jesus' name. Amen.

DAY 263

Inspiration:

"But let all those rejoice who put their trust in You; Let them ever shout for joy, because You defend them; Let those also who love Your name be joyful in You." ~ Psalm 5:11, New King James Version

"Then the angel said to them, "Do not be afraid, for behold, I bring you good tidings of great joy which will be to all people." ~ Luke 2:10, New King James Version

Insight:

"Joy to the world, the Lord is come. Let earth receive Her King!" Doesn't the first stanza of this favorite Christmas hymn invoke thoughts and feelings of rejoicing for the season? The truth is that we have a reason to live and express joyfulness everyday because of God's greatest gift sent to us. External stimuli does not bring joy; it is an inner resource that fuels our passion for living and giving.

Today, let the same joy that many experience only once a year reign in your heart and manifest itself tangibly in the act of giving that is shared with others. Show that the Spirit of Christ is alive and well and is not limited to a season or a day because it lives in the hearts of all who receive Him.

Prayer to Ignite Action:

Dear Lord, my joy comes from and is found in You, and that same joy is accessible and available to all people who accept Jesus Christ as their personal Lord and Savior. Since You have filled me with unspeakable joy, I will make every effort to share joy with someone else in my living and giving as evidence of Your salvation and presence flowing in me for the world to see. In Jesus' name. Amen.

DAY 264

Inspiration:

"Now to Him Who, by (in consequence of) the [action of His] power that is at work within us, is able to [carry out His purpose and] do superabundantly, far over and above all that we [dare] ask or think [infinitely beyond our highest prayers, desires, thoughts, hopes, or dreams]--To Him be glory in the church and in Christ Jesus throughout all generations forever and ever. Amen (so be it)." ~ Ephesians 3:20-21, Amplified Bible

Insight:

It takes courage to dream, cast vision, and set goals worthy of being measured and accomplished with God's help. If we don't dare to dream, we cheat ourselves out of the creativity that comes with casting vision. If we care not to cast vision, then we rob ourselves of the wonderment that comes with setting goals to achieve our vision. If we succumb to fear that keeps us from setting goals, then we'll never know the exhilarating fulfillment that follows the accomplishment of our goals. And if we don't accomplish any goal that was worthy of setting in the first place, then we'll live a life void of value and empty of expectations that give purpose to all of life's pursuits. God is indeed "able to do exceeding abundantly above all that we ask or think according to the power that works within us" (Ephesians 3:20), but we've got to put that power to work fearlessly. Take courage, and expect God to reveal Himself to you through your thoughts, words and actions today!

Prayer to Ignite Action:

Father God, I am awed by the promise of Your power that is available to work in and through those who receive and are energized by it. I accept Your wondrous power and believe that it will overshadow my own as it manifests in my dreams, vision casting and goal-setting. I know You are able to do much more than I could ever do alone in my own strength, but with Your supernatural ability superimposed upon my natural ability, there is nothing impossible. I'm expecting great things today! In Jesus' name. Amen.

DAY 265

Inspiration:

"What a God we have! And how fortunate we are to have him, this Father of our Master Jesus! Because Jesus was raised from the dead, we've been given a brand-new life and have everything to live for, including a future in heaven--and the future starts now! God is keeping careful watch over us and the future. The Day is coming when you'll have it all--life healed and whole." ~ 1 Peter 1:3-5, The Message Bible

Insight:

We have so much to live for, and even more to thank God for when we put things in proper perspective. When we focus upon Him and the inheritance of salvation we receive after accepting Jesus as the Christ (the Messiah or Anointed One), we realize that everything else pales in comparison to the gift of abundant life here on earth and eternal life without end in His presence. All anxiety, grief, disappointment and fear cannot compare to the exchange of peace, comfort, assurance and courage that God gives us. Serving Him makes life worth living, and there's even more to come because of the inheritance that is reserved for us in heaven as well.

Prayer to Ignite Action:

Father God, I rejoice in You and in the inheritance of salvation, health and wholeness that I have now and in eternity. What a privilege it is to know, love and serve You--a privilege that I will extend to others today as I am led to them by You. The promise of spending life now and an eternity with You is good news worth sharing. In Jesus' name. Amen.

DAY 266

Inspiration:

"...The LORD be exalted, who delights in the well-being of his servant."
~ Psalm 35:27b, New International Version

"Dear friend, I pray that you may enjoy good health and that all may go well with you, even as your soul is getting along well." ~ 3 John 2, New International Version

Insight:

McDonald's coined a popular phrase with which many of us are familiar: "You deserve a break today!" Well, there may be more truth than we think to that statement, and certainly much more can be derived from it. We need not wait for others to recognize or acknowledge what we fail to do ourselves. We must take the necessary time to be refreshed, retooled and refueled, and that can only happen when we take a mental, emotional and/or physical break by giving ourselves permission to do so and then following through with a plan of action. We not only deserve a break (so that we avoid reaching our breaking point), but we also deserve to give ourselves the very best that life has to offer in terms of developing our spirit, mind and body. Doing what is in the best interest of the growth and development of our tripartite being is a spiritual principle and precedent that we should not only observe, but that we most definitely deserve.

Go ahead...give yourself a break and take care of your most valuable asset...YOU! Then you can better serve those around you who need and desire what you have to offer.

Prayer to Ignite Action:

Father, You take pleasure in our well being and prosperity as we care for our spirit, mind and body. Let me also be disciplined enough to do what is needed for my own health and well being, and adjust my attitude so that the discipline to care for myself is transformed into consistent behavior and habits that I can delight in, too. Strengthen me so that I can set needed boundaries in my life to help me to become whole and strong spiritually, mentally and physically. I will also make myself accountable to You and trusted others as I enjoy my journey to holistic health. In Jesus' name. Amen.

DAY 267

Inspiration:

"God 'will give to each person according to what he has done.' To those who by persistence in doing good seek glory, honor and immortality, he will give eternal life." ~ Romans 2:6-7, New International Version

"I press toward the goal for the prize of the upward call of God in Christ Jesus." ~ Philippians 3:14, New King James Version

Insight:

Life is not all peaches and cream. There are times when a lot of energy is called for to keep moving forward while learning from the difficulties that confront us. The mere fact that we are alive is a reminder that there is more to life than what we have already experienced, and nothing or no one should prevent us from pressing toward the mark for the prize that God has already set before us (Phil. 3:14). That mark may be difficult to reach, but it is still possible to attain if we replace our resistance with persistence knowing that with God, all things are possible.

Prayer to Ignite Action:

Heavenly Father, I am reminded in Your Word of the effort and persistence needed to reach my destiny on earth and my eternal reward in heaven. Although life is not always easy, it becomes easier when my focus is directed upward and onward. Today, I am determined to persevere and move forward in pursuit of You and Your will for my life. In Jesus' name. Amen.

DAY 268

Inspiration:
"Thank [God] in everything [no matter what the circumstances may be, be thankful and give thanks], for this is the will of God for you [who are] in Christ Jesus [the Revealer and Mediator of that will]." ~ 1 Thessalonians 5:18, Amplified Bible

Insight:
We are instructed in 1 Thessalonians 5:18 to give God thanks in everything. Have you ever wondered why the scripture tells us to give thanks in, rather than for, everything? I believe it is because the attitude of our heart determines how we will respond rather than react to circumstances and people that may challenge us to our very core. An attitude of gratitude gives us the power to stick and stay when we may want to kick and walk away. Giving God thanks in the midst of what is uncertain and unexpected opens an avenue for us to change our perspective while allowing God to bring new opportunities and relationships our way. An "even so" thanksgiving will release a "nevertheless" praise that will elevate our mentality as we focus on a brand new reality. Come what may, let's decide to allow an "even so" thanksgiving to permeate our day!

Prayer to Ignite Action:
Father, today I will give thanks in every situation that occurs, no matter what, as an expression of my gratitude to You. I'll thank You in good times and bad...in sickness and health...in recession and abundance...in my heart, words and actions. I appreciate all Your blessings toward me, for You are still at work in times of sunshine and rain. Being thankful at all times in every circumstance, places me in the center of Your will. In Jesus' name. Amen.

DAY 269

Inspiration:

"Whatever your hand finds to do, do [it] with your might; for [there is] no work or device or knowledge or wisdom in the grave where you are going."
~ Ecclesiastes 9:10, New King James Version

Insight:

The easiest thing in the world is to do nothing and blame others or obstacles for the reason life seems to pass us by. But it takes courage, determination, visionary thinking, and unwavering resolve to take hold of life and our destiny by refusing to settle for less than what we are able to contribute to and gain from life with specific, measurable goals in mind. Let's not allow others or even our own thoughts, words or deeds to deter us from living an incredibly blessed life so that we can be a blessing to those around us. The only excuse for not participating in life occurs when we can no longer breathe. The fact that we are still living is God's gift and grace as a reminder that we have a charge to keep, a God to glorify and lives of others to edify.

Prayer to Ignite Action:

Heavenly Father, only what we do now will count for an eternity. Let me be filled to overflowing with Your Spirit today so that I can live with the mission and motive of loving You, being a good steward of every resource charged to my keep, and building up the lives of others around me. I will accomplish all that I am capable of today because I am empowered to do so. In Jesus' name. Amen.

DAY 270

Inspiration:

"As for you, my son Solomon, know the God of your father, and serve Him with a loyal heart and with a willing mind; for the LORD searches all hearts and understands all the intent of the thoughts. If you seek Him, He will be found by you; but if you forsake Him, He will cast you off forever." ~ 1 Chronicles 28:9, New King James Version

"Commit your works to the LORD, And your thoughts will be established." ~ Proverbs 16:3, New King James Version

Insight:

Everything begins with just one single thought. That lets us know just how important it is to evaluate the thoughts we allow to enter our consciousness, and to eliminate and replace any thoughts that are contrary to our dreams which should coincide with God's will and Word. Thoughts of good rather than evil, health rather than sickness, wealth rather than poverty, success rather than failure, and productivity rather than the lack thereof, will determine how our words and actions help to manifest what we think. Our thoughts can either work for or against us.

Prayer to Ignite Action:

Dear God, today I commit my works to You in humility and reverence so that my thoughts will be established. Since wherever thoughts wander the body swiftly follows, I pray that I will meditate on only that which is fruitful and productive so that my actions will also be fruitful and productive. Search my mind and heart so that my intentions will be tested and found to be pure and undefiled in Your sight, I pray. In Jesus' name. Amen.

DAY 271

Inspiration:

"Remember me for this, O my God, and do not blot out what I have so faithfully done for the house of my God and its services." ~ Nehemiah 13:14, New International Version

"But he who does the truth comes to the light, that his deeds may be clearly seen, that they have been done in God." ~ John 3:21, New King James Version

"Then I heard a voice from heaven saying to me, 'Write: 'Blessed [are] the dead who die in the Lord from now on.' 'Yes,' says the Spirit, 'that they may rest from their labors, and their works follow them.'" ~ Revelation 14:13, New King James Version

Insight:

No one can play the part of being you or me, because we were each created as an original masterpiece intricately sculpted and innately woven with exactly what we need to fulfill our unique destiny. It is absurd to emulate someone else's personality or to covet another person's life, gift, career, or possessions, for then we give up the right to be who God designed us to be and will never discover the potential that can only be released by the courageous act of our will. When we are true to ourselves, the state of being who we really are will lead to doing what only we can do to impact our generation and the world while we live. And if we really live by just being who God called us to be, then our life will continue to speak even after it has ended on earth and entered eternity.

Prayer to Ignite Action:

Heavenly Father, You have created each of us with the ability to pursue meaningful work using our natural and spiritual gifts to make a difference as we serve a purpose greater than ourselves alone. Thank You for the knowledge Your Word gives to assure that the work we do will outlive and outlast us, and follow us into eternity. I pray for discernment in knowing what I am called to do in every season of my life, as well as the determination to stay focused on "being" (enjoying the journey along the way) while I am "doing" Your will. In Jesus' name. Amen.

DAY 272

Inspiration:

"After looking at the way things are on this earth, here's what I've decided is the best way to live: Take care of yourself, have a good time, and make the most of whatever job you have for as long as God gives you life. And that's about it. That's the human lot. Yes, we should make the most of what God gives, both the bounty and the capacity to enjoy it, accepting what's given and delighting in the work. It's God's gift!" ~ Ecclesiastes 5:18-19, The Message Bible

Insight:

If we want to experience true satisfaction and fulfillment in our daily tasks and activities, then we must determine to put the best of who we are and what we have into all that we do. When we seek to live, work, and play wholeheartedly, then what we receive in return is a reflection of the effort we invested. Not only will we be satisfied and fulfilled in the process, but others cannot help but take notice of the level of commitment to excellence that is exhibited which may cause them to do the same. Living in such a way as to fully engage ourselves in what we do to honor God transforms daily routines that have to be done into purpose-driven assignments that will influence someone. Wow--what a way to live!

Prayer to Ignite Action:

Dear Lord, You have given humanity the gift to choose the life we desire. From You also comes the wisdom so that we may know how to live, work, and play while maintaining balance. Today, I exercise the right to decide to engage fully in every facet of the life I have chosen by Your grace. I appreciate what could be viewed as monotonous and routine, and choose to view it from the vantage point of being miraculous and rewarding because of the investment I make so that positive results will follow. I will make the most of what You've given me by delighting in the gift of living and all the possibilities that come with it. In Jesus' name. Amen.

DAY 273

Inspiration:

"And let the beauty and delightfulness and favor of the Lord our God be upon us; confirm and establish the work of our hands--yes, the work of our hands, confirm and establish it." ~ Psalm 90:17, Amplified Bible

Insight:

There is immense beauty all around us. In fact, the Bible tells us that the heavens declare the glory of the Lord as does the earth. We don't have to look far to see the beauty of the Lord, for every time we look in the mirror, His reflection looks back at us. Everything around us utters the voice of God to remind us that we really have no reason to complain or to take life for granted by not living it fully in all its richness.

What can and will you do today to celebrate and share God's beauty in your life? Will you live the abundant life that Jesus came to give you with more intentionality and vibrancy? Allow the beauty in and around you to shine brightly in all you do. Others may begin to do the same by following your example.

Prayer to Ignite Action:

Father, all of creation declares the beautiful reflection of You, the Creator. Everything and everyone exists as evidence of Your glory and splendor. As I look at who and what is in front of and all around me today--including myself--open my eyes to see the depth of beauty that is beneath the surface of every living thing. Let me take in the beauty that I see and reflect it back to whoever I meet today as I seize opportunities to follow You and lead others. In Jesus' name. Amen.

DAY 274

Inspiration:

"The Spirit Himself bears witness with our spirit that we are children of God, and if children, then heirs--heirs of God and joint heirs with Christ, if indeed we suffer with [Him], that we may also be glorified together. For I consider that the sufferings of this present time are not worthy [to be compared] with the glory which shall be revealed in us." ~ Romans 8:16-18, New King James Version

"...but the people who know their God shall be strong, and carry out [great exploits]." ~ Daniel 11:32b, New King James Version

Insight:

Did you know that as an heir of God and a joint heir with Jesus Christ, that you have royal blood running through your veins? You have access to the riches of God's Word, which contain keys to unlock the vast treasury of God's wisdom, knowledge, understanding, power, and might that is from the inner resource of God's Spirit as we connect to Him through prayer and putting biblical principles to work in our lives. There is nothing you can't achieve if it is in the will of God and backed up by the authority of the Word of God. In fact, you and I were born to do great exploits and to believe and achieve what others may think is impossible and improbable. Don't let the critics and skeptics keep you from dreaming, envisioning, goal-setting, and following through with what you know God has ordained for you. Go after God's best, and don't you dare settle for anything less!

Prayer to Ignite Action:

Dear God, because I am Your heir and a joint heir with Jesus Christ, I am entitled to all the rights and privileges of sonship--the same rights and privileges that are also extended to all who belong to the family of God. Thank You for including the benefits of my inheritance in the Bible to be read, meditated on, and practiced in my life. I will pursue Your promises and my purpose with enthusiasm in expectation of living fully and accomplishing great exploits for You. In Jesus' name. Amen.

DAY 275

Inspiration:

"Now [in Haran] the Lord said to Abram, Go for yourself [for your own advantage] away from your country, from your relatives and your father's house, to the land that I will show you." ~ Genesis 12:1, Amplified Bible

"And Peter answered Him, Lord, if it is You, command me to come to You on the water. He said, Come! So Peter got out of the boat and walked on the water, and he came toward Jesus. But when he perceived and felt the strong wind, he was frightened, and as he began to sink, he cried out, Lord, save me [from death]! Instantly Jesus reached out His hand and caught and held him, saying to him, O you of little faith, why did you doubt?" ~ Matthew 14:28-31, Amplified Bible

Insight:

Pursuing purpose can be a daunting task, but it is also exhilarating and enlightening as we allow ourselves to be stretched and removed from our places of comfort and familiarity. There is such peace, joy and fulfillment in knowing that God will lead us to the places where we should go one step at a time, even though we may not see the big picture or know all the details. Often times, God will test our faith and obedience before He shows us the next step.

Abram (whose name was later changed to Abraham) was told to leave everything that brought him comfort, familiarity, and security at the time--his father's house--and to go to a land where he'd never been before. Peter was compelled by Jesus to get out of the comfort and security of the boat to do something that he had never done before--walk on water. The similarities between these two patriarchs and their stories include bidding them both to leave their comfort zone and to follow the path where God the Father and Jesus Christ the Son had gone before. The lesson we learn from both scenarios is that we can go wherever God leads and do whatever He tells us to do because He knows and will show us the way, and it has been paved for us as long as we have faith without doubting and keep our eyes focused forward.

Prayer to Ignite Action:

Dear Lord, there are times when I know You are compelling me to leave my comfort zone to go where I've never gone or to do what I've never done before. I admit that those times have been fearful, but they were necessary for the growth and development of my faith, intellect, and skills. Let me not be dissuaded or discouraged by fear of failure or of the unknown. Like Abraham and Peter, I will trust You explicitly, for You would never lead me astray. In Jesus' name. Amen.

DAY 276

Inspiration:

"You will show me the path of life; in Your presence [is] fullness of joy; At Your right hand [are] pleasures forevermore." ~ Psalm 16:11, New King James Version

Insight:

Psalm 16:11 reminds us that joy is always available to us when we seek and live in God's presence. Not only that, but it is God's desire that we experience both joy and pleasure, not just when we get to Heaven, but in the here and now. Isn't that good news?

I've discovered five ways in which to receive joy:
1. Seek to be filled by asking for and receiving the Holy Spirit. (John 15:11; Galatians 5:22-23)
2. Choose to give God praise. (Psalm 27:6 & 32:11)
3. Surround yourself with like-minded, joy-filled people. (Psalm 35:27)
4. Attend a God-believing, Bible-teaching and people-loving church. (Psalm 42:4)
5. Give joy away to someone else every day. (Philippians 2:2)

Prayer to Ignite Action:

Father, what a wonderful God You are! You bless us even when we're undeserving, and You show us what is in store for all who desire to know and follow the path that leads to fulfilled purpose and pleasures now and forever in Your presence. Our feet are only on the right path when we listen for and follow after Your voice as it speaks in a myriad of ways. Let the radiance of Your light and the richness of Your joy be seen in me and imitated by others today, I pray. In Jesus' name. Amen.

DAY 277

Inspiration:

"That is what the Scriptures mean when they say, 'No eye has seen, no ear has heard, and no mind has imagined what God has prepared for those who love him.'" ~ 1 Corinthians 2:9, New Living Translation

Insight:

Purpose often unfolds as a result of our childhood dreams. If the insatiable desire to become something great or to do something special never left our heart or mind's eye since childhood, then God more than likely gave us that innate desire in order to accomplish His purpose for our lives. We can hold on to and pursue it if it is believable, achievable, and realistic given our natural abilities and talents, present or available resources as well as where we are and what responsibilities we currently have in life's journey. We should never stop dreaming, no matter how old we are or how much we have or have not accomplished in our past. Go ahead and dream big enough for God to intervene and accomplish what ears have not heard and eyes have not seen!

Prayer to Ignite Action:

Heavenly Father, You have so much in store for those who love You-- more than we could ever possibly imagine. I love You, Lord, and I know that Your love for me is boundless and endless. Thank You for loving me enough to give me a glimpse of my future as revealed in my dreams and by the desires of my heart. Keep the fire ablaze in me so that the passion for fulfilling my purpose motivates me to keep dreaming and moving forward. In Jesus' name. Amen.

DAY 278

Inspiration:

"If you are wise and understand God's ways, prove it by living an honorable life, doing good works with the humility that comes from wisdom." ~ James 3:13, New Living Translation

Insight:

There is a line in the Forest Gump movie when the main character quoted something that his mother said: "Life is like a box of chocolates. You never know which one you're gonna get." What we can be assured of is that life, with all of its twists and turns, will be exactly what we make of it, and how we choose to view it and use it can make us either bitter or better. Rather than concentrating on the challenges and difficulties, let's choose to contemplate and create new opportunities that would not have existed unless life had presented them to us in unexpected ways. If what Forest Gump's mother said is true, then we should embrace life in all its richness, fullness and unexpectedness just as we would a box of chocolates. (By the way, I absolutely LOVE chocolate! I visited Hershey Park in Hershey, PA and Cadbury World in Bourneville, UK, so I've tasted firsthand just how good chocolate, and life's opportunities, can be!)

Prayer to Ignite Action:

Father, You are the Originator and Sustainer of life. You rain on the just and the unjust--the good and the evil--and nothing happens that You do not allow. Although life may be unpredictable, I am certain that You are aware of the ups, downs, and turnarounds that will come my way. I pray that the unpredicted and unexpected circumstances that occur today will be used as a catalyst to draw me closer to You. As I commune with You more closely, please cultivate humility and honor in me so that I can honor You in my life's work. In Jesus' name. Amen.

DAY 279

Inspiration:
"When I consider Your heavens, the work of Your fingers, The moon and the stars, which You have ordained, What is man that You are mindful of him, And the son of man that You visit him? For You have made him a little lower than the angels, And You have crowned him with glory and honor. You have made him to have dominion over the works of Your hands; You have put all [things] under His feet." ~ Psalm 8:3-6, New King James Version

Insight:
We have the power of choice and intelligence of mind that automatically distinguishes us above every other created being on earth. However, if we do not properly exercise our right to choose and nurture our intellect, we will weaken these God-given gifts and relegate ourselves to a life beneath our inheritance. Let's choose to be strong by tapping into the power of God while claiming the blessed promises of His Word as the principles that will guide our choices and behavior.

Prayer to Ignite Action:
Dear God, You have so much love for and faith in man that You placed us in ranking order beneath the angels who dwell with You and above the rest of creation to exercise dominion over the earth and not over another human being. You have given to us the power to choose, the wisdom to choose wisely, and Your Word as the roadmap to our destiny as we live by its principles. Thank You for loving and empowering me to do the right thing today. In Jesus' name. Amen.

DAY 280

Inspiration:

"Even though troubles come down on me hard, your commands always gave me delight. The way you tell me to live is always right; help me understand it so I can live to the fullest." ~ Psalm 119:143-144, The Message Bible

Insight:

Every moment is precious, profound, and particularly positioned to be used as the pavement on the path toward our purpose. Think of past failures as the foundational pavement that propels us to keep marching on the right track. Our past should be used as the training ground for learning from mistakes, mishaps and misunderstandings so that they become the momentum for moving forward without looking back. Yesteryear and yesterday are history. All we have is right now--this moment--to maximize our potential for God's glory.

Prayer to Ignite Action:

Heavenly Father, Your Word undergirds me with the strength to do what is right and the wisdom to resist what is wrong. As I decide to be disciplined and determined enough to put my past behind me and to live in the moment with a futuristic orientation, it is Your Word that keeps me grounded. I love learning more about Your ways as Your Word instructs me. I can live a full and meaningful life because of Your teachings. In Jesus' name. Amen.

DAY 281

Inspiration:
"Pride goes before destruction, and haughtiness before a fall." ~ Proverbs 16:18, New Living Translation

"And you who are younger must follow your leaders. But all of you, leaders and followers alike, are to be down to earth with each other, for--God has had it with the proud, But takes delight in just plain people. So be content with who you are, and don't put on airs. God's strong hand is on you; he'll promote you at the right time." ~ 1 Peter 5:5-6, The Message Bible

Insight:
Those who are proud at any age will not gain favor with God or other people. There is a quality, however, that is appealing and attractive to our Creator as well as to those with whom we may relate, and that is humility. Pride is the antithesis of humility, and it is still the downfall of many. Rather than allowing arrogance to rear its ugly head, we must pursue God's nature as well as the grace to embody humility with godly confidence. When our lives are characterized by the qualities that represent the excellence that God is to our world, promotion will be our reward.

Prayer to Ignite Action:
Oh God, You reject and oppose those who are proud, but Your loving favor is extended to those who are humble before You. I ask for Your forgiveness for the times when pride has driven a wedge between my relationship with You and others. Cleanse me so that humility can fill the space of my heart. Let Your nature govern my thoughts, conversation, and conduct today. In Jesus' name. Amen.

DAY 282

Inspiration:

"May you always be filled with the fruit of your salvation--the righteous character produced in your life by Jesus Christ--for this will bring much glory and praise to God." ~ Philippians 1:11, New Living Translation

Insight:

Although perfection is unattainable in this life, excellence is certainly within our grasp. Consequently, we should avoid the frustration that comes with possessing perfectionist tendencies and embrace the freedom that comes with striving to accomplish every endeavor to the best of our abilities with the resources we have. Knowing that we have done everything within our God-given power to reach our short- and long-term goals without compromising our integrity or character guarantees peace of mind and fulfillment.

Prayer to Ignite Action:

Heavenly Father, my heart's desire is to always embody the excellence of Your character that serves as the foundation of my integrity. As I yield more of myself to You, I am filled in return with more of You. Therefore, I am strengthened by You to accomplish all that is set before me today and to live by a moral code that influences everything I say and do. Pleasing You fills me with peace and contentment. In Jesus' name. Amen.

DAY 283

Inspiration:
"His lord said to him, 'Well [done], good and faithful servant; you were faithful over a few things, I will make you ruler over many things. Enter into the joy of your lord.'" ~ Matthew 25:21 & 23, New King James Version

Insight:
In Matthew 25:18-30, Jesus gives us a principle to practice in the Parable of the Talents. We are admonished to use before we lose what He has entrusted to us as good stewards. Not only do we jeopardize the loss of resources because of our own lack of use, misuse or abuse, but the parable also shows us that what could have been a blessing in our hands could possibly be given to someone else who will not only use the resource, but also multiply the resource in order to gain a profit.

What gift has been placed in your hands, and how well are you managing it? Are the human and natural resources at your disposal being maximized or minimized for the Master? You and I have a responsibility to use and make the most of all of our T.A.G.S. (Talents, Abilities, Gifts and Skills). When we do, we'll hear God say, "Well done, good and faithful servant. Enter into the joy of your Lord!"

Prayer to Ignite Action:
Father, thank You for giving me talents, abilities, gifts and skills that are to be used and multiplied for the sake of honoring You and blessing other people. Today, I pray for the grace to maximize every human and natural resource that I have. Help me to be a faithful steward over all that has been entrusted to me. My earnest desire is to hear You say, 'Well done, my good and faithful servant. You've been faithful over a few things, so I will make you ruler over many. Enter into the joy of your Lord.' In Jesus' name. Amen.

DAY 284

Inspiration:

"Not that I am implying that I was in any personal want, for I have learned how to be content (satisfied to the point where I am not disturbed or disquieted) in whatever state I am." ~ Philippians 4:11, Amplified Bible

"The LORD will open to you His good treasure, the heavens, to give the rain to your land in its season, and to bless all the work of your hand. You shall lend to many nations, but you shall not borrow." ~ Deuteronomy 28:12, New King James Version

Insight:

The apostle Paul stated that he had learned to be content in all things. That is easier said than done, yet it is possible to display this attitude and reap the joy that peaceful contentment brings. It is important to note, however, that being content does not mean that one is satisfied with the present condition. Instead, being content places one in a position not to complain but to remain thankful knowing that now is enough until God changes the season of our lives. God's promise of provision will remain and sustain us, regardless of the season we're in, when we've learned to be content.

Prayer to Ignite Action:

Father, 1 Timothy 6:6 says, "Now godliness with contentment is great gain." Today, I am content because I know that my sufficiency inwardly and outwardly comes from You. Every need is met and I am not lacking anything. Thank You for providing for my every need in each season of my life and for blessing the works of my hands. Because of Your goodness, I confess that I am a lender, not a borrower. I am blessed to be a blessing today. In Jesus' name. Amen.

DAY 285

Inspiration:

"And don't for a minute let this Book of the Revelation be out of mind. Ponder and meditate on it day and night, making sure you practice everything written in it. Then you'll get where you're going; then you'll succeed. Haven't I commanded you? Strength! Courage! Don't be timid; don't get discouraged. GOD, your God, is with you every step you take." ~ Joshua 1:8-9, The Message Bible

Insight:

Success does not occur by happenstance but rather, it is the product of diligent, purposeful effort and the convergence of opportunity and courageous action. We cannot depend upon others to do what we must do for ourselves, nor should we blame the lack of success on circumstances or critics. Once we define what success means to us personally, we must go after it with conviction that comes from knowing that God is the architect of the plan of our lives, and we must build a successful life based on the specifications of His Word.

Prayer to Ignite Action:

Lord God, Your Word gives me the foundation of what I need to succeed in life. Help me to digest every word and to apply it to every area of my life--spiritually, mentally, emotionally, physically, socially and financially--as I meditate upon each principle and precept. I thank You for the courage and strength to wait for and to listen to Your wisdom so that I can promptly obey. I will not be timid or discouraged today, for I know that You are with me, empowering me to succeed. In Jesus' name. Amen.

DAY 286

Inspiration:

"[And it is, indeed, a source of immense profit, for] godliness accompanied with contentment (that contentment which is a sense of inward sufficiency) is great and abundant gain." ~ 1 Timothy 6:6, Amplified Bible

Insight:

Nothing can grant us favor with God and man as well as bless our own lives faster than having a heart filled with gratitude. I have learned that contentment brings with it great gain, and that showing appreciation opens doors of opportunity that surpass the imagination. It is true that our attitude determines our altitude, but I've also learned that our gratitude in life determines our latitude in life--that is, how thankful we are will have an affect or effect upon the breadth and width of abundance that we experience in life.

Prayer to Ignite Action:

Oh, Lord, today I express my gratitude to You for who You are and all You've done in my life. I am thankful for who You created me to be, all You've allowed me to do and the many doors of opportunity and windows of favor that were opened for me and those I've prayed for through the years. I am content with the life that I have, and if You never did another thing for me, I would have no reason to complain. Your goodness, faithfulness, lovingkindness, and tender mercies are enough to fill me with thanksgiving for the rest of my life. In Jesus' name. Amen.

DAY 287

Inspiration:

"For you were called to freedom, brethren; only do not use your freedom as an opportunity for the flesh, but through love be servants of one another." ~ Galatians 5:13, Revised Standard Version

"So then, as occasion and opportunity open up to us, let us do good [morally] to all people [not only being useful or profitable to them, but also doing what is for their spiritual good and advantage]. Be mindful to be a blessing, especially to those of the household of faith [those who belong to God's family with you, the believers]." ~ Galatians 6:10, Amplified Bible

Insight:

Although I have had a wonderfully blessed life thus far, I have decided that the next half of my life will be my best and most blessed ever! I am living each day as if it were my last before Jesus comes while enjoying every moment, relationship, person, and place to the fullest with no holds barred. After all, Jesus came that we might live a life of abundance--that is, that we might enjoy our time and existence on earth to the full until it overflows--and I intend to do just that while allowing the blessings of my life to spill over into the lives of others.

Today is another opportunity to live with passion and laser sharp focus. Don't waste a second of God's precious time given to you for safe keeping. Guard your time by using it fully and phenomenally to express who you were created to be, and let your zeal for God and zest for life serve others like never before.

Prayer to Ignite Action:

Father, this is a day filled with new opportunities and occasions to live and give with newfound fervor and zeal. Let the love of God in me be poured out upon others by God-inspired words spoken and deeds done. I offer myself to be used fully and phenomenally by You today, and I will enjoy the journey along the way. In Jesus' name. Amen.

DAY 288

Inspiration:

"Not that I have already obtained all this, or have already been made perfect, but I press on to take hold of that for which Christ Jesus took hold of me." ~ Philippians 3:12, New International Version

Insight:

What is 'that' which motivates you to awaken each morning and to press forward despite the challenging circumstances or people that you may encounter? What is 'that' which drives you to keep on pushing past limitations with anticipation and expectation? What is 'that' which keeps the flame of desire burning in your heart as you guard and fan the flames that others may try to extinguish? When you discover what 'that' is, you will know and continue to pursue after 'that' with renewed vigor and vitality that defies the vicissitudes of life. 'That' will become your magnificent obsession--the force that drives you and the destiny that awaits you.

Prayer to Ignite Action:

Heavenly Father, I am chasing after 'that' which first took hold of me today. You invested time and resources into my life so I can find and follow after what motivates me to wake up every morning--the vision of my future and destiny here on earth and in Heaven with You. Thank You for showing me the plan You have for my life, and for giving me the tenacity to press onward to attain it. In Jesus' name. Amen.

DAY 289

Inspiration:

"In all your ways acknowledge Him, And He shall direct your paths." ~ Proverbs 3:6, New King James Version

"I will instruct you and teach you in the way you should go; I will guide you with My eye." ~ Psalm 32:8, New King James Version

Insight:

Live your life with purpose, on purpose. Only you can decide what priorities will govern your daily choices, actions, and words. As you trust in and depend upon God for guidance and direction and follow the promptings of the Holy Spirit, you'll find that opportunities will come easily, and those that don't only provide an avenue for opportunities to be created where there weren't any before. It is wonderful to experience the creative energy to forge new paths in order to live the life you've always dreamed about to bring God pleasure and serve others in the process. There's really no greater joy than that.

Prayer to Ignite Action:

Father, I acknowledge that You are my God. Direct my paths and give me divine instructions to guide me in every decision I make with every step that I take. Broaden my perspective so that I can see new ways and use innovative methods of accomplishing the tasks that are set before me today. Let the motives of my heart be pure so that I reflect the desire to please You and serve others without pretense or offense. In Jesus' name. Amen.

DAY 290

Inspiration:

"For we are God's masterpiece. He has created us anew in Christ Jesus, so we can do the good things he planned for us long ago." ~ Ephesians 2:10, New Living Translation

"I can do all things through Christ who strengthens me." ~ Philippians 4:13, New King James Version

Insight:

We are the creative masterpiece of God, created to do good in a world that is often unapologetically evil. When God created the heavens and the earth, He was so pleased that He made a declarative statement to reinforce how good His created works were. However, He saved the pinnacle of His masterpiece--the creation of humanity--until last. We are inherently good, not because of our human nature, but because we have been made in the image and likeness of our God to reflect His nature and mannerisms...and that is indeed good!

Prayer to Ignite Action:

Dear Lord, I thank You for valuing me enough to masterfully create me and to instruct me to be and do good. It is only Your nature living inside me that transforms me into who I was predestined to be. Because of Christ Jesus, my spirit and mind are renewed. I can do all things through Him who strengthens me today. In Jesus' name. Amen.

DAY 291

Inspiration:

"Let me tell you why you are here. You're here to be salt-seasoning that rings out the God-flavors of this earth. If you lose your saltiness, how will people taste godliness? You've lost your usefulness and will end up in the garbage. Here's another way to put it: You're here to be light, bringing out the god-colors in the world. God is not a secret to be kept. We're going public with this, as public as a city on a hill." ~ Matthew 5:13-14, The Message Bible

Insight:

My husband and I were blessed to visit Israel years ago, bringing to life all the biblical passages we'd read about as we stood in the exact places of their origin. We kept it moving, from spending the night in Nazareth to staying in Jerusalem, to praying at the Wailing Wall. We walked side by side with Israelis, Orthodox Jews, bedouin shepherds and visitors from all over the world as we visited the market places within the city walls. We touched the same massive rock upon which Abraham placed his son, Isaac, who was about to be sacrificed at Mount Moriah had God not provided for him a ram in the bush. And we had the unique opportunity to visit Jericho, the tomb of Lazarus, the Garden of Gethsemane and the birthplace of Jesus. My husband even rode a camel while I took his picture!

We were continuously moving about from place to place, helping to baptize people in the Jordan River, sharing in communion with strangers who quickly became friends and family in Christ with whom we ate fish and broke loaves of bread along the Sea of Galilee, and stood at the banks of the Dead Sea. I was quickly reminded of the lifestyle that Jesus and those who were with Him lived--one of simple faith--daily relying on the Spirit of God to direct their every step as they "kept it moving."

While constant and purposeful action keeps us focused on doing God's work, our consistent and prayerful attitude keeps us focused on being in God's will. My husband says it this way: "The work of God will produce frustration and fatigue, but the will of God will produce fruitfulness and fulfillment." Shakespeare's question is one that is appropriate to ask ourselves: "To be or not to be?" Today, let's choose "to be" as God's light shines through you and me.

Prayer to Ignite Action:

Father, many times I get so caught up in doing work that I fail to be in the center of Your will. Today, I choose to be the seasoning of salt and the beam of light that is to shine in dark places. Let my life and lifestyle make others thirsty for You. I will be the change I desire to see, for it is my being that will impact my doing as I stay focused on the mission of sharing my faith. In Jesus' name. Amen.

DAY 292

Inspiration:

"You have granted me life and favor, And Your care has preserved my spirit." ~ Job 10:12, New King James Version

"For You, Lord, will bless the [uncompromisingly] righteous [him who is upright and in right standing with You]; as with a shield You will surround him with goodwill (pleasure and favor)." ~ Psalm 5:12, Amplified Bible

Insight:

There is absolutely no time like the present to be present. Fully embrace who you are (assets and flaws) and decide how you can add value to wherever you are (i.e., work, home, school, community, church, etc.). Take in the richness of each moment with your senses, and spiritually discern how you can both give and gain from the people and places that surround you. Choose to be a teacher and a student of life and watch how many doors of opportunity and favor will open just for you, starting right now.

Prayer to Ignite Action:

Dear Lord, I embrace all that I am--assets and attributes, flaws and frailties--and trust You to mold me into Your unique masterpiece. Use my tests as testimonies of your faithfulness, and my gifts as the gateway for others to see and seek after You. Let my life add value to the people and environment around me as Your favor surrounds me like a shield. In Jesus' name. Amen.

DAY 293

Inspiration:

"For God has not given us a spirit of fear and timidity, but of power, love, and self-discipline." ~ 2 Timothy 1:7, New Living Translation

"Do not stifle the Holy Spirit." ~ 1 Thessalonians 5:19, New Living Translation

Insight:

I learned this valuable lesson in my life a long time ago: Action cures fear, so do it now! So often we over analyze and talk ourselves out of doing what our gut tells us is the right thing. That gut feeling is really the Spirit of God that is nudging us to follow Him despite what we feel, and to choose His way regardless of what others say. Fear is really an emotion that paralyzes us, preventing us from moving forward into a blessed future. God has given us a triple force to combat the spirit of fear--love, power, and self-discipline.

Don't let the enemy's tactic of fear keep you from doing great exploits and experiencing the abundant life that Jesus promised. Action cures fear; do it now and live out your dream!

Prayer to Ignite Action:

Father, You have given me everything I need to defeat the enemy of fear--love, power, and self-discipline. Today, I will let my actions cure and obscure my fears as I listen to and follow the leading of Your Spirit. I praise You, because You have given me the faith to move with decisive action. In Jesus' name. Amen.

DAY 294

Inspiration:

"God's kingdom isn't a matter of what you put in your stomach, for goodness' sake. It's what God does with your life as he sets it right, puts it together, and completes it with joy." ~ Romans 14:17, The Message Bible

"Do not fear, little flock, for it is your Father's good pleasure to give you the kingdom." ~ Luke 12:32, New King James Version

Insight:

I often reflect upon the faithfulness of our Heavenly Father who loves us so much that He desires to give us all that we desire to live a good and godly life. God takes pleasure in the fact that we belong to Him, and as such, gives us access to inherit the riches of His kingdom--riches that include righteousness, peace, and joy that will benefit us now and in an eternity spent in His presence. We have the keys to an abundant supply of whatever we need to be refilled and refueled.

Are you running on full, half-full, or empty in your life? Perhaps it's time to reconnect with God who is the Source of every resource you need. If necessary, schedule a personal retreat that will yield both natural and eternal dividends in the spiritual, mental, emotional, social, and physical areas that need attention in your life. Spending time away with God, apart from your regular routine and relationships, may keep your life from falling apart. He has the keys to the kingdom where everything you need is available in abundance.

Prayer to Ignite Action:

Dear God, Your love for humanity baffles my mind! It is too wonderful for me to comprehend how You could give us access to the true riches of Your kingdom--a life filled with righteousness, peace, and joy. You take pleasure in what gives us pleasure when we choose to serve You with our life's choices and works. I desire to live uprightly before You and to have a balanced life. Please reveal to me the areas where I am out-of-balance and help me to reconnect with You in a time of personal retreat so that I can be renewed in Your presence. In Jesus' name. Amen.

DAY 295

Inspiration:

"Summing it all up, friends, I'd say you'll do best by filling your minds and meditating on things true, noble, reputable, authentic, compelling, gracious--the best, not the worst; the beautiful, not the ugly; things to praise, not things to curse. Put into practice what you learned from me, what you heard and saw and realized. Do that, and God, who makes everything work together, will work you into his most excellent harmonies."
~ Philippians 4:8-9, The Message Bible

Insight:

I discovered a long time ago that we will only receive what we believe, and we believe exactly what we perceive as determined by our subjective thoughts and how we process them. Our perception, then, becomes our reality.

What we must do is ensure that our perceptions are rooted and grounded in the truth of God's Word with a perspective that views the world through a God-inspired purpose that ignites our passions daily. Our actions are a direct result of the thoughts that we allow to linger, so let's choose to think accordingly and make this a great day!

Prayer to Ignite Action:

Heavenly Father, You have given humanity the ability to think rationally and to process information based on what is perceived. Today, I pray for discernment to perceive information based on the truth of Your Word rather than my senses alone. Help me to meditate on thoughts that will bring out the best and not the worst in me and others. Speak to me through my mind as I focus on all that is beautiful, noble, virtuous, and praiseworthy. In Jesus' name. Amen.

DAY 296

Inspiration:

"For if you keep silent at this time, relief and deliverance shall arise for the Jews from elsewhere, but you and your father's house will perish. And who knows but that you have come to the kingdom for such a time as this and for this very occasion?" ~ Esther 4:14, Amplified Bible

Insight:

You've heard the saying, "I'm waiting for my ship to come in." That statement is an excuse for sitting on the sidelines and not getting involved in life. We shouldn't wait for perfect conditions to occur in order for us to "cash in" on what life has to offer. Instead, we should create opportunities to give of ourselves and our resources in order to leave a legacy that future generations can build upon with the knowledge that we were created, as was Esther, "for such a time as this."

Each new day carries with it the chance to contemplate, create, and celebrate life as we embrace the abundance that it affords us. We can live out our best days right now without waiting for some event or person to give us the hookup. Besides, we become the hookup that others are looking for and need when we are determined to point them to God by the way we live.

Prayer to Ignite Action:

Father, I am so grateful to be alive here and now, for such a time as this. I pray that I can be a living example of Your love, goodness, and mercy wherever I go today. I will look for opportunities to share who You are to me and what You've done for me with someone else. This is the day for me to be the hookup that others need as I live intentionally and give generously. In Jesus' name. Amen.

DAY 297

Inspiration:

"So Jesus answered and said to them, "Assuredly, I say to you, if you have faith and do not doubt, you will not only do what was done to the fig tree, but also if you say to this mountain, 'Be removed and be cast into the sea,' it will be done. And whatever things you ask in prayer, believing, you will receive." ~ Matthew 21:21-22, New King James Version

Insight:

One of the principles I've learned in my life is that faith and doubt cannot coexist if we expect to see results manifested. Trying to mix the two is like trying to mix oil and water. No matter how much you shake the two ingredients up in the same container, once the ingredients settle, they still are totally separate from one another. So it is when we confess God's word with faith, yet allow doubt to linger in our minds at the same time. The only way to experience faith in action is just that, to exercise our faith by acting upon God's Word and will for our lives while eliminating the doubt so that it does not distract or deter us from seeing results.

Prayer to Ignite Action:

Lord God, You've told us how to receive the answers to the prayers we've requested by asking in faith without doubting. Today, I relinquish all doubt and focus my faith on the promises found in Your Word. Let my faith rise as a memorial before You to be remembered as I ask and believe You to answer every request of my heart that agrees with Your will. In Jesus' name. Amen.

DAY 298

Inspiration:
"God created human beings; he created them godlike, Reflecting God's nature. He created them male and female." ~ Genesis 1:27, The Message Bible

"No, we neither make nor save ourselves. God does both the making and saving. He creates each of us by Christ Jesus to join him in the work he does, the good work he has gotten ready for us to do, work we had better be doing." ~ Ephesians 2:10, The Message Bible

Insight:
I remember these lyrics from a song I heard years ago: "Everything is beautiful in its own way..." Beauty is indeed in the eye of the beholder, but what we behold is an image that is a reflection of what we think about ourselves and others. We must, therefore, pay careful attention to the patterns of thought that color the way we see ourselves and renew our minds so that we can think about and see ourselves as we were originally created to be before sin, negativity, timidity, and shame ever entered the picture.

Take time today to consider and celebrate the beauty of who you are based on the fact that you were created in the beautiful image and likeness of God who makes no mistakes...only masterpieces.

Prayer to Ignite Action:
Heavenly Father, You are the One who I adore. I can't imagine living without You, for my relationship with You makes life beautiful. I am so blessed to know that You took the time to create me in Your image and to design my life's purpose before I ever took one breath. Just as no two people are alike, each person's vocation is as distinct as the individual to whom You've assigned it. Thank You for seeing the worth, value and beauty in me that is to be shared with the world in my own unique way. In Jesus' name. Amen.

DAY 299

Inspiration:

"Hope deferred makes the heart sick, But desire fulfilled is a tree of life."
~ Proverbs 13:12, New American Standard Bible

"You have given him his heart's desire. And You have not withheld the request of his lips. Selah." ~ Psalm 21:2, New American Standard Bible

Insight:

God is so awesome in that He has created us to live for a reason which often times is revealed by the desires of our heart. Listening to your deepest heart's cry and tuning in to what gives you the most joy while doing what comes easy to you, points the way to the path upon which we should walk. That which comes easy is as natural to us as is the air that we breathe. However, what is second nature to us is against nature and difficult for others, because each person is God's original design built with the exact specifications of personality, purpose, spirit, and skill that cannot be duplicated.

When we find out why we were created and focus on who we were meant to be and what we were designed to do, we will find true fulfillment and pleasure. Others will even take notice and share in the blessing of our passion for living life. Getting and staying in a position and posture of purpose is what keeps our passion alive.

Prayer to Ignite Action:

Father, my heart's desire is a clue from You of what I am called to do. Thank You for showing me what is possible, and for setting my heart ablaze with the passion to fulfill my desire as You allow it to manifest. I thank You for every natural talent, ability, gift, and skill that is as distinct as my spirit, personality, and purpose. I will continue to do what You've called me to do and to be who I was originally created to be by Your grace. In Jesus' name. Amen.

DAY 300

Inspiration:

"The right word at the right time is like a custom-made piece of jewelry, And a wise friend's timely reprimand is like a gold ring slipped on your finger. Reliable friends who do what they say are like cool drinks in sweltering heat—refreshing! Like billowing clouds that bring no rain is the person who talks big but never produces. Patient persistence pierces through indifference; gentle speech breaks down rigid defenses." ~ Proverbs 25:11-15, The Message Bible

Insight:

It has been said that people retain only 7% of what is said. The remaining 93% is remembered by what people hear and see (inflections, tone of voice and body language based on word choices and actions). For that very reason, it is imperative that we give careful attention not just to what we say, but most importantly, to how we translate what we say in the way we live. Whether we realize it or not, people are always watching us and making decisions to follow what we do more than what we say. We are leaders in our own right, no matter what our occupation, vocation, or title may be.

Here's what I know for sure: The Holy Spirit gives us the inner fire for others to admire so that we can inspire them to go even higher. Now, that's what my daughter, Lesley, would call "in-reach for outreach!"

Prayer to Ignite Action:

Dear Lord, You are the Master of all wisdom, knowledge, and understanding, all of which are needed to communicate Your plan to us. Allow me to master the art of communicating effectively in verbal and nonverbal ways as well as with the advances of technology that are available without misconstruing the message. Help me to listen and to speak with empathy and to genuinely seek to understand the needs and desires of others without just seeking to be understood from my point of view. I pray that Your Holy Spirit will empower me to inspire others who are searching for a relationship with You. In Jesus' name. Amen.

DAY 301

Inspiration:

"Workouts in the gymnasium are useful, but a disciplined life in God is far more so, making you fit both today and forever. You can count on this. Take it to heart." ~ 1 Timothy 4:8-9, The Message Bible

Insight:

Have you stopped to think about how well you've been treated lately-- not just by others, but more importantly, by yourself? We are tempted to work our fingers to the bone for others, particularly if you have a nurturing nature as many women do, and a providing, protecting nature as do most men. However, if we do not expend the necessary energy to care for our own holistic health, we are really doing ourselves and those closest to us a disservice. Jesus instructed us to "love our neighbor as ourselves" as the second greatest commandment given. Yet, in order to do so, we must truly take an introspective look at how well we love, respect, and value our mind, body, and spirit so that we can extend the same "balanced" care and concern to those in our sphere of influence. We must inspect what we are doing and expect more of ourselves by caring for our inner and outer temple so that God can truly use us in more ways than we could possibly imagine. Doing so requires proper self-love that will overflow to those watching, listening to, and following us as we follow Christ.

Prayer to Ignite Action:

Dear Lord, forgive me for not paying close attention to the care of my own spirit, mind, and body. Neglecting any part of me is what leads to a life that is out-of-balance and unhealthy. I know that we are called as Christians to love and care for our neighbors by serving them, but we are not to do so at the expense of neglecting ourselves. Today, I pray for the decision-making ability, discipline, and determination to respect and take care of the business of my spirit, mind, and body. By faith and with Your help, I am holistically healthy and whole. In Jesus' name. Amen.

DAY 302

Inspiration:

"But I tell you, Love your enemies and pray for those who persecute you, To show that you are the children of your Father Who is in heaven; for He makes His sun rise on the wicked and on the good, and makes the rain fall upon the upright and the wrongdoers [alike]." ~ Matthew 5:44-45, Amplified Bible

Insight:

Life is a gift from God to be enjoyed fully, and to learn valuable lessons internally and externally as we share them with others. It is not the good times, I've found, that I learn from and appreciate the most. Rather, I have grown and matured holistically by leaps and bounds from the ups and downs that have ebbed and flowed through my life's journey, and there's still much more to be experienced. Into every life, a little rain must fall. What matters most is the way we choose to view and pursue life with the intent of extracting meaning and value that motivates us to keep on moving forward, knowing that God is still at work even in the rain.

Prayer to Ignite Action:

Heavenly Father, You are good to all and Your grace is extended to everyone who will accept it. I receive Your grace today, for it enables me to do what I cannot do in my own strength. Today, I choose to love and to receive love, to learn and to teach, and to grow and encourage others to grow along with me. In Jesus' name. Amen.

DAY 303

Inspiration:

"For He looked down from the height of His sanctuary, from heaven did the Lord behold the earth, To hear the sighing and groaning of the prisoner, to loose those who are appointed to death, So that men may declare the name of the Lord in Zion and His praise in Jerusalem. When peoples are gathered together, and the kingdoms, to worship and serve the Lord...The children of Your servants shall dwell safely and continue, and their descendants shall be established before You." ~ Psalm 102:19-22 & 28, Amplified Bible

Insight:

I had the opportunity to pronounce a prayer of comfort at the funeral service of my best childhood friend's father. His daughter and I literally grew up together, slept at each other's house, played together, got in trouble together, and shared stories we will cherish and keep to ourselves forever. Our families were right next door to each other, and our parents and siblings looked out for each other in ways that few neighbors would do in our present day and time. We all knew the names of every family on the street, and many of them attended the funeral service. Although this was a time of loss for family and friends, there were no tears shed because we knew that he had accepted the Lord and he lived a full life of 83 years. A flood of memories washed over us during and after the service, and especially at the repast as we all ate, laughed, and recalled our fondest neighborhood stories.

Sometimes it takes the loss of a life to bring our own life's lessons into perspective. Living well, laughing often and loving fully despite what we see, hear and/or experience should be the order of each new day. In doing so, we will find an abundance of joy and fulfillment of purpose that will extend from us to others and make our world a better place in which to live.

Prayer to Ignite Action:

Dear Lord, death is a natural part of the process and progress of life.

Although it is difficult, accepting and dealing with the pain of losing a loved one allows us to grieve and heal, not with the passing of time, but because we are undergirded by Your strength and comforted by Your Spirit and a support system of trusted loved ones and friends who surround us. Today, I pray for those who may be experiencing loss in their lives. Allow me to be the hands and feet of Jesus today, for in helping others to heal, I also receive help and healing for myself. I celebrate the gift of life and laughter today--a gift that is meant to be shared with others. In Jesus' name. Amen.

DAY 304

Inspiration:
"There's an opportune time to do things, a right time for everything on earth." ~ Ecclesiastes 3:1, The Message Bible

"Behave yourselves wisely [living prudently and with discretion] in your relations with those of the outside world (the non-Christians), making the very most of the time and seizing (buying up) the opportunity." ~ Colossians 4:5, Amplified Bible

Insight:
There is no time like the present, and that time is now. Today live as if each moment of time is an incredible inkling of inspiration infused into your subconscious and conscious mind as a reminder of God's precious commodity given to be used and maximized with wisdom and skill. The allocation of your time can be spent working fervently, serving faithfully, moving forward fearlessly, living fruitfully or resting...finally.

As each new day approaches, seize it with all the strength and savvy you can muster and choose to be a good steward of every moment within its span of time.

Prayer to Ignite Action:
Father, time is a precious commodity given to humanity to be used with discretion and managed wisely. I ask for specialized wisdom and skill so that I will know without hesitation how to make the most of every moment of time. Help me to identify and eliminate time wasters in my life and to pinpoint with precision what needs to be done and when. In Jesus' name. Amen.

DAY 305

Inspiration:

"A man [who has] friends must himself be friendly, But there is a friend [who] sticks closer than a brother." ~ Proverbs 18:24, New King James Version

"A friend is always loyal, and a brother is born to help in time of need." ~ Proverbs 17:7, New Living Translation

"You use steel to sharpen steel, and one friend sharpens another." ~ Proverbs 27:17, The Message Bible

Insight:

We never know what a day may hold, but we certainly know Who holds the day! Life is filled with unexpected and unexplainable pain with unforeseen potholes on our pathway toward purpose. Not long ago, our family attended the homegoing celebration of the life of an 80 year old mother of one of our pastors. During her eulogy, she was referred to as a "refreshing friend" to all who knew her.

We all need to be refreshed by those who are true friends indeed, and to be a refreshing friend to others as we share in life's joys and sorrows. Refreshing friendships will allow us to support one another in times that are good, bad, happy or sad, and that makes our path a little easier to traverse. Today, let's make every effort to share our gratitude and appreciation with those who have been "a refreshing friend."

Prayer to Ignite Action:

Oh Lord, I thank You for being a friend to me that is closer than any sister or brother could ever be. I also am grateful for every person You've placed in my life who has been a refreshing friend. You have strategically placed different people in my life at the exact time when I needed them most. From my true friends, I have learned valuable lessons, received encouragement and benefited from times of intense sharpening. True friends are there not just for a season, but for a lifetime. Thank You that I can be the same kind of friend in return in our relationship of reciprocity. Today, I will be sure to tell my friends "thank you." In Jesus' name. Amen.

DAY 306

Inspiration:

"We, however, will not boast beyond measure, but within the limits of the sphere which God appointed us--a sphere which especially includes you. For we are not overextending ourselves (as though [our authority] did not extend to you), for it was to you that we came with the gospel of Christ; not boasting of things beyond measure, [that is], in other men's labors, but having hope, [that] as your faith is increased, we shall be greatly enlarged by you in our sphere, to preach the gospel in the [regions] beyond you, [and] not to boast in another man's sphere of accomplishment." ~ 2 Corinthians 10:12-16, New King James Version

Insight:

Although the business and busyness of life keep our hands to the plow, so to speak, we must remember to stay within our sphere of influence where there is grace, peace, and joy which causes us to be fruitful and fulfilled even in the midst of what may seem to be a hectic schedule. God only gives us grace to function in our area of anointing. Anything outside of the limits of that sphere will produce frustration and fatigue. We must learn how to "stay in our lane" while maintaining balance in our lives for the sake of our own holistic health--a lesson that becomes more and more important as we grow older and wiser.

Prayer to Ignite Action:

Father, thank You for the confidence I have in You--confidence that allows me to operate in the grace that You have given me. That grace is apportioned to me so that I can function well in the sphere of influence that has been assigned to me. Today, I purpose to stay in my lane, knowing that Your grace is sufficient for me as long as I do not overstep the limits of the sphere You've given me. I will experience fruitfulness and fulfillment because I will not overextend myself beyond what I am capable of doing, with Your help. In Jesus' name. Amen.

DAY 307

Inspiration:

"One night Joseph had a dream, and when he told his brothers about it, they hated him more than ever. 'Listen to this dream,' he said...Soon Joseph had another dream, and again he told his brothers about it. 'Listen, I have had another dream,' he said. 'The sun, moon, and eleven stars bowed low before me!' This time he told the dream to his father as well as to his brothers, but his father scolded him. 'What kind of dream is that?' he asked. 'Will your mother and I and your brothers actually come and bow to the ground before you?'" ~ Genesis 37:5-6, 9-10, New Living Translation

"Then his brothers came and threw themselves down before Joseph. 'Look, we are your slaves!' they said. But Joseph replied, 'Don't be afraid of me. Am I God, that I can punish you? You intended to harm me, but God intended it all for good. He brought me to this position so I could save the lives of many people.'" ~ Genesis 50:18-20, New Living Translation

Insight:

Joseph was a young teenager when God allowed him to have a series of dreams that foretold of his future--a future that would save the same siblings who were jealous and envious of him and his dream. They would later realize that when God inspires a dream in the heart of one who serves him, that nothing will stop it from becoming a reality.

No matter how old, young or accomplished we have been or are at the moment, we should still have a dream that motivates us to move forward in hot pursuit of God's Master plan--a plan that sometimes unfolds from a mere seed of inspiration planted in our heart. Focusing on a dream that honors God, edifies others and fulfills our deepest desires will give new meaning to life and add value to the world around us. Don't abort your God-implanted dream, especially when others don't understand or support it. Once you receive it as a seed planted in the fertile ground of your heart, water it with your faith. When you dare to believe it, you will find the self-discipline to achieve it and God will bring it to fruition.

Prayer to Ignite Action:

Father, You are the originator of dreams and the inspiration. Remind me of the dreams that You planted within my heart as a seed of the promise that is to be fulfilled in my life. Help me filter out every dream and idea that is not inspired by You so that my focus may become clear and unencumbered. Give me the fortitude not to be distracted by dream-robbers who will try to steal, kill, or destroy what is safely hidden in my heart. I thank You for empowering me with the tenacity and toughness to stay the course in the face of adversity and opposition, for I know that what You have promised will come to pass so that I may be a blessing to many. In Jesus' name. Amen.

DAY 308

Inspiration:

"He created them male and female, and blessed them and called them Mankind in the day they were created." ~ Genesis 5:2, New King James Version

"I will praise You, for I am fearfully [and] wonderfully made; Marvelous are Your works, And [that] my soul knows very well." ~ Psalm 139:14, New King James Version

"But now, thus says the LORD, who created you, O Jacob, And He who formed you, O Israel: 'Fear not, for I have redeemed you; I have called [you] by your name; You [are] Mine.'" ~ Isaiah 43:1, New King James Version

Insight:

The way we see ourselves is sometimes skewed based on what others have told us or what we believe about ourselves. For that reason, we should search God's Word to see what He has already spoken concerning us, and therefore, delete the former mental script and replace it with the definition of who God says we are.

Our prayer to God is that He indeed opens our eyes so that we can see ourselves from His vantage point and not from our own or from the perspective of others. When we choose to see who and whose we really are, there is nothing that we cannot do as it pertains to the purpose and potential that God has predestined for us to fulfill.

Prayer to Ignite Action:

Heavenly Father, today I pray that the veil would be removed from my eyes so that I can see clearly who I am through Your eyes. Where there was once hurt and pain, I thank You that I now see healing and wholeness. Give me forward vision as well so that I can see my future and position myself today not to be controlled or held captive by my past. I see myself as being saved and free from low-level thinking and mediocre living. I will hold on to the new vision that You have given me for the sake of living my best life and showing others how to do the same. In Jesus' name. Amen.

DAY 309

Inspiration:

"There hath no temptation taken you but such as is common to man: but God [is] faithful, who will not suffer you to be tempted above that ye are able; but will with the temptation also make a way to escape, that ye may be able to bear [it]." ~ 1 Corinthians 10:13, King James Version

"He gets angry once in a while, but across a lifetime there is only love. The nights of crying your eyes out give way to days of laughter." ~ Psalm 30:5, The Message Bible

Insight:

When facing overwhelming obstacles and obstructions in our way, we must remember the promise found in 1 Corinthians 10:13. Overwhelming obstacles and obstructions can be overcome and transformed into opportunities to share what we have endured as well as what lessons we have learned with others. When we look through the lens of learning from challenging circumstances, our perspective will be changed and our situation can be rearranged--all because we decided to step up rather than give up when difficulties arose.

There are some hurdles that God may choose to remove as He creates an escape route for us. However, other hurdles are strategically placed in our race of life because God has already equipped us with the strength and stamina to leap over them. Whatever the scenario, the outcome is the same: "...Weeping may endure for a night, but joy comes in the morning." (Psalm 30:5, NKJV)

Prayer to Ignite Action:

Dear Father, I am grateful for the promise that You will make a way for me to escape temptations that come--either by removing them altogether or by giving me the strength to withstand the temptation as it is transformed into a test for my good. Most of all, I thank You that this too shall pass. Although obstacles that come seem difficult, I know that by faith I have already overcome. I am a winner with You on my side. In Jesus' name. Amen.

DAY 310

Inspiration:

"The fear of the LORD [is] to hate evil; Pride and arrogance and the evil way And the perverse mouth I hate." ~ Proverbs 8:13, New King James Version

"For the Lord shall be your confidence, firm and strong, and shall keep your foot from being caught [in a trap or some hidden danger]." ~ Proverbs 3:26, Amplified Bible

Insight:

Some people mistake confidence for arrogance. The difference between the two is that confidence exudes our choice to utilize our natural talents and skills without cowering to others' negative opinions or statements regarding what we know we are gifted to accomplish to fulfill a cause greater than ourselves that drives us. Arrogance, on the other hand, is steeped in pride and self-promotion at the expense of others. Godly confidence is healthy, for it allows our trust and expectation to rest in God's ability to work in and through us to accomplish His good pleasure which will honor His name, benefit others and allow us to pursue purpose.

Prayer to Ignite Action:

Father, forgive me for the times when I did not place my confidence in You where it belongs. I do not want to come across as being arrogant to anyone, and especially not to You because that is what You despise. Fill me with humility and love as I lean and depend on You to preserve, protect, and provide for me. You are awesome in all You do, and I place my trust and expectation in You, my King and my God. In Jesus' name. Amen.

DAY 311

Inspiration:

"So teach [us] to number our days, That we may gain a heart of wisdom."
~ Psalm 90:12, New King James Version

"Whoever observes the [king's] command will experience no harm, and a wise man's mind will know both when and what to do." ~ Ecclesiastes 8:5, Amplified Bible

Insight:

A familiar stanza of an old song says, "One day at a time, sweet Jesus. That's all I'm asking from You." The reality is that we don't have to ask God for that gift at all, because He has already given it to us when He allows our eyes to open yet again. Another way to restate that request would be to ask God to "Teach us to live wisely and well!" (Psalm 90:12b, The Message Bible Translation) as was Moses' petition. Moses received the revelation that in order for him to make the best use of every opportunity of each new day, he needed God to give Him the wisdom to know what to do as well as when and how to do it. Such wisdom carries with it the ability to perceive and distinguish between what is urgent, important and trivial by maximizing every moment that matters, relishing every relationship that is relevant, and accomplishing every assignment that is appointed to us by God.

Prayer to Ignite Action:

Heavenly Father, I pray that You would teach me how to live wisely and well so that I know what to do, how to do it, and when. Help me to know the difference between what is urgent, what is important, and what needs to be delegated to someone else so that I can manage my responsibilities well today. I receive a heart of wisdom to benefit me and others. In Jesus' name. Amen.

DAY 312

Inspiration:

"A man's gift makes room for him, And brings him before great men." ~ Proverbs 18:16, New King James Version

Insight:

Every day provides a wealth of opportunities for us to make use of our brightest ideas, best gifts, boldest courage, and most bountiful amount of compassion. By doing so, we leave a deposit in the lives of those who cross our path and others whom we may never meet. When we use our God-given gifts boldly, we will find ourselves in the company of great men and women who are in need of the service that only we can provide. When those doors of favor open, it is because we have prepared ourselves for divine opportunity to arrive at our doorstep.

Prayer to Ignite Action:

Father, I hear You calling me closer to You. Your love has captivated my heart. I pursue Your presence, for that is where I find joy and pleasures forevermore. As I spend time with You, I pray that You would inspire me with creative ideas to use my gifts and talents boldly for You. As I sharpen my skills in preparation to be used in greater ways, I will anticipate the doors of opportunity that will be opened just for me. Thank You for giving me favor with You as well as with great men and women so that we can partner together to expand Your kingdom and add value to others. In Jesus' name. Amen.

DAY 313

Inspiration:

"The king's heart is in the hand of the Lord, as are the watercourses; He turns it whichever way He wills. Every way of a man is right in his own eyes, but the Lord weighs and tries the hearts." ~ Proverbs 21:1-2, Amplified Bible

Insight:

God's will is His expressed desire for us, and as we become more intimate in knowing God through prayer and meditating in His Word, we discover that His heart is in direct alignment with His Word and will concerning us. In like manner, our heart should agree with God's Word and will as well. Then, we'll know that the desires emanating from our hearts are purely motivated by God's established purpose and not our own selfish ambitions. There's no need to feel guilty or condemnatory about desires that are already approved and ordained by our heavenly Father.

Prayer to Ignite Action:

Father God, search my heart and remove any wicked way in me. All I want and ever need is in You, and I desire to live my life to glorify You. Let my dreams, ambitions, relationships, and passions be tempered and refined by the work of Your Spirit in me. Let my heart be turned in the direction of Your will today and always. I want to love what You love, and abstain from anything that displeases You. In Jesus' name. Amen.

DAY 314

Inspiration:
"You will succeed in whatever you choose to do, and light will shine on the road ahead of you." ~ Job 22:28, New Living Translation

"May he grant your heart's desires and make all your plans succeed." ~ Psalm 20:4, New Living Translation

"Commit your actions to the LORD, and your plans will succeed." ~ Proverbs 16:3, New Living Translation

Insight:
We are empowered by the Spirit of God to excel and to propel others to do the same. How can we go about following that path? It's not as difficult as some think. All we have to do is to initiate a strong desire to achieve God's best, and then acquire the necessary skills to move forward without making excuses or settling for less. Once we desire more, we'll require more so that the status quo of yesteryear and the mediocrity of yesterday can no longer satisfy the inner drive that compels us to unleash the greatness inside of us today. The Greater One predestined us to represent Him with excellence in word and deed, and He has already empowered us to succeed!

Prayer to Ignite Action:
Father, I thank You for the spirit to succeed that is in me, for it comes from You. Because You live in me, I can do great things. In my weakness You are strong, and when I am unsure of the next step, You see the way ahead and compel me to follow You. Help me to release the latent potential that is ready to soar as I strive for excellence as Your ambassador today. In Jesus' name. Amen.

DAY 315

Inspiration:

"Hope deferred makes the heart sick, But [when] the desire comes, [it is] a tree of life." ~ Proverbs 13:12, New King James Version

Insight:

Hope as defined by Merriam Webster's Dictionary is trust, reliance, and a desire accompanied by expectation or belief in fulfillment. To hope, then, is to cherish a desire with confident anticipation and expectation of obtaining it. Hope is a small word, but when placed in our hearts, it expands and serves as the motivating factor to believe that our dreams will come true. However, action is the moving force that transforms dreams into manifested reality. Dreaming is good, but doing is even better because it allows God to display His power and creativity in order to achieve greatness in and through us.

Prayer to Ignite Action:

Heavenly Father, I am grateful for the gift of hope, for it is the spark that sets fire to my desires and dreams. I confidently hope in You, knowing that in You I shall never be disappointed. I hope in Your Word, for it promises salvation that has been extended not only to me, but to my entire household. I confidently believe, anticipate and expect to see the manifestation and fulfillment of every God-inspired desire and dream within me. In Jesus' name. Amen.

DAY 316

Inspiration:

"God told Abram: 'Leave your country, your family, and your father's home for a land that I will show you. I'll make you a great nation and bless you. I'll make you famous; you'll be a blessing. I'll bless those who bless you; those who curse you I'll curse. All the families of the Earth will be blessed through you." ~ Genesis 12:1-3, The Message Bible

"Then the LORD said, 'Shall I hide from Abraham what I am about to do? Abraham will surely become a great and powerful nation, and all nations on earth will be blessed through him. For I have chosen him, so that he will direct his children and his household after him to keep the way of the LORD by doing what is right and just, so that the LORD will bring about for Abraham what he has promised him." ~ Genesis 18:17-19, New International Version

Insight:

God told Abraham to leave everything that was familiar to him in order to go to a land that God would show him. What amazes me about this text is that Abraham left his father's house and his kindred--a life of idol worship that he was used to--to follow a God he did not know without receiving specific details about his new address. God did not tell Abraham what direction in which to go or give him a map or a GPS system. He just said, "Go," and that was enough for Abraham to obey without seeing or knowing God for himself. No wonder he was (and is) known as the father of faith!

How many of us are willing to leave what we have become accustomed to so that God can enlarge our territory and increase our capacity to become more and to accomplish even greater works for His glory for the sake of the next generation? Now is the time not just to fully use our faith, but to pass it on to our children and our children's children.

Prayer to Ignite Action:

Lord God, although Abraham is known as the father of faith, those who belong to the family of God are known as the seed of Abraham, and therefore, partakers of the same promise. Today, I thank You that I am blessed to be a blessing; my name and reputation are great because I represent You; nations and other families shall be blessed through me; and I will pass on what I know about You and Your Word to the generation that follows me, beginning with those in my own household and community. In Jesus' name. Amen.

DAY 317

Inspiration:

"Then said the Lord to me, You have seen well, for I am alert and active, watching over My word to perform it." ~ Jeremiah 1:12, Amplified Bible

Insight:

I believe that God will watch over His Word to perform it, but also that we must do our part in giving Him something to work with in the process. We can achieve all that is within the sphere of influence that God has granted us given the skills and abilities that we have and seek to develop, as well as the purpose He has predestined for us to fulfill. All of our efforts should be concentrated toward the desired end that God has in mind for us so that we seek to fulfill His plan for our lives rather than our own. There is freedom in knowing and empowerment in doing God's will, which brings Him pleasure and us inexpressible joy.

Prayer to Ignite Action:

Dear Lord, You are faithful and true to Your Word. Everything You speak can be trusted, for Your track record throughout the ages proves that You will perform what has been spoken in due time. Help me to stand by the words I've spoken to make them good, and let the integrity of my heart determine my decisions and dictate my actions today, I pray. In Jesus' name. Amen.

DAY 318

Inspiration:

"Talk no more so very proudly; Let no arrogance come from your mouth, For the LORD [is] the God of knowledge; And by Him actions are weighed." 1 Samuel 2:3, New King James Version

"Who are those who fear the LORD? He will show them the path they should choose." ~ Psalm 25:12, New Living Translation

Insight:

In order for any action to be effective, it must first begin as a decisive thought that makes an impression upon our will. Every aspect of our soul (which includes the mind, will, intellect, emotions and imagination), has the potential to engage in meaningful ways so that our actions will have a lasting impact upon us and those assigned to us. One action, whether right or wrong, can either positively affect or negatively infect those who are within our circle of influence. Therefore, we should use wisdom and discretion in every choice we make, because our choices and actions will leave an indelible mark upon others who are watching, listening to, and following us.

Prayer to Ignite Action:

Father, I stand in reverence and in holy awe of You. I am amazed by Your goodness and grace towards all of Your creation. You are full of knowledge, and possess a vast supply of information that all of humanity needs to make wise choices which will lead to right actions. Please speak to my mind and soul, and conform my will to Yours. Let my thoughts become Your thoughts, and transform my ways so that they are aligned with Yours. Help me to lead by example today. In Jesus' name. Amen.

DAY 319

Inspiration:

"But [like a boxer] I buffet my body [handle it roughly, discipline it by hardships] and subdue it, for fear that after proclaiming to others the Gospel and things pertaining to it, I myself should become unfit [not stand the test, be unapproved and rejected as a counterfeit]." ~ 1 Corinthians 9:27, Amplified Bible

Insight:

We don't need to wait for someone else to do for us what we can do for ourselves, especially when it comes to wanting and needing to live a valuable and meaningful life that utilizes the best gifts that God has given us. Sometimes that means that we need to sharpen our mental faculties, hone our skills and abilities, as well as ensure that we are physically fit so that we can live and give at an optimum level. The discipline to be self-motivated and determined to make an indelible mark upon the world around us, is within our power. Let's use it before we lose it!

Prayer to Ignite Action:

Dear God, as a teacher to others in any subject or area, I must first be disciplined in the same area myself. Let me first be a partaker of everything that is conducive to living this Christian life before I share it with others so that I will be authentic, sincere, and genuine in communicating who Jesus is not just with my words, but by the example of a godly and healthy lifestyle. Assist me in my efforts to be disciplined as Your disciple so that others can follow the habits and behaviors that I model. In Jesus' name. Amen.

DAY 320

Inspiration:

"And the Lord came down to see the city and the tower which the sons of men had built. And the Lord said, Behold, they are one people and they have all one language; and this is only the beginning of what they will do, and now nothing they have imagined they can do will be impossible for them." ~ Genesis 11:5-6, Amplified Bible

Insight:

My husband often says that we must be careful of the picture that we paint upon the canvas of our minds. That picture becomes the mental "image" that will rule the "nation" of the mind, which is a country all to itself. Thus, the "imagination" is a power that can be used for good or evil, blessing or cursing, for ourselves and others. Today, let's be more alert and aware of the thoughts in our conscious and subconscious minds, and sublimate that power so that we become wiser, stronger, healthier, and better equipped to accomplish the will of God and to attract the human and natural resources necessary to be our best selves. Our imagination is the key to our elevation when it is yielded to God.

Prayer to Ignite Action:

Father, the Tower of Babel shows us just how easy it is to accomplish anything within the scope of our imagination when we are in one accord. However, You came down from Heaven to confuse and separate the language of the people of Babel because their motive for building the tower was wrong. Thank You for teaching me this valuable lesson, Lord. You are not obligated to accomplish every dream and desire etched upon the canvas of our mind and the landscape of our heart. You know and test the intents of our hearts which are the real motivation behind all that is said and done. Let the meditation of my heart be acceptable in Your sight, oh, Lord. Sanctify my imagination and the intent of my heart so that I am in sync with what You desire for me. In Jesus' name. Amen.

DAY 321

Inspiration:

"I press toward the goal for the prize of the upward call of God in Christ Jesus." ~ Philippians 3:14, New King James Version

"For as the body without the spirit is dead, so faith without works is dead also." ~ James 2:26, New King James Version

Insight:

I had the opportunity to serve as the facilitator for an in-service training session on "Goal Setting for Results." The anatomy of a goal allows us to examine the goal itself ("WHAT"), its benefits ("WHY"), and the strategy needed to accomplish it ("HOW"). We must set goals in our personal and professional lives that are believable, attainable, and measurable using this anatomy if the goal is to be reached and results are to follow. Dreams and hopes alone will not produce results. Intentions and expectations, although good, are not enough. Real decisions, raw determination, and relentlessly doing what needs to be done as we chart our course along the way will cause a goal that began as a mere visionary thought, to be translated into an assertive action plan replete with objectives that are to be met within a specific time frame. Remember..."faith without works is dead."

Prayer to Ignite Action:

Father, I've learned that to see real results in and around me, I must activate my faith and be assertive in adding works to my faith. I pray for Your guidance in channeling my faith in the direction of Your word and will so that I will not pray amiss or labor in vain. I thank You for the wisdom to plan strategic goals that will produce the end result that You have in mind for me. You designed a specific destiny for me, and I pray that I will be motivated to stay the course with joy. In Jesus' name. Amen.

DAY 322

Inspiration:

"Perseverance must finish its work so that you may be mature and complete, not lacking anything. If any of you lacks wisdom, he should ask God, who gives generously to all without finding fault, and it will be given to him. But when he asks, he must believe and not doubt, because he who doubts is like a wave of the sea, blown and tossed by the wind."
~ James 1:4-6, New International Version

Insight:

Here is a phrase that stops procrastination in its tracks and ends excuses from prohibiting progress: "Persevere and get it done!" Isn't that the answer to whatever ails us in our holistic health, wealth, relationships, and career choices? Stop vacillating like the waves of the sea and make up your mind to accomplish the goal that will move you closer toward your God-ordained destiny. Ask God for the wisdom and the willpower to do what needs to be done to experience elevation in every area of your life. Don't doubt what God is able to do, and refuse to second guess yourself. Persevere and get it done!

Prayer to Ignite Action:

Father, You are the ultimate example of finishing the work that was first begun. Wisdom was at Your beck and call when the world was created, and for six days You worked until creation was finished, and on the seventh day You rested. You began the plan of salvation before mankind would accept redemption through the birth, death, and resurrection of Your Son. Jesus, the Author and Finisher of our faith, declared, "It is finished" and fulfilled Your plan to reconcile our relationship with You. I pray for the wisdom and willpower to finish the work that I have started, and to set goals to reach the destiny that You have planned for me. Give me the perseverance to "get it done" today, I pray. In Jesus' name. Amen.

DAY 323

Inspiration:

"If they obey and serve him, they will spend the rest of their days in prosperity and their years in contentment." ~ Job 36:11, New International Version

"But godliness with contentment is great gain." ~ 1 Timothy 6:6, New International Version

Insight:

Sometimes we desire to do the work of the Holy Spirit in changing individuals or circumstances in order to bring about contentment. We can only change ourselves and not others by transforming our perspective as we learn to be content despite what we see, hear, or feel. Rather than viewing people and problems as obstructions, see them as opportunities to advance to a new place and position of contentment with great gain, knowing that God has a bigger and better plan working together for our good.

Prayer to Ignite Action:

Dear God, You have taught me that I am only responsible for my own decisions and actions. I cannot change the hearts of others, but I can work on myself and allow Your Holy Spirit to lead me in adjusting my attitude and actions. Help me to listen, to obey, and to live contently today, for the benefits that I'll reap will be evident for me and others to see. In Jesus' name. Amen.

DAY 324

Inspiration:
"And he called his ten servants, and delivered them ten pounds, and said unto them, Occupy till I come." ~ Luke 19:13, King James Version

Insight:
Jesus teaches us in The Parable of the Pounds about the principle of investment which is easier to do when one has cultivated a strong work ethic. He teaches us what the kingdom of Heaven is by allowing us to see that faith and works go hand-in-hand, and our works should exemplify excellence as we "occupy" or "do business" (as the New King James Version translation states) until the Master comes.

Today is unlike any other day in that it is brand new and filled to the brim with unseen possibilities and untapped potential that can only be accessed when we are unafraid to seize all the opportunities that God sends our way. Dare not only to dream, but to be determined to delve into the doorway of destiny that awaits the fearless and the faithful by exercising an excellent work ethic. The reward for doing so is unparalleled fulfillment, not only for us, but for those who are assigned to us.

Prayer to Ignite Action:
Father, You did not create anyone or anything to exist just to take up time or space, but everyone and everything is to occupy until Jesus returns. I have a purpose to fulfill because of the investment that has been made in me. Today, I am determined to occupy time and space by working fervently to make an investment in the lives of others for Your kingdom. I invite You to work in and through me so that I and those assigned to me can fulfill destiny. In Jesus' name. Amen.

DAY 325

Inspiration:

"And may you have the power to understand, as all God's people should, how wide, how long, how high, and how deep his love is. May you experience the love of Christ, though it is too great to understand fully. Then you will be made complete with all the fullness of life and power that comes from God." ~ Ephesians 3:18-19, New Living Translation

Insight:

"Love is a many splendid thing," as they say, and indeed it is when it comes from the Source of all love--God. He alone enables us to know and comprehend the height, depth, width and breadth of His love so that it flows in and through us to others. Because of His agape love, we can unconditionally accept that we belong to God and are created to love and to be loved in return. When we see through His eyes rather than the eyes of others and our own, the world and the people in it seem more beautiful and so do we. As Christians, God's love supersedes our own and emanates from our hearts to touch the hurting and point them to the same hope in the Savior that we have found. Stop looking for love in all the wrong places and start embracing the true splendor of God's love from the inside out.

Prayer to Ignite Action:

Heavenly Father, I marvel at the depths of Your matchless love. It is bountiful and boundless, extravagant and endless. I will never be able to fully understand it, but I am so grateful to be able to generously receive it. Let the power of Your love flow through me and touch those around me today as I represent who You are to the world. In Jesus' name. Amen.

DAY 326

Inspiration:
"And be not conformed to this world, but be ye transformed by the renewing of your mind, that ye may prove what is that good and acceptable, and perfect will of God." ~ Romans 12:2, King James Version

Insight:
Joyce Meyer often says, "Where the mind goes, the man follows." What a simple, yet profound statement. Our thoughts play the lead role in the dance of life, causing our bodies to function much like a puppet on a string. The mind is very powerful. We are not what we do, but what we think. What we accomplish in life is only a byproduct of how rich or poor our thoughts are.

What are you allowing to play on the movie screen of your mind? Living differently begins with thinking differently, and the quality of our life is directly linked to the quality of our thoughts. A transformed mindset will produce the results that you desire to see.

Prayer to Ignite Action:
Father God, I give You permission to transform my thoughts as my mind is renewed by reading and meditating on biblical principles. I want to be found in Your will. Teach me how to reject negative thoughts and to receive and entertain a positive mindset today as I create new patterns of thinking for abundant living. In Jesus' name. Amen.

DAY 327

Inspiration:

"Do not be deceived: 'Evil company corrupts good habits.'" ~ 1 Corinthians 15:33, New King James Version

Insight:

Habits are good when they benefit us and others. However, they can become corrupt when influenced by wrong character and keeping company with wrong thoughts and people. We must always evaluate ourselves and the relationships around us so that our habits will reflect the best of what God desires for our lives.

Routines can be good or detrimental, based on whether or not they are good for us. It is definitely wise to be habitual about spending time with God, reading and studying the Bible, carving out time for our family and special friends, devising and following through with a daily "things to do list," and making better choices regarding nutrition, exercise and the amount of sleep we need. These routines are not only right, but will yield the right kind of results and opportunities for success in our personal, spiritual, and professional lives. And lest we forget, we need just the right amount of spontaneity in the midst of our right routines to keep our lives, relationships, and work from being mundane.

Prayer to Ignite Action:

Dear Lord, I desire to keep good company with You through prayer, worship, Bible study and having the right thoughts and people in my life to influence my habits and ways that are good and beneficial for me and those closest to me. Today, I will examine myself and my relationships to discern unhealthy patterns so that they can be eliminated and replaced with good habits with Your help. In Jesus' name. Amen.

DAY 328

Inspiration:

"For the word of God [is] living and powerful, and sharper than any two-edged sword, piercing even to the division of soul and spirit, and of joints and marrow, and is a discerner of the thoughts and intents of the heart." ~ Hebrews 4:12, New King James Version

Insight:

It is amazing just how much power we possess within our grasp by the thoughts that we allow to permeate our decisions and actions. We can choose to think the best and thereby attract who and what is best for us in terms of people and possessions when our thoughts are governed by biblical principles. God wants us to be good stewards of managing our mind as well as money, relationships, and time, and He shows us how in His Word. Everything we say and do is a direct reflection of what we think, so we must guard our minds by filtering out what is unfruitful and meditating on those things that will cause God's best to manifest in and around us.

Prayer to Ignite Action:

Heavenly Father, Your Word is able to discern the thoughts of my mind and the intentions of my heart. I will allow Your Word to permeate my mind and heart today so that it governs all that I think, say, and do. As I read and ponder the principles in the Bible, I will use them as the tools I need to effectively manage everything You've given me to cause Your best to manifest for me and others within my area of influence. In Jesus' name. Amen.

DAY 329

Inspiration:

"Your words were found, and I ate them, And Your word was to me the joy and rejoicing of my heart; For I am called by Your name, O LORD God of hosts." ~ Jeremiah 15:16, New King James Version

Insight:

When watching the news or reading the morning paper, one can become easily alarmed with the state of our community, city, nation, and world. Joy, hope, and expectation can dwindle, if it were not for the fact that as Christians, we derive our joy from and place our hope in our unchangeable God and His infallible Word. We can find all the inspiration we need when considering and being grateful for His amazing grace, unfathomable favor, unending mercy and unconditional love. That is enough to keep on living, moving and abiding in Him, trusting that we will be infused with inspiration from within that will override whatever we see or hear around us.

Prayer to Ignite Action:

Dear Lord, I praise You because of Your consistent display of faithfulness toward us even though we don't deserve it. Thank You for allowing those who love and serve You to be an example of righteousness in the midst of a world that often shows no moral consciousness. Empower us as Your people to live by the standard of Your Word and to walk our talk today as an example to make our world a better place in which to live. As I and others live out our faith, may we ignite others to do the same. In Jesus' name. Amen.

DAY 330

Inspiration:

"Dear friends, don't be surprised at the fiery trials you are going through, as if something strange were happening to you. Instead, be very glad--for these trials make you partners with Christ in his suffering, so that you will have the wonderful joy of seeing his glory when it is revealed to all the world." ~ 1 Peter 4:12-13, New Living Translation

Insight:

Life is no bed of roses, but we can smell the roses along our life's journey in the midst of the unpleasant aromas that will surely come our way. Knowing that difficulties will arise shouldn't be a surprise. Rather, difficulties should serve as resistance to push us to soar above problems with the dynamic duo of perseverance and a positive attitude. These two traits alone will change our perspective and allow us to trudge through any trial while remaining triumphant. Besides, each difficulty will soon give way to a brand new day with opportunities to show and share lessons learned from what was experienced the day before.

Prayer to Ignite Action:

Father, in the midst of the best and worst of life, You are always with me. There is no trial too difficult for You to handle while I persevere through it with a positive mental attitude. Broaden my perspective so that I can see, understand, and appreciate the lessons that life's difficulties can teach me so that I can be strengthened, matured, and challenged to help others who may be experiencing trials in their lives. In Jesus' name. Amen.

DAY 331

Inspiration:
"The LORD your God will delight in you if you obey his voice and keep the commands and decrees written in this Book of Instruction, and you turn to the LORD your God with all your heart and soul." ~ Deuteronomy 30:10, New Living Translation

Insight:
Whereas we may see ours and others' shortcomings, God sees who He created us to be and what we were predestined to accomplish for Him. We, too, should focus more on who and whose we are while valuing the uniqueness of God's masterpiece--you and me! God loves us so much that He delights in us, especially when we live by the principles of His Word.

There is so much untapped potential within us that is just bursting to be unleashed, but it's up to us to discover and deploy it without waiting for someone else to do it for us. When we embrace the greatness that comes from the Greater One within us with grace and gratitude, we will no longer tolerate being around people or in places that devalue the investment that God has deposited in us, or the new-found confidence that we have in who He has created us to be. Instead, we will surround ourselves with people in environments where we are appreciated and celebrated and reciprocate the same sentiments wherever we go.

Prayer to Ignite Action:
Dear God, it is wonderful to know that I am full of value and worth in Your sight, and that You delight in me as I seek to follow Your Word and will for my life. I am safe, secure, and confident in Your love for me and the purpose that You created me to fulfill. Thank You for leading me to people and places that are conducive for my personal and professional growth as I seek to add value to the people that surround me in the places where I am to go today. In Jesus' name. Amen.

DAY 332

Inspiration:

"So, beloved, since you are expecting these things, be eager to be found by Him [at His coming] without spot or blemish and at peace [in serene confidence, free from fears and agitating passions and moral conflicts]."
~ 2 Peter 3:14, Amplified Bible

Insight:

Have you ever been disappointed because your expectations of people or life's events were unmet? The easy thing to do would be to give up and stop setting expectations altogether. However, when expectations are not set, and goals are not aimed for and measured by ourselves as well as those who may serve in our sphere of leadership influence, then we'll get exactly what we expect--nothing!

Allow determination to override disappointment by ensuring that expectations are both believable and achievable so that we do not set up ourselves and others for failure, but rather for favor as a result of accomplishing realistic goals. There's nothing better than knowing and feeling the satisfaction of personal accomplishment and the affirmation that accompanies a job well done in our personal and professional lives.

Prayer to Ignite Action:

Father, You are my Creator and Counselor--the God who designed me and my future and provides wisdom that I need to set realistic expectations for myself first, and then for others as necessary. I am empowered by You to be encouraged and to be an encourager--to be motivated and to be a motivator--to set believable goals that can be achieved and to help others to do the same today. In Jesus' name. Amen.

DAY 333

Inspiration:

"Knowing what is right is like deep water in the heart; a wise person draws from the well within. Lots of people claim to be loyal and loving, but where on earth can you find one? God-loyal people, living honest lives, make it much easier for their children." ~ Proverbs 20:5-7, The Message Bible

Insight:

No person, place, or thing can hinder us from moving forward and taking advantage of every God-ordained opportunity that comes our way, unless we give away our power of choice. Rather than fighting against what we cannot change, we must choose instead to embrace and create new changes that are within our power and sphere of influence. Today came our way as a gift in which to contemplate, create, and celebrate. Now we can fully employ our mental and physical capacities and enjoy the spiritual, emotional, and relational benefits that will support our power of choice.

Prayer to Ignite Action:

Dear Lord, today is a present from You to be cherished and lived fully while enjoying every moment. There is nothing and no one that can prevent me from taking advantage of today's possibilities because I choose to take responsibility for what is within my power to do and to change. I am grateful for the wisdom You've given me to know the difference between right and wrong, and to follow my moral convictions today. I believe that the decisions I make now are defining my destiny and creating a legacy for those I am called to mentor. In Jesus' name. Amen.

DAY 334

Inspiration:

"Joyful are those you discipline, LORD, those you teach with your instructions." ~ Psalm 94:12, New Living Translation

"If you reject discipline, you only harm yourself; but if you listen to correction, you grow in understanding." ~ Proverbs 15:32, New Living Translation

"When you produce much fruit, you are my true disciples. This brings great glory to my Father." ~ John 15:8, New Living Translation

Insight:

There is a word that begins with "d" that some people must think to be a bad word because they stay as far away from it as they can. "Discipline" is a word that demands both accountability and responsibility. Just as God sometimes disciplines us, parents must also impart discipline to their children along with instruction and encouragement for effective child rearing to take place. Employers must provide a structure for corrective discipline and motivation in the workplace to create order and to maintain momentum. If we can recognize, render, and respond to discipline in our homes and places of employment, why is it so difficult to initiate and continue to implement self-discipline for the sake of our spiritual, emotional, mental, and physical health?

I believe 3 John 2 speaks to the idea of self-discipline when it states, "Beloved, I wish above all things that you would prosper and be in health, even as thy soul prospers." (King James Version) The word "soul" in the Greek is the word "psyche" which is translated as "soul, life, mind and heart" in the King James version. The soul consists of the seat of our feelings, desires, affections, and aversions. This is the essence of who we are and from which everything else emanates, which affects our decisions and actions, and therefore, our destiny.

The word "disciple" can be derived from the word "discipline," for to follow one's teachings, the student or pupil must pattern his or her life after that of the teacher. To be a true disciple, one must possess self-discipline, and that is what Jesus modeled and mandated for us as His followers.

Prayer to Ignite Action:

Father, discipline doesn't always seem pleasant, but it is necessary for growth and development. Today, I accept the lessons You desire to teach me so that I may mature in my understanding of life and pass on to others what I have learned. Help me to be self-disciplined enough to make the right decisions regarding my spiritual, emotional, mental, and physical health today, I pray. In Jesus' name. Amen.

DAY 335

Inspiration:

"Then Jesus was led by the Spirit into the wilderness to be tempted there by the devil. For forty days and forty nights he fasted and became very hungry. During that time the devil came and said to him, 'If you are the Son of God, tell these stones to become loaves of bread.' But Jesus told him, 'No! The Scriptures say, 'People do not live by bread alone, but by every word that comes from the mouth of God.'" ~ Matthew 4:1-4, New Living Translation

"When the devil had finished tempting Jesus, he left him until the next opportunity came." ~ Luke 4:13, New Living Translation

Insight:

Temptation comes and goes, ebbs and flows into our lives just as the tide rises and falls. Not even Jesus was exempt from the temptations of the enemy, which came to try Him when He was at His weakest point after fasting for forty days and nights without bread or water. There are three principles that we can learn from this passage found in Matthew 4:1-11 and Luke 4:1-13.

1) God will never tempt us, but He will surely test us. (Jesus was led by the Spirit into the wilderness to be tempted. Whereas God was and is not the Source of temptation, nor can He be tempted with or by evil, He allowed His Son, Jesus, to be placed in a position to be tempted by Satan. The very character and nature of Jesus was revealed not through Satan's temptations, but through the testing of who He was and what He knew to be true.)

2) The Word of God will sustain us through life's temptations and trials. (Satan tempted Jesus three times in the wilderness, and each time Jesus replied with, "It is written..." to signify that God's Word is the answer to every ailment and that although the flesh may be weak, the Spirit of God within us is stronger and can overcome the flesh.)

3) When we focus on our assignment, our determination will deter the

enemy "for a season." (Satan left Jesus for a time after discovering that his temptations could not allure Him. Jesus was so determined to fulfill destiny that He had no time to be deterred, so Satan was deterred instead.)

Determination is the key to overcoming temptation and adversity to live triumphantly and abundantly.

Prayer to Ignite Action:

Heavenly Father, I know that temptations will come and go because of the fact that Jesus experienced them Himself. Yet, I also realize that the power to resist temptation is already within me as I trust You for the strength not to yield to it. Your Word is the foundation upon which I stand today. As temptations come, I will declare what You have already spoken with confidence. Today, the battle against temptation is won and I have already overcome. In Jesus' name. Amen.

DAY 336

Inspiration:

"Here's another old saying that deserves a second look: 'Eye for eye, tooth for tooth.' Is that going to get us anywhere? Here's what I propose: 'Don't hit back at all.' If someone strikes you, stand there and take it. If someone drags you into court and sues for the shirt off your back, gift-wrap your best coat and make a present of it. And if someone takes unfair advantage of you, use the occasion to practice the servant life. No more tit-for-tat stuff. Live generously." ~ Matthew 5:38-42, The Message Bible

Insight:

Jesus reminded us to do more than what is expected of us. For example, He said if someone asks for your shirt, give that person your coat, too. If a person asks you to go with them one mile, don't just stop there, but go two! He even says something that is quite alarming to many in that if a person hits you on one cheek, then offer the other as well. Now, that is challenging to say the least, isn't it?

The bottom line is this: as disciples (pupils or students) of Jesus Christ, we have a responsibility to live in a way that most resembles what our Savior would do in any given situation. Jesus did not do just enough to get by, but rather, He gave all that He had to give. He sacrificed Himself to fulfill His Father's will and to meet the needs of those He came to serve. We, too, are called not to be served, but to serve and to give our life back to God as a sacrifice of obedience and devotion. God will then use our life to glorify His name and to edify those assigned to us as we give all that we are and have to share our faith with a world that is in desperate need of Him.

Prayer to Ignite Action:

Father, Your expectations of me are higher than my own, and I am striving to reach the mark You've set for me with laser-sharp focus. Help me to take the higher road in my thoughts, words and deeds today as I practice servant leadership. Though others may choose to be vengeful or vindictive, I implore You to grant me the grace to be patient, loving, kind and yet firm as necessary so that my responses will represent Christ who lives in me. In Jesus' name. Amen.

DAY 337

Inspiration:

"The conclusion, when all has been heard, is: fear God and keep His commandments, because this applies to every person. For God will bring every act to judgment, everything which is hidden, whether it is good or evil." ~ Ecclesiastes 12:13-14, New American Standard Bible

Insight:

After summing up all of life's triumphs and tragedies, wisdom prevailed in Solomon's musings as penned in Ecclesiastes 12:13-14. He had experienced life from one end of the spectrum to the other while seeking to extract wisdom from every person, place, and predicament he could survey. At one point, Solomon became so disconcerted with life that he proclaimed it to be vanity. However, in all of his observing, he finally concluded that living is vain unless we have learned who God is, who we are, and what our purpose for living is.

It is our reasonable service to offer God our lives as a loving, willing response to the sacrifice of His Son, Jesus Christ. That offering is an admission to God that we are dependent upon Him to lead, guide, and direct our steps, trusting Him to work through us to fulfill His purpose for our lives. God is pleased when we enjoy our lives abundantly while serving Him and seizing every opportunity to experience joy while fulfilling our purpose.

Prayer to Ignite Action:

Dear God, thank You for showing me the true meaning of life which is to love You, to love others as I love myself, and to know and fulfill my purpose. When all is said and done, I will be held accountable for everything that I have said and done. With that in mind, help me to discern what to do and what not to do as I live to please You and serve others. In Jesus' name. Amen.

DAY 338

Inspiration:

"Bless our God, O peoples! Give him a thunderous welcome! Didn't he keep us out of the ditch? He trained us first, passed us like silver through refining fires, brought us into hardscrabble country, pushed us to our very limit, Road-tested us inside and out, took us to hell and back; Finally he brought us to this well-watered place." ~ Psalm 66:8-12, The Message Bible

Insight:

Instead of focusing on and being frustrated about what happened in the past, choose to be liberated and lavished by the love and mercy of God that is extended today in the freedom to pursue new opportunities and be grateful. No one can stop, curse or reverse what God has already blessed from the onset, and you are included in His original plan and blessing. Today, be grateful for the well-watered place that you are in because you are alive and able to live in the moment and move forward in determining a better future. Today, decide to position yourself to display your greatness for God's glory.

Prayer to Ignite Action:

Lord God, nothing that has happened in my past has taken You by surprise. You know what will unfold today while holding my future in Your hands. I cannot change what has been, but I can determine how I will live and be grateful for my life now and in the future. I praise You for preserving me in the midst of my past challenges, and for upholding me today. I will continue to depend on You. In Jesus' name. Amen.

DAY 339

Inspiration:
"Don't become so well-adjusted to your culture that you fit into it without even thinking. Instead, fix your attention on God. You'll be changed from the inside out. Readily recognize what he wants from you, and quickly respond to it. Unlike the culture around you, always dragging you down to its level of immaturity, God brings the best out of you, develops well-formed maturity in you." ~ Romans 12:2, The Message Bible

Insight:
There is nothing like knowing that our life is to be lived for a purpose greater than ourselves to bring God pleasure and to benefit others. Everything we think, say and do will impact our quality of life as well as the life of those assigned to us now and in the future. In fact, our works will speak for us not just in this life, but well into eternity.

My husband says it this way: "Every decision we make will either affect or infect those closest to us." We must, therefore, choose to affect persons positively so that we don't infect them inadvertently by our own negativity.

Prayer to Ignite Action:
Father, today I choose not to conform to the world around me, but to fix my attention on You so that I can be transformed from the inside out. Help me to respond to Your lovingkindness towards me in the way that I give of myself to You and the people sent my way today. Bring the best out of me for others to see and emulate. In Jesus' name. Amen.

DAY 340

Inspiration:

"There is a river whose streams make glad the city of God, the holy place where the Most High dwells. God is within her, she will not fall; God will help her at break of day." ~ Psalm 46:4-5, New International Version

"There the Lord will be our Mighty One. It will be like a place of broad rivers and streams. No galley with oars will ride them, no mighty ship will sail them." ~ Isaiah 33:21, New International Version

Insight:

There is indeed a stream that flows from God's rich river of resources into our lives. Sometimes that stream trickles into the recesses of a particular nook or cranny that may have gone unnoticed. At other times, that same stream may flow in such a way that the goodness of God gushes over us in plain view for everyone to see. Today, let's choose to be grateful for the stream of blessings that God allows, and rejoice in the fact that He chooses to allow that stream to continue to flow without ceasing so that we know beyond a shadow of a doubt that every good and perfect gift comes from God, regardless of how large or small it might be.

Prayer to Ignite Action:

Gracious God, You are the One who gives to all of us generously without partiality. You choose to bless the just and the unjust as You see fit. I am thankful for the stream of blessings that flow in my life--sometimes as a trickle and at other times as a deluge of rain. You have lavished me with Your love in so many ways, and I appreciate Your unchanging character and nature that remains the same yesterday, today and forever. In Jesus' name. Amen.

DAY 341

Inspiration:

"The steps of a [good] man are ordered by the LORD, And He delights in his way." ~ Psalm 37:23, New King James Version

Insight:

The Bible tells us that "the steps of a good man (or woman) are ordered by the Lord." The operative word that I'd like to focus on in this scripture is "ordered." Synonyms for "ordered" include "systemized, methodized, arranged, and organized" so that things are placed in their proper order in relation to each other. Our steps are ordered by God because He knows the predestined plan He has for us, but it is our choice as to whether we will walk in the footprints He has already set for us. Step lively now, with confidence and conviction, as you follow God's leading for your life.

Prayer to Ignite Action:

Father God, I have peace of mind knowing that my steps today are ordered by You. The path that I choose to take has already been prepared and planned beforehand by You. I willingly surrender myself to You to be led in the way that I should go so that I can learn what I must for continued growth. Please be my leader and guide today. In Jesus' name. Amen.

DAY 342

Inspiration:

"I knew you before I formed you in your mother's womb. Before you were born I set you apart and appointed you as my prophet to the nations." ~ Jeremiah 1:5, New Living Translation

"And he called his ten servants and delivered them ten pounds, and said unto them, Occupy till I come." ~ Luke 19:13, King James Version

"...making the most of every opportunity, because the days are evil." ~ Ephesians 5:17, New International Version

Insight:

It's been said that, "Time waits for no one." While some may be waiting, wondering or perhaps wandering like the children of Israel in the wilderness, time just keeps on rolling along just as the waves roll on the shore. That is evidence enough to know that Jesus' words to us are true. Rather than waiting for some sign or miracle to take place, let's "occupy until He comes" by finding needs and filling them. Although it is wonderful to have, it is not absolutely necessary to garner the approval and affirmation of others to do what God has equipped and empowered us to do before we were placed in our mother's womb. Discover purpose and fulfill it by becoming the sign and miracle that others may be looking for, even if you need to reinvent yourself and develop a meaningful strategy to accomplish your God-inspired goals.

Prayer to Ignite Action:

Dear Lord, now is the time to live fully and well by making the most of every opportunity given to make an investment in life and not just a withdrawal. You have deposited talents, abilities, gifts, and skills in me that I must use as my deposit into the world. Help me to identify ways in which I can be most useful, but most of all, empower me to identify people in whose lives I can make a difference. In Jesus' name. Amen.

DAY 343

Inspiration:

"Tell those rich in this world's wealth to quit being so full of themselves and so obsessed with money, which is here today and gone tomorrow. Tell them to go after God, who piles on all the riches we could ever manage--to do good, to be rich in helping others, to be extravagantly generous. If they do that, they'll build a treasury that will last, gaining life that is truly life." ~ 1 Timothy 6:17-19, The Message Bible

Insight:

There are two old sayings that go something like this: "Everything that glitters ain't gold," and "Don't judge a book by its cover." My mother-in-law spins a different perspective by asserting that, "Every shut eye ain't sleep!" These adages caution us to ensure that our perspective is sharp, keen, and discerning, requiring us to stay alert so that we aren't lured into situations and relationships that aren't the best fit for who we are and all that we bring to the table of life.

Take the time today and from this moment forward to look through the lenses of possibility with a perspective that creates new opportunities to display who God designed you to be as well as all that He empowered you to do for the expansion of His kingdom here on earth. Think and live outside of the box and enjoy the richness of life that your new mindset and actions will bring. You'll live an extravagant life that will extend to those who cross your path, and that kind of life will follow into eternity.

Prayer to Ignite Action:

Loving Father, You have given me life to enjoy richly--not to accumulate an abundance of possessions to heap on myself--but to live to honor You willingly and to serve others generously. I pray for a keen sense of discernment so that I am aware of Your will for my life as well as the needs of others that I am equipped to fulfill today. In Jesus' name. Amen.

DAY 344

Inspiration:

" 'No weapon forged against you will prevail, and you will refute every tongue that accuses you. This is the heritage of the servants of the LORD, and this is their vindication from me,' declares the LORD." ~ Isaiah 54:17, New International Version

Insight:

As children of God, we inherit a vast number of promises found in His Word. One of those promises assures us that no weapon, device, scheme or plan that is formed against us will prosper. It does not tell us that nothing will ever come against us because the Christian life is a euphoric utopia. Rather, we are encouraged to know that the opposition that comes will not overpower or overtake us.

Thus, I am reminded that God has given us weaponry of our own according to 2 Timothy 1:7 to counteract the opposition that may come our way: 1) power; 2) love; and 3) a sound mind. We have the power to choose to serve God and fulfill His plan for our lives. We have the spirit of love that will cast out fear and remove torment. And we have a sound mind that stabilizes and fortifies everything that we do as we think daily with "the mind of Christ" which makes us an expert as He uses our gifts of expertise to show His glory. The weaponry from God is a winning combination that will defeat the odds and obstacles that may come against us.

Prayer to Ignite Action:

Dear Lord, I am Your child, and as such, inherit the rich and precious promises found in Your Word. Today, I stand on the promise that no weapon that is forged against me will amount to anything. You have freely given me power, love, and a sound mind to confront and conquer all odds, obstacles, and opposition. Thank You for equipping me with what I need to succeed in life. In Jesus' name. Amen.

DAY 345

Inspiration:
"This I recall to my mind, Therefore I have hope. [Through] the LORD's mercies we are not consumed, Because His compassions fail not. [They are] new every morning; Great [is] Your faithfulness. 'The Lord [is] my portion,' says my soul, 'Therefore I hope in Him!' The Lord [is] good to those who wait for Him, To the soul [who] seeks Him." ~ Lamentations 3:21-25, New King James Version

Insight:
Just as God allows us to experience a brand new day with the dawning of the sun, He also grants us another chance today to hit the target that we may have missed yesterday. His mercies toward us are new every morning because we evidently used up our allotted portion the day before. Thankfully, God's love for us is unfailing.

Each day is too precious to waste by wallowing in past failures or wading in past accomplishments. What we focus on today matters most. Today, be sure to value each moment by seeking God, seizing life, and serving people fully with love and appreciation.

Prayer to Ignite Action:
Dear Lord, I am so grateful for the multitude of mercies that You measure out to us each morning--mercies that are as new and fresh as the day itself. As a recipient of Your mercies, I will be conscious of how I spend this day. I ask for Your help so that I can declare Your faithfulness to others by the way I live today. In Jesus' name. Amen.

DAY 346

Inspiration:

"And let us consider one another in order to stir up love and good works, not forsaking the assembling of ourselves together, as [is] the manner of some, but exhorting [one another], and so much the more as you see the Day approaching." ~ Hebrews 10:24-25, New King James Version

Insight:

There are so many modern conveniences due to the technological advances of the 21st century that the internet superhighway has in many cases replaced the bridge of face-to-face fellowship and communication. That is not to say that emails, phone texts, social media networks, and internet or phone chat messages are wrong. In actuality, these are tools that can be used to promote the Gospel as well as businesses, and are certainly convenient for conveying messages quickly. However, nothing is as encouraging and effective as meeting face-to-face, particularly during times of worship. There is something to be said about coming together with people who have common faith and values to hear teaching and preaching that is based on biblical principles conveyed with practical applications. When the family of God worships together, faith increases, love multiplies, gifts are deployed as people are encouraged and equipped to serve, needs are met and unity prevails. Most of all, God is glorified because we have not forsaken the opportunity to assemble ourselves in a place of worship as the body of Christ.

Prayer to Ignite Action:

Heavenly Father, Your Word exhorts us not to forsake the opportunity to assemble ourselves to worship. We are encouraged to love one another enough to make sure that we are consistent in attending our chosen place of worship--an environment where love and good works can be clearly seen and expressed beyond church walls into the community and world. Thank You for reminding me today of the importance of my local church and the need for me to stay connected by attending and being involved consistently. In Jesus' name. Amen.

DAY 347

Inspiration:

"Looking away [from all that will distract] to Jesus, Who is the Leader and the Source of our faith [giving the first incentive for our belief] and is also its Finisher [bringing it to maturity and perfection]. He, for the joy [of obtaining the prize] that was set before Him, endured the cross, despising and ignoring the shame, and is now seated at the right hand of the throne of God." ~ Hebrews 12:2, Amplified Bible

Insight:

Have you discovered why you exist? God has placed you on earth for a particular reason to fulfill a unique purpose according to His timing and season. There's no greater joy than to know that you are living out your purpose and impacting the lives of others each day. Such fulfillment makes life worth living and the vicissitudes of life's valleys worth traveling through as we, like Jesus, fine-tune our focus and fix our attention on the destiny that is set before us. That destiny becomes the source of our joy and the motivation that keeps us moving forward.

Prayer to Ignite Action:

Dear Lord, You are an example of true servanthood, perseverance, focus, and motivation for mission. Although You endured hostile, unjust treatment from others while on earth, You pushed past the pain because of the joy of fulfilling Your purpose--to redeem the souls of humanity--before returning to Your rightful place at the righthand of Your Father in Heaven. You served a purpose that was greater than anything I could possibly fathom. I, too, believe that my purpose is greater than me. Today, I will focus on the joy of fulfilling my destiny as it motivates me to keep on going, no matter what. In Jesus' name. Amen.

DAY 348

Inspiration:

"Have you never heard? Have you never understood? The LORD is the everlasting God, the Creator of all the earth. He never grows weak or weary. No one can measure the depths of his understanding. He gives power to the weak and strength to the powerless. Even youths will become weak and tired, and young men will fall in exhaustion. But those who trust in the LORD will find new strength. They will soar on high on wings like eagles. They will run and not grow weary. They will walk and not faint." ~Isaiah 40:28-31, New Living Translation

Insight:

Life has its share of challenges which may show up at the most unexpected times and in the most unexpected places. Yet, it is our perspective and expectations regardless of the wrench thrown in the cogs that determines how we will respond. Whatever we perceive is what we will believe and receive. We can change our reality based on our perception and perspective, and thus, change ourselves when we focus on the opportunities that can be birthed from challenges that arise. Sometimes, challenges come for a reason to propel us into a new season. If our perspective and expectation levels are high, then like an eagle over the challenge we can fly!

Prayer to Ignite Action:

Everlasting God, Creator of all the earth, You are awesome and full of wisdom and strength. There is never a moment when You slumber or sleep. You know and see all, and are ready to rescue and recover those who are weak and powerless. You give energy to those who are exhausted when they seek You. As I pray today, I am trusting You for the strength and power to authentically be who You've called me to be and to boldly do what You've equipped me to do. I thank You for the ability to soar above every challenge with a winning attitude and a plan of action as You instruct me. In Jesus' name. Amen.

DAY 349

Inspiration:

"Since, then, you have been raised with Christ, set your hearts on things above, where Christ is seated at the right hand of God. Set your mind on things above, not on earthly things." ~ Colossians 3:1-2, New International Version

Insight:

Negative emotions and energy certainly do not come from God who is the Giver of every good and perfect gift. We must exchange negative emotions and energy for a positive God-given purpose to passionately pursue. When God places purpose within us, our desire serves as the fuel to fulfill it. When there is a vision that is larger than us, it drives us to become all that we were predestined to be, and to accomplish all that we can within the scope of that vision with the gifts and abilities we were given.

Colossians 3:1-2 tells us what kinds of things to think about so that negativity will not become a permanent resident in our minds. Raising the standard, and therefore, the consciousness of our thoughts by setting our minds and hearts on what pleases God, teaches two very valuable lessons:

1) Positivity is positively infectious and its affect is quite contagious; and 2) The quality of our thoughts will determine the kind of relationships as well as the environment that we will attract.

Raise the bar in your thoughts today, and expect excellent results to follow.

Prayer to Ignite Action:

Gracious God, although You have endowed me with the ability to think about whatever I choose, Your Word tells me what I should focus on for my own good. Today, I choose to tune my thoughts to a higher frequency so that I focus on the things that honor You. As I raise my standard of thinking, I will also raise my standard of living that will be reflected in my relationships, home, workplace and wherever else I must be today. I am expecting great results to follow because I am raising the bar in my thought life. In Jesus' name. Amen.

DAY 350

Inspiration:
"There is no fear in love; but perfect love casts out fear, because fear involves torment. But he who fears has not been made perfect in love."
~ 1 John 4:18, New King James Version

Insight:
Too often, some people spiritualize their problems, justify their words and actions, and avoid the obvious simply because of fear--fear of criticism, rejection, failure, and the perceptions or opinions of others-- perhaps thinking that by doing so, the difficulties in their lives and relationships will just work out by God's grace (but that's not always the case).

I've learned this simple equation from observation and experience: Fear of Confrontation + Lack of Communication = Frustration

The antithesis of that equation is to do exactly the opposite of everything that has produced no fruit or results in your life. Today, instead of being controlled by fear, decide to be consumed by faith and love. Choose to edify rather than criticize, and to confront rather than to avoid the obvious. Surround yourself with those who will accept and celebrate you rather than tolerate or reject you. Rather than seeking a spiritual solution to every problem, look for the practical things to do that you may have missed along the way. Then you can accomplish more than you've ever dreamed of by empowering yourself and enhancing the relationships in your life.

Prayer to Ignite Action:
Dear God, my faith in You overrides all fear and replaces it with love. Let the evidence of my faith and love be clearly heard and seen in my conversation and conduct. I pray that the nature of Your character will be developed in me so that I can become more like Christ by applying biblical principles in the right context. Help me to be practical by doing my part to listen to and obey the instructions that You give which will show up in the way I treat others today. In Jesus' name. Amen.

DAY 351

Inspiration:

"Then he said, "There was once a man who had two sons. The younger said to his father, 'Father, I want right now what's coming to me.' So the father divided the property between them. It wasn't long before the younger son packed his bags and left for a distant country. There, undisciplined and dissipated, he wasted everything he had...The son started his speech: 'Father, I've sinned against God, I've sinned before you; I don't deserve to be called your son ever again.' But the father wasn't listening. He was calling to the servants, 'Quick. Bring a clean set of clothes and dress him. Put the family ring on his finger and sandals on his feet...My son is here--given up for dead and now alive! Given up for lost and now found!' And they began to have a wonderful time...The older brother stalked off and refused to join in. His father came out and tried to talk to him, but he wouldn't listen...His father said, 'Son, you don't understand. You're with me all the time, and everything that is mine is yours--but this is a wonderful time, and we had to celebrate. This brother of yours was dead, and he's alive! He was lost, and he's found!'" ~ Luke 15: 11-13, 21-22, 24, 28, 31-32, The Message Bible

Insight:

Like the story of The Prodigal Son in Luke chapter 15:11-32, many have experienced what it's like to go astray in search of independence, freedom and the right to do "their own thing." But our loving Heavenly Father, who created us with the power to choose our own path, waited patiently for us to return to Him and to realize that what we were in search for was ours all along. Sometimes we have to go through seasons of difficulty in order to get to and seize our destiny with a newfound sense of belonging and ownership that make the entire journey worth traveling in the end. What makes the journey bearable and bountiful at the same time is knowing that no matter how challenging the roads and curves of life may be, there is an Omniscient, Omnipresent and Omnipotent God who will never leave or forsake us. Now that is GOOD NEWS!

Prayer to Ignite Action:

Forgiving Father, the story of the Prodigal Son and his older brother remind us of devastating effects of sin that results in stripping us of our value, worth and sense of belonging-until we come to our senses and accept Your unconditional love and forgiveness. You love us in and out of sin--a love that is not predicated upon the works that we do to earn it; it is freely given to all who will acknowledge and receive it. Thank You for being such a loving and forgiving God. The confession of my sin to You not only guarantees my forgiveness, but it also wipes the stain of sin from my life never to be remembered or counted against me again. I now realize that Your love and acceptance of me was there all the time. I'm so happy to be in Your family. In Jesus' name. Amen.

—

DAY 352

Inspiration:

"Judge not, that you be not judged. For with what judgment you judge, you will be judged; and with the measure you use, it will be measured back to you. And why do you look at the speck in your brother's eye, but do not consider the plank in your own eye? Or how can you say to your brother, 'Let me remove the speck from your eye'; and look, a plank [is] in your own? Hypocrite! First remove the plank from your own eye, and then you will see clearly to remove the speck from your brother's eye." ~ Matthew 7:1-5, New King James Version

Insight:

We cannot blame other people or circumstances for our lack of progress in life. Rather than making excuses, we should strive to evaluate ourselves and make the necessary adjustments so that we will not be judged by the same measure that we have used to judged others so quickly. Just as a farmer tests and tastes his crops before offering them to others, so must we test our own character and convictions, and be the first partaker of the lessons and the judgment that we would pass onto others.

An old adage says, "If we can't stand the heat, get out of the kitchen." Similarly, if we can't measure up to the judgment we pass on others, then we shouldn't pass judgment. We have enough work on our hands to keep us busy for a lifetime when we determine to work on ourselves.

Prayer to Ignite Action:

Dear Lord, forgive me for judging others presumptuously when I have things in my own life that need to be addressed. Convict me of my wrong and strengthen me so that I can choose the right way in which to think, speak, and act. I will not point fingers at other people to blame them for something that I should take responsibility for in my own life. Help me to work on and to judge myself and to apologize to those I have unfairly criticized. Thank You for answering my prayer as I work on me today. In Jesus' name. Amen.

DAY 353

Inspiration:

"But my servant Caleb has a different attitude than the others have. He has remained loyal to me, so I will bring him into the land he explored. His descendants will possess their full share of that land." ~ Numbers 14:24, New Living Translation

"Finally, all of you should be of one mind. Sympathize with each other. Love each other as brothers and sisters. Be tenderhearted, and keep a humble attitude." ~ 1 Peter 3:8, New Living Translation

Insight:

Our attitude determines much more than our altitude (or how far we can go). It also determines our inner and outer health, beauty, peace, purpose, and passion. Attitude is related to everything and everyone that is attached to us and every assignment that will impact us and influence others. Adorning ourselves with the proper attitude should be a necessary part of our daily wardrobe that we should refuse to leave home without. The perfect way to cultivate the right attitude is to start the day with scripture meditation and prayer, asking God for His help.

Prayer to Ignite Action:

Heavenly Father, I ask You today to lead me as I start my day by meditating on Numbers 14:24 and 1 Peter 3:8. Just as Caleb stood out among others because he had a different attitude and spirit, help me to get Your attention as well as remain loyal in my love, service and attitude towards You and others. Today, help me to have empathetic eyes, listening ears, a compassionate heart and a humble attitude. I can adjust my attitude as necessary because You are with me. In Jesus' name. Amen.

DAY 354

Inspiration:

"Where [there is] no vision, the people perish: but he that keepeth the law, happy [is] he." ~ Proverbs 29:18, King James Version

Insight:

We exert our most diligent effort in and behind the things we are most passionate about. It is important to realize where our passions lie, and that they are in direct alignment with God's purpose for our lives. God places passion in our heart for the vision that He gives us for our lives. Acting upon that passion by utilizing our gifts, abilities and the resources at our disposal will cause astounding results to follow as God gives the increase and allows our vision to come to life. There is great peace in knowing that when we're in God's divine will, everything we need to fulfill our vision--people, resources and favor--will be granted as His kingdom is expanded and lives are transformed in the process.

Prayer to Ignite Action:

Father, You are the God of prevision and provision who sees the future and provides for every need now to support our vision and destiny. Thank You for planting a vision in my heart to connect me to my purpose. As I meditate on Your Word, help me to keep it in my heart so that I may know and obey Your precepts. May what I learn undergird the vision You've given me so that it continues to progress with momentum motivated by a mission to serve You and bless other people. In Jesus' name. Amen.

DAY 355

Inspiration:

"If you decide that it's a bad thing to worship GOD, then choose a god you'd rather serve--and do it today. Choose one of the gods your ancestors worshiped from the country beyond The River, or one of the gods of the Amorites, on whose land you're now living. As for me and my family, we'll worship GOD." ~ Joshua 24:15, The Message Bible

"Choose my instruction rather than silver, and knowledge rather than pure gold." ~ Proverbs 8:10, New Living Translation

"Choose a good reputation over great riches; being held in high esteem is better than silver or gold." ~ Proverbs 22:1, New Living Translation

Insight:

God gave us a wonderful gift when He equipped us with the power of choice. We can choose to serve God and live life abundantly to the full until it overflows. We can choose to surround ourselves with the caliber and quality of friends that will celebrate, strengthen and sharpen us. We can choose to let go of unhealthy habits and hindrances that prevent us from maturing and moving forward. We can choose to learn from the lessons and relationships in life that may have been unpleasant at the time, but were necessary in building character within us. We can choose to do all these things and more, or we can choose to take the lesser road and settle for mediocrity. The choice is ours, so let's choose wisely.

Prayer to Ignite Action:

Dear Lord, I choose to serve, hear from, and follow You explicitly today. Instruct me in the decisions I should make throughout the day so that I may continue to develop spiritually, intellectually, physically, and socially. Although others may make choices contrary to mine, help me to stay focused and to stand firm on the foundation of Your Word and my code of ethics as the basis for every decision made. I will choose wisely today. In Jesus' name. Amen.

DAY 356

Inspiration:

"Now to him who is able to do immeasurably more than all we ask or imagine, according to his power that is at work within us." ~ Ephesians 3:20, New International Version

Insight:

My husband, Bishop L. W. Francisco III, serves as Senior Pastor of Calvary Community Church in Hampton, VA. He often reminds our congregation to visualize the person we desire to become as well as the goals we want to achieve by first painting an "image" on the "nation" of our mind. Thus, the word "imagination" challenges us to be conscious of the pictures that we allow to run repetitiously on the canvas of the mind, for the mind is the womb where images and ideas take shape to form a vision before it is birthed into manifestation. When we internalize and visualize our vision and commit to working our God-given plan, we can expect growth and maturation to follow what we dared to imagine.

Prayer to Ignite Action:

Heavenly Father, thank You for the creativity that flows in me to imagine the vision that I desire for my personal and professional life. I pray that the vision that I imagine is in alignment with the purpose You predestined for me. Please inspire and empower me to think and act strategically as Your Spirit leads me in making my God-given vision my reality. In Jesus' name. Amen.

DAY 357

Inspiration:
"And after he had dismissed the multitudes, He went up into the hills by Himself to pray. When it was evening, He was still there alone." ~ Matthew 14:23, Amplified Version

"And He said to them, [As for you] come away by yourselves to a deserted place, and rest a while--for many were [continually] coming and going, and they had not even leisure enough to eat. And they went away in a boat to a solitary place by themselves." ~ Mark 6:31-32, Amplified Version

Insight:
Taking a break from the routine and the mundane can actually help to keep us sane. Even Jesus realized that although He was consumed with doing His Father's will, He needed to take the time to rest to be renewed in mind, body, and spirit. Jesus told His disciples after many days of ministry work and travel that they needed to "come apart and rest for a while" so that they wouldn't come or fall apart. May we all become sensitized to the need to rest and renew our bodies and relationships so that we can reap the benefits both now and in the future. Relax and live abundantly, because life is about so much more than what consumes us during the day.

Prayer to Ignite Action:
Heavenly Father, You have created me to be a tripartite being consisting of spirit, mind, and body. Each part of me is equally important and deserves proper nurture and self-care. I ask for the discernment and discipline needed to rest on my own and relax with family and friends, to eat healthily and exercise regularly, and to renew my mind and spirit through prayer, Bible study, attending my local church, and using my gifts and resources to serve others. Thank You for loving me enough to remind me to care for my holistic health and well-being. In Jesus' name. Amen.

DAY 358

Inspiration:
"O LORD our Lord, how excellent is thy name in all the earth." ~ Psalm 8:9, King James Version

Insight:
Excellence in the Hebrew is translated as "great, majestic and noble" which clearly speaks of Who He is. Since we are made in His image and likeness, our character should exemplify excellence which is further displayed in everything that our hands undertake. Seeking to emulate and inundate ourselves with an excellent spirit exalts God and causes others to take notice.

Today, I pray that we all seek to be endowed and infused afresh with God's Spirit so that the excellence factor can be multiplied in our lives.

Prayer to Ignite Action:
Father, Your name, character and works are excellent. No one and nothing else can compare to Your glory and splendor. You do all things well, and because You live in me, I can also do all things well. Today, I will strive to excel in all I do. Empower me to reject mediocrity and the status quo, and to go the extra mile by doing more than is required. Let Your spirit of excellence engulf and engage me today. In Jesus' name. Amen.

DAY 359

Inspiration:

"Do not call to mind the former things, Or ponder things of the past. Behold, I will do something new, Now it will spring forth; Will you not be aware of it? I will even make a roadway in the wilderness, Rivers in the desert." ~ Isaiah 43:18-19, New American Standard Bible

Insight:

It is so easy to stay within our comfort zone and to do what we've always done without thinking because it has become automatic and routine. The challenge for every believer is to reach for higher heights and deeper depths, not just in our relationship with God, but in the utilization of our gifts. When we truly surrender all that we are and have to our Creator, then He in return will grant creativity and challenge us to move beyond our comfort zone into the unfamiliar and unknown. In order to experience real change and growth, we must be willing to discover and courageously pursue new ideas and goals that will intentionally stretch us beyond our normal capabilities and learning propensities. Only then will we expand our knowledge, engage wisdom, enhance our skills, and embrace the essence of all that we are and can accomplish as God's ambassadors.

Let's not become so accustomed to old patterns, behaviors, routines, and methods of doing things that we miss out on opportunities that will provoke us to passionately pursue "the new."

Prayer to Ignite Action:

Father, You are the God of our past, present, and future. You know where I have been, where I am now, and where I am going. Although the past is gone, I have the gift of today to savor here and now with an expectation of seeing You manifest something new and refreshing. You promised to make a road in the wilderness and a river in the desert, so I know that nothing will stop the shift that will take place to exchange the old for the new in my life. In Jesus' name. Amen.

DAY 360

Inspiration:

"Then Joseph hurried from the room because he was overcome with emotion for his brother. He went into his private room where he broke down and wept." ~ Genesis 43:30, New Living Translation

"God met me more than halfway, he freed me from my anxious fears. Look at him; give him your warmest smile. Never hide your feelings from him." ~ Psalm 34:4-5, The Message Bible

"The king was overcome with emotion. He went up to the room over the gateway and burst into tears. And as he went, he cried, 'O my son Absalom! My son, my son Absalom! If only I had died instead of you! O Absalom, my son, my son.'" ~ 2 Samuel 18:33, New Living Translation

Insight:

Some people become accustomed to hiding their emotions. Whereas we are not to be led solely by our emotions, they are a God-given gift to allow us to release what is necessary so that issues can be acknowledged and dealt with rather than ignored and denied. Hidden emotions cause the truth to be hidden from ourselves and others, but not God. Let's allow our emotions to be exposed to our All Knowing God, and trusted others as necessary, so that our destiny is not blocked but brought closer into view.

Prayer to Ignite Action:

Heavenly Father, You created all of us with the capacity to love and be loved. The ability to express emotions is a blessing, for it puts me in touch with what I am truly feeling and why so that I can identify and manage my emotions appropriately. Help me not to suppress my feelings but to temper them so that I will not be controlled by or make decisions solely based on them. Thank You for giving me this special gift so that I can know myself and relate to others better. In Jesus' name. Amen.

DAY 361

Inspiration:

"If a ruler loses his temper against you, don't panic; A calm disposition quiets intemperate rage." ~ Ecclesiastes 10:4, The Message Bible

"A fool always loses his temper, But a wise man holds it back." ~ Proverbs 29, New American Standard Bible

Insight:

Unexpected twists and turns, puddles and potholes are to be found as we traverse the road of life. Yet, we cannot allow the foreseen and spur of the moment occurrences to keep us from moving ahead, even when our emotions dictate otherwise. The reality is that we have the power to command our emotions to succumb to our will, which is stronger than our feelings. Do not allow what we feel to take precedence over what is real. Positive action keeps us from being stagnated or stalemated as a result of yielding to our emotions, so let's keep it moving!

Prayer to Ignite Action:

Dear Lord, the ability to feel and express happiness, sadness, fear, guilt, and shame reminds me that I am alive and well, and able to respond to people and situations in the way that I choose. I pray for discernment and self-discipline so that I can be a good steward and manage each emotion with grace from You. My emotions will not get the best of me today. In Jesus' name. Amen.

DAY 362

Inspiration:

"I will bless the Lord at all times; His praise shall continually be in my mouth. My life makes its boast in the Lord; let the humble and afflicted hear and be glad. O magnify the Lord with me, and let us exalt His name together. I sought (inquired of) the Lord and required Him [of necessity and on the authority of His Word], and He heard me, and delivered me from all my fears." ~ Psalm 34:1-4, Amplified Bible

Insight:

A thankful heart is one that is filled with an abundance of overflowing gratitude as a result of being dependent upon and appreciative of God's handiwork regardless of circumstances that may change. It is a heart that chooses to trust God rather than man, knowing that He is the Giver of all good and perfect gifts which may come in and through unexpected people and situations. When we cultivate thankfulness in our heart, the fruit that is produced is evident in peace, contentment, and unwavering faith that gives stability and certainty, assuring us that the way to win is to begin and end each day by valuing God's ways and thoughts above our own and determining to thank Him at all times.

Prayer to Ignite Action:

Heavenly Father, I thank You from the bottom of my heart for being my God. You are great and mighty, holy and worthy, marvelous and majestic in all Your ways. I worship You because You are Sovereign. I am grateful to be called Your own. Today, I simply want to express my admiration of You, and my appreciation for all the wonderful works You've done and continue to perform not just for me, but for all the world. There is none like You, and no one else can love and care for me as You do. Thank You. In Jesus' name. Amen.

DAY 363

Inspiration:

"Hear my cry, O God; Attend unto my prayer. From the end of the earth I will cry to You, When my heart is overwhelmed; Lead me to the rock that is higher than I. For You have been a shelter for me, A strong tower from the enemy. I will abide in Your tabernacle forever; I will trust in the shelter of Your wings. Selah." ~ Psalm 61:1-4, New King James Version

"There hath no temptation taken you but such as is common to man: but God [is] faithful, who will not suffer you to be tempted above that ye are able; but will with the temptation also make a way to escape, that ye may be able to bear [it]." ~ 1 Corinthians 10:13, King James Version

Insight:

It has been said that "where there's a will, there's a way." Although that is not a Bible verse, there are biblical implications inferred by that statement. No matter what confronts us on a daily basis, it is with the act of our will working in concert with our mind and heart, that we choose to move beyond life's obstacles. The converse also is true in that the mind, heart and will can also keep us from seeing the vast possibilities that are before us because we "choose" not to see and pursue a way out.

Let's look for our "way of escape" when the cares of this life seem to overwhelm us, for that is the outlet that God can use to turn obstacles into opportunities created for our good. God always makes a way!

Prayer to Ignite Action:

Father, You are the God who can make a way where there seems to be no way. In the midst of the most critical of circumstances, You are able to provide a means of escape so that I am not overwhelmed. I am never without hope as long as my trust is confidently in You--the Rock that is Higher than I. In Jesus' name. Amen.

DAY 364

Inspiration:

"And God shall wipe away every tear from their eyes; there shall be no more death, nor sorrow, nor crying. There shall be no more pain, for the former things have passed away." ~ Revelation 21:4, New King James Version

Insight:

I have learned the most valuable lessons of my life as a result of either unexpected or unexplainable pain. Pain is a natural part of both the process and progress of life, and we must learn how to confront rather than ignore it. Learning how to cope with and learn from the painful circumstances in our lives can be just the fuel needed to motivate us to sublimate that energy and propel us toward a greater focus for our future. Pain, when approached from this perspective, can be the launching pad for purpose as it is utilized to move forward.

Prayer to Ignite Action:

Dear God, You are Jehovah Rapha--the God who Heals. There is no sorrow or pain that is too great for Your hand to heal. I thank You for the comfort, strength, and peace of the Holy Spirit that is an ever present help in troublesome times. Today, I ask for the sensitivity to be able to cope with and learn from pain that may be present around me. Let me be Your eyes, ears, hands, and feet as a carrier of hope and healing to those who are hurting today. In Jesus' name. Amen.

DAY 365

Inspiration:

"God rules: he brings this one down to his knees, pulls that one up on her feet." ~ Psalm 75:7, The Message Bible

"Likewise, you who are younger and of lesser rank, be subject to the elders (the ministers and spiritual guides of the church)--[giving them due respect and yielding to their counsel]. Clothe (apron) yourselves, all of you, with humility [as the garb of a servant, so that its covering cannot possibly be stripped from you, with freedom from pride and arrogance] toward one another. For God sets Himself against the proud (the insolent, the overbearing, the disdainful, the presumptuous, the boastful)--[and He opposes, frustrates, and defeats them], but gives grace (favor, blessing) to the humble." ~ 1 Peter 5:5, Amplified Bible

Insight:

We cannot fully become who or accomplish what God has designed for our lives unless we rid ourselves of the destructive force of pride. Humility is the key to attaining authentic and holistic prosperity, for it allows our focus to be placed upon serving God and others rather than just ourselves. Pride is selfishly ambitious and motivated by a hidden agenda. Humility, however, is selfless because it is motivated by love and concern for other people. Pride is destructive in that it tears down individuals to lift up the one who is haughty and puffed up. Humility is constructive in that it builds up individuals by putting the needs of others ahead of oneself. It is obvious why God promotes the humble and demotes the proud and arrogant.

Possessing humility as a character trait is necessary to live a meaningful and significant life, for that is what attracts favor from God and people. What are you doing to ensure success in your life? Cultivating godlike character traits such as humility will definitely get God's attention.

Prayer to Ignite Action:

Heavenly Father, I desire to continue to develop character traits such as humility in my life. Purge any inkling of pride or selfish ambition from my heart. I want to be motivated to fulfill my purpose because of my love for You and the people I am called to influence. Help me to be humble in my attitude and in my service today. Please give me the heart of a humble servant so that I can follow the example of Jesus who came not to be served, but to serve. In Jesus' name. Amen.

ABOUT DR. NATALIE A. FRANCISCO

Dr. Natalie A. Francisco has served as co-pastor of Calvary Community Church and co-founder of Calvary Christian Academy in Hampton, VA, alongside her husband, Bishop L. W. Francisco III. She has also served extensively in full-time ministry for over 27 years in areas of leadership in both the Music and Arts and Christian Education departments of her local church. The culmination of her years of experience in relating to women and children of all ages have been instrumental in affording her the opportunity to author four books: *Wisdom for Women of Worth & Worship: Lessons for a Life of Virtue, Value & Victory; Parenting and Partnering with Purpose: Linking Homes, Schools and Churches to Educate Our Children; A Woman's Journal for Joyful Living: Successful Steps to Holistic Health;* and *I'm Just Saying! Daily Devotional Inspiration and Insight for Men and Women* (all published by St. Paul Press). In addition, she has served as a writer for several magazines and co-authored the book, *Becoming A Steward Leader: Essential Insights from Stewardship Thought Leaders and Practitioners* (Christian Leadership Alliance).

As founder and executive director of the Women of Worth Conference and the Women of Worth and Worship Institute (WOWWI), Dr. Francisco seeks to provide godly and practical instruction to women who desire to learn and implement biblical truths and principles from her life's lessons. As a personal mentor and a consultant, she strives to equip others to excel as principle-led leaders in marriage, ministry and the marketplace. This is accomplished via her books, conferences, seminars, retreats, and several eight-week sessions held throughout the year on location as requested as well as online for registered participants across the country and around the world.

With over fifteen years of television experience alongside her husband, Dr. Francisco also is a contributor to the Shaping Families radio broadcast sponsored by Third Way Media. She offers pastoral insight and biblical solutions while addressing difficult, real life issues that families often face. The broadcast is aired weekly on several radio stations nationwide and can also be heard online. Additionally, Dr. Francisco serves as director on various community and financial services boards, and as an advisory board member of Wisdom Women Worldwide and Women in Ministry International founded by Dr. Suzan Johnson Cook.

Although Dr. Francisco has served as a motivational speaker, teacher, worship leader and author, her greatest joys are found in serving God, spending time with her family and friends, and practicing self-care.

CONTACT DR. NATALIE A. FRANCISCO

To register for a Women of Worth & Worship Institute course offered onsite or online which includes eight-week sessions with intensive teaching utilizing any or all of her books (Wisdom for Women of Worth and Worship, Parenting and Partnering with Purpose and A Woman's Journal for Joyful Living) as the curriculum guide:

Dr. Natalie A. Francisco Women of Worth & Worship, LLC
2311 Tower Place
Hampton, VA 23666
Email: wowwi@nataliefrancisco.com

To visit the Women of Worth & Worship, LLC website:
www.nataliefrancisco.com

To request Dr. Natalie A. Francisco for church, educational or corporate speaking engagements, conferences, consultations, seminars or workshops:
Dr. Natalie A. Francisco
Calvary Community Church
2311 Tower Place
Hampton, VA 23666
(757) 825-1133 ext. 200
Email: wowwi@calvarycommunity.org
Website: www.calvarycommunity.org

To visit Dr. Francisco's book websites:
www.awomansjournalforjoyfulliving.com
www.wisdomforwomenofworthandworship.com
www.parentingandpartneringwithpurpose.com
www.imjustsayingthebook.org